Maya Programming with Python Cookbook

Master complex workflows and conquer the world with Python and Maya

Adrian Herbez

PUBLISHING

BIRMINGHAM - MUMBAI

Maya Programming with Python Cookbook

First published: July 2016

Production reference: 1260716

Published by Packt Publishing Ltd.

Livery Place

35 Livery Street

Birmingham B3 2PB, UK.

ISBN 978-1-78528-398-7

www.packtpub.com

Credits

Author
Adrian Herbez

Reviewer
Brian Escribano

Acquisition Editor
Subho Gupta

Content Development Editor
Rashmi Suvarna

Technical Editors
Pramod Kumavat

Gaurav Suri

Copy Editor
Dipti Mankame

Project Coordinator
Judie Jose

Proofreader
Safis Editing

Indexer
Hemangini Bari

Graphics
Kirk D'Penha

Production Coordinator
Shantanu N. Zagade

Cover Work
Shantanu N. Zagade

About the Author

Adrian Herbez is an accomplished software engineer and educator with a background in virtual worlds and gaming. He has worked as a web developer at Linden Lab (the creators of *Second Life*) and a senior software engineer at Sony Computer Entertainment, America, where he developed games and interactive content for PlayStation Home. He also served as the lead gameplay engineer for KIXEYE's *War Commander*. Adrian has also taught at the Academy of Art University in San Francisco in a number of different departments over the years, covering Maya, web development, and game programming.

He is currently the cofounder and president of Jamwix, a game and media start-up. So far, Jamwix has released *CineMagic: Hollywood Madness*, a mobile game for iOS and Android as well as the first feature-length movie for virtual reality (*The Banshee Chapter: Oculus Rift Edition*).

Adrian holds a master's degree in Fine Arts from the University of California, Irvine, from the Arts, Computation, and Engineering department, and has served as a juror for IndieCade, the international festival of independent gaming, for a number of years.

I would like to thank my students for spurring me on to seek out the heart of every topic, and for always inspiring me with their enthusiasm and creativity. I have also been fortunate enough to benefit from a number of wonderful teachers, including Terry Calais, Randy Pausch, and Simon Penny, as well as my longtime friend and mentor, Frank Garvey. I've learned a great deal from each of them, and my life would be much diminished without their guidance and insight.

I'd also like to thank my business partners, Bill Booth and Blair Erickson, for jumping into the deep end with me in starting our company, and for being patient with me on those days when I came into the office bleary-eyed after a long night of writing.

And most of all, I'd like to thank my wonderful partner, Carrie, for being so supportive and for always helping me to go farther and to achieve more in everything I do.

About the Reviewer

Brian Escribano has over 13 years of experience working in Education, TV, and Games. He builds world class character rigs and animation pipelines for companies such as Nickelodeon, Mirada, Spark Unlimited, and Bioware. With his deep scripting knowledge of Python and MEL, Brian brings a wealth of expertise and experience to any team that he works with.

www.PacktPub.com

eBooks, discount offers, and more

Did you know that Packt offers eBook versions of every book published, with PDF and ePub files available? You can upgrade to the eBook version at www.PacktPub.com and as a print book customer, you are entitled to a discount on the eBook copy. Get in touch with us at customercare@packtpub.com for more details.

At www.PacktPub.com, you can also read a collection of free technical articles, sign up for a range of free newsletters and receive exclusive discounts and offers on Packt books and eBooks.

https://www2.packtpub.com/books/subscription/packtlib

Do you need instant solutions to your IT questions? PacktLib is Packt's online digital book library. Here, you can search, access, and read Packt's entire library of books.

Why subscribe?

- Fully searchable across every book published by Packt
- Copy and paste, print, and bookmark content
- On demand and accessible via a web browser

Table of Contents

Preface

This book is a guide to using the Python scripting language to automate tasks in, and build tools for, Maya. The first two chapters provide an overview of Python scripting in Maya and the basics of UI creation. From there, chapters three through seven each cover a different problem domain, in roughly the same order that they are encountered in real-world projects. We start with modeling, moving through texturing, rigging, animation, and rendering. The last three chapters cover topics needed to flesh out scripts into full tool pipelines, including file input and output and communicating with the world outside of Maya via the Web. In the last chapter, we'll cover a few more advanced topics, such as script nodes and script jobs.

Each chapter provides several examples of how to achieve specific tasks in that domain, will full code listing and explanation. Each example stands on its own, and the reader should feel free to move around within the book as needed.

What this book covers

Chapter 1, Getting Started with Maya, covers the basics of using Maya's script editor and getting set up to write scripts of your own. It also covers the differences between Maya Embedded Language (MEL) and Python. The basic parts of Maya's built-in commands are covered, along with the different modes (create, query, and edit) in which they can be invoked.

Chapter 2, Creating User Interfaces, introduces the reader to creating user interfaces for their scripts. It covers creating windows, adding layouts, and filling them with controls. Nested layouts and custom menus are also explained.

Chapter 3, Working with Geometry, covers using Python to work with geometric data. It starts with how to retrieve information about models, both polygonal and NURBS. It also covers creating new curves and new faces, as well as manipulating existing data to deform a model.

Chapter 4, Giving Things a Coat of Paint – UVs and Materials, deals with getting models ready for rendering, both working with UV data as well as creating and applying shading networks.

Chapter 5, Adding Controls – Scripting for Rigging, covers topics related to using scripting for rigging, including how to create bones and edit their properties. It also covers how to create set-driven key relationships and how to set up inverse kinematics (IK).

Chapter 6, Making Things Move – Scripting for Animation, deals with querying and setting keyframe data to create and modify animation. It also covers copying keyframes from one object to another and using code to create custom expressions.

Chapter 7, Scripting for Rendering, covers topics related to actually generating frames. The examples show how to create lights and cameras, and how to render images. It also covers using the Python Imaging Library (PIL) to combine images after they've been rendered.

Chapter 8, Working with File Input/Output, covers the topics needed to build larger toolchains by importing and exporting custom data. Reading and writing both text-based and binary formats is covered.

Chapter 9, Communicating with the Web, covers how to retrieve information from the Web for use in Maya. The parsing of both XML and JSON data is covered, as well as sending POST data to a website.

Chapter 10, Advanced Topics, covers several more advanced topics, including script jobs and script nodes. It also covers how to create a custom context to make scripts that work more like Maya's built-in tools.

What you need for this book

To get the most out of this book, you'll need a copy of Maya and a programmer-friendly text editor. There are a great number of text editors out there, and many people have strong opinions on which they prefer. At a minimum, you'll want an editor that saves in plain text and offers the option to display line numbers. You'll also likely want an editor that offers syntax highlighting for Python.

All of the code for this book was written using Sublime Text (`https://www.sublimetext.com/`), an excellent and low-cost text editor that is great for Python, as well as many other tasks. You don't have to use that though; any text editor that allows you to edit plain text will work just fine.

Almost all of the examples in the book rely on nothing more than Python and Maya, but there is one example that uses PIL. To install PIL, you'll likely want to use PIP, a package manager that makes installing Python packages easy. You can get that at `https://pip.pypa.io/en/stable/`.

Who this book is for

This book is for anyone that wants to use Python to get more out of Maya. It's expected that you have a decent familiarity with Maya's interface and toolset. Knowledge of Python or other programming languages is helpful, but not required.

Sections

In this book, you will find several headings that appear frequently (Getting ready, How to do it..., How it works..., There's more..., and See also).

To give clear instructions on how to complete a recipe, we use these sections as follows:

Getting ready

This section tells you what to expect in the recipe and describes how to set up any software or any preliminary settings required for the recipe.

How to do it...

This section contains the steps required to follow the recipe.

How it works...

This section usually consists of a detailed explanation of what happened in the previous section.

There's more...

This section consists of additional information about the recipe in order to make the reader more knowledgeable about the recipe.

See also

This section provides helpful links to other useful information for the recipe.

Conventions

In this book, you will find a number of text styles that distinguish between different kinds of information. Here are some examples of these styles and an explanation of their meaning.

Code words in text, database table names, folder names, filenames, file extensions, pathnames, dummy URLs, user input, and Twitter handles are shown as follows: "We can include other contexts through the use of the `include` directive."

A block of code is set as follows:

```
import maya.cmds as cmds

print("Imported the script!")
def makeObject():
    cmds.polyCube()
    print("Made a cube!")
```

New terms and **important words** are shown in bold. Words that you see on the screen, for example, in menus or dialog boxes, appear in the text like this: "Open the script editor by going to **Windows | General Editors | Script Editor**."

 Warnings or important notes appear in a box like this.

 Tips and tricks appear like this.

Reader feedback

Feedback from our readers is always welcome. Let us know what you think about this book—what you liked or disliked. Reader feedback is important for us as it helps us develop titles that you will really get the most out of.

To send us general feedback, simply e-mail `feedback@packtpub.com`, and mention the book's title in the subject of your message.

If there is a topic that you have expertise in and you are interested in either writing or contributing to a book, see our author guide at `www.packtpub.com/authors`.

Customer support

Now that you are the proud owner of a Packt book, we have a number of things to help you to get the most from your purchase.

Downloading the example code

You can download the example code files for this book from your account at `http://www.packtpub.com`. If you purchased this book elsewhere, you can visit `http://www.packtpub.com/support` and register to have the files e-mailed directly to you.

You can download the code files by following these steps:

1. Log in or register to our website using your e-mail address and password.
2. Hover the mouse pointer on the **SUPPORT** tab at the top.
3. Click on **Code Downloads & Errata**.
4. Enter the name of the book in the **Search** box.
5. Select the book for which you're looking to download the code files.
6. Choose from the drop-down menu where you purchased this book from.
7. Click on **Code Download**.

Once the file is downloaded, please make sure that you unzip or extract the folder using the latest version of:

- WinRAR / 7-Zip for Windows
- Zipeg / iZip / UnRarX for Mac
- 7-Zip / PeaZip for Linux

The code bundle for the book is also hosted on GitHub at `https://github.com/PacktPublishing/Maya-Programming-with-Python-Cookbook`. We also have other code bundles from our rich catalog of books and videos available at `https://github.com/PacktPublishing/`. Check them out!

Downloading the color images of this book

We also provide you with a PDF file that has color images of the screenshots/diagrams used in this book. The color images will help you better understand the changes in the output. You can download this file from `http://www.packtpub.com/sites/default/files/downloads/MayaProgrammingwithPythonCookbook_ColorImages.pdf`.

Errata

Although we have taken every care to ensure the accuracy of our content, mistakes do happen. If you find a mistake in one of our books—maybe a mistake in the text or the code—we would be grateful if you could report this to us. By doing so, you can save other readers from frustration and help us improve subsequent versions of this book. If you find any errata, please report them by visiting http://www.packtpub.com/submit-errata, selecting your book, clicking on the **Errata Submission Form** link, and entering the details of your errata. Once your errata are verified, your submission will be accepted and the errata will be uploaded to our website or added to any list of existing errata under the Errata section of that title.

To view the previously submitted errata, go to https://www.packtpub.com/books/content/support and enter the name of the book in the search field. The required information will appear under the **Errata** section.

Piracy

Piracy of copyrighted material on the Internet is an ongoing problem across all media. At Packt, we take the protection of our copyright and licenses very seriously. If you come across any illegal copies of our works in any form on the Internet, please provide us with the location address or website name immediately so that we can pursue a remedy.

Please contact us at copyright@packtpub.com with a link to the suspected pirated material.

We appreciate your help in protecting our authors and our ability to bring you valuable content.

Questions

If you have a problem with any aspect of this book, you can contact us at questions@packtpub.com, and we will do our best to address the problem.

1
Getting Started with Maya

This chapter will cover everything you need to get the most out of the rest of the book, as well as give you a feel for the differences between MEL and Python, as follows:

- ▶ Using the script editor to investigate functionality
- ▶ Running code from the script editor
- ▶ Importing Maya's built-in Python functionality
- ▶ Accessing documentation for a specific command
- ▶ Understanding Create, Query, and Edit flags
- ▶ Adding custom folders to your script path
- ▶ Writing and running an external script
- ▶ Calling a MEL script with Python

Introduction

In this chapter, we'll cover the basics of scripting with Maya and Python. If you've been scripting for Maya for a while, a lot of what's covered will likely be familiar. If you're new to Maya scripting, this chapter will get you set up with everything you'll need to know to get the most out of the rest of the book.

Using the script editor to investigate functionality

The script editor is your primary tool in order to learn about Maya's script-based functionality, as well as a great place to test small snippets of code outside a full script. One of the most useful aspects of the script editor is that it will show you the commands that correspond to the actions that you take within Maya's interface.

This is one of the best ways to learn about the commands involved in your day-to-day Maya tasks. For example, let's use it to find out how to make a polygonal cube with **Maya Embedded Language** (**MEL**):

How to do it...

1. Open the script editor by going to **Windows | General Editors | Script Editor**.

2. You'll likely note that there is a lot of text already displayed, even if you've only recently opened Maya. To make things easier to see, go to **Edit | Clear History** from within the **Script Editor** window's menu.

3. Now try making a polygon cube by holding down space to bring up the hotbox and going to **Create | Polygon Primitives | Cube**.

4. Use the interactive creation tool to specify the poly cube's dimensions.

5. Observe the output in the top half of the script editor. You should see something like the following:

```
setToolTo CreatePolyCubeCtx;
polyCube -ch on -o on -w 5.502056 -h 3.41434 -d 7.451427 -sw 5 -sd
5 -cuv 4 ;
// Result: pCube1 polyCube1 //
```

How it works...

The output that Maya provides is presented as the MEL commands that correspond to the action that you've just taken. That can be a great way to find out which commands you'll need to use in your own scripts. In this case, it's the `polyCube` command, which will create a polygonal cube. Every command in Maya comes in two flavors—the MEL version and the corresponding Python command.

The script editor shows you commands in MEL syntax, which tends to take the form of:

```
commandName -option1Name option1Value -option2Name option2Value;
```

The MEL syntax borrows a lot from batch scripting wherein it relies on strings of option names (generally referred to as "flags") and corresponding values. The corresponding Python command generally has the following syntax:

```
commandName(option1Name=option1Value, option1Name=option1Value)
```

As you can see, the MEL and Python versions are fairly similar, but with some key differences:

- In the MEL version, flag names are indicated with a dash, and their values follow directly after, whereas in Python, options are given with the "optionName=value" syntax
- Python encloses all the flags in parentheses, whereas MEL does not
- MEL requires a semicolon (;) at the end of each line, whereas Python does not

Another big difference between MEL and Python is how they treat whitespace characters (spaces, tabs, and newlines). MEL, like most languages, doesn't care about whitespace; statements are terminated with semicolons, and blocks of code are defined with matched sets of curly brackets.

Python, however, uses whitespace characters to control program flow. This is often one of the strangest things about Python to people who are new to the language, but not to programming. In Python, blocks of code are defined by indentation. You can use either tabs or spaces, but the key thing is that you're consistent. In Python, every time you increase the number of tabs (or spaces) at the start of a line, it's equivalent to adding an opening curly bracket, and every time you decrease that number, it's equivalent to a closing curly bracket. This can often be confusing, as the structure of your program is defined by characters that may not actually be visible. If you're new to Python and having trouble keeping track of your whitespace, you might want to change your editor settings to display whitespace characters. Most programmer-friendly text editors include such an option, and it can be a big help.

The specific list of options for each command can be found in the built-in Python documentation, accessible from within Maya by going to **Help | Python Command Reference**. For most commands, you'll find a long list of options.

To make things even more complicated, every option has both a short name and a long name. For example, the polyCube allows you to specify the number of subdivisions along the X axis. You can use either the long name, "subdivisionsX" or the short name, "sx" to set it.

For example, all of the following will result in the creation of a 1x1x1 polygonal cube with five subdivisions along the X-axis.

The MEL versions are:

```
polyCube -sx 5;
polyCube -subdivisionsX 5;
```

The Python versions are:

```
maya.cmds.polyCube(sx=5)
maya.cmds.polyCube(subdivsionsX=5)
```

Feel free to use either the short or long version for your arguments. You can also mix and match, using short names for some arguments and long names for others.

In practice, it's generally best to use short names for common arguments (ones that you're likely to remember) and long names for more obscure / more rarely used arguments. Remember that just because your code seems completely sensible to you right now, it may look confusing when you revisit it 6 months (or 6 years!) from now. Make it easy for your future self by using long names (and including comments) when necessary.

There's more...

You may be wondering why Maya offers two different methods for scripting, MEL and Python. That's a simple case of backwards compatibility. MEL came first and was available in Maya long before Python support was added. Back then, you had to use MEL for day-to-day tasks, and if that couldn't provide you with what you needed, you had to dive into the C++ API (which was quite involved and hard to work with on non-Windows systems). Python unites both approaches, but MEL is still supported to allow older scripts to work. It's also possible that you might get better performance with MEL than with Python, as the Python functionality is a wrapper around MEL. Python is a much nicer language to work with though, so it's generally a worthwhile trade-off.

Note that the script editor doesn't (by default) show you everything that you do. Under normal circumstances, Maya shows you a slightly filtered output based on what you are most likely to be interested in. This is usually a good thing, but there are times when you'll want to disable it. To show *all* the output, go to the script editor and select **History | Echo all Commands**. This will cause Maya to output *everything* to the script editor. This generally means much, much more output than you want, but can sometimes be helpful. In practice, you'll generally want to leave that option off except when you're trying to replicate a given piece of functionality in a script, and the default output isn't giving you any insight into what Maya is doing.

See also

If you have Maya setup to use interactive mode for the creation of primitive shapes, you must have seen the following in the output presented in the Script Editor:

```
setToolTo CreatePolyCubeCtx;
```

Contexts are an alternative way of getting input from the user, and we'll have more to say about them in *Chapter 10, Advanced Topics*.

Running code from the script editor

Not only is the Script Editor a great way to see which commands correspond to the actions you take in Maya's UI, but it is also a convenient way to write small bits of code. While you will certainly want to use a text editor to write your scripts, it is still important to be comfortable using the script editor to run small sections of code, either to test it out before inclusion in a larger script or to get more information about the current scene.

Getting ready

Make sure that you have the script editor open and that you've switched to the Python tab in the input (bottom) section.

How to do it...

Type the following into the input section:

```
import maya.cmds

maya.cmds.polyCube()
```

Once you've done that, execute it by either pressing the Execute button at the top of the Script Editor or just by pressing *Control + Enter*.

Your code will disappear from the input section, a new polygon cube will be created, and the results will be pasted into the output ("History") section of the script editor.

To keep your code from disappearing automatically, highlight it first with Command-A (to select everything), then press *Command + Enter*. This will cause Maya to run just the selected code without clearing out the input section.

How it works...

Although the `polyCube` command does the actual work, we have to first import the Maya library for Python before we can use it. To do this, we have to first use `import maya.cmds`.

The script editor is a great way to try out small snippets of code, but the fact that successful code is deleted can get rather frustrating. For any real script development, you'll want to use a programmer-friendly text editor.

There's more...

One handy thing about the script editor is that you can save code from the editor to the shelf. To do this, enter some code into the input section, then go to **File | Save Script to Shelf...** from the **Script Editor** menu. Maya will ask you to provide a name for the script and then (after a bit of time), a new button will appear in the "Custom" shelf. Pressing that button will execute the corresponding code.

Although most of your scripting work will involve writing separate scripts, it can sometimes be useful to copy-paste commands from the history (top) section of the Script Editor to the input (bottom) section and save it all to the shelf. This is a bit like recording an action in Photoshop and can be a quick and dirty way to create a new shortcut for commonly used functionality.

Importing Maya's built-in Python functionality

Python is a really useful language, but it doesn't actually offer that much out of the box other than some basic commands for manipulating simple data. In order to do truly interesting things, you'll generally need to extend Python's built-in functionality with one or more libraries, including the one that provides access to Maya's functionality.

How to do it...

First, let's import the main Maya scripting library for Python, `maya.cmds`:

```
import maya.cmds as cmds
```

Once we've done that, we can use `cmds` instead of `maya.cmds`. For example, if we have this code:

```
maya.cmds.polyCube()
```

We can instead use the following:

```
cmds.polyCube()
```

That might seem like a minor change, but in the course of a full script, it can save you a great deal of typing. Less typing means fewer typos, so it's well worth doing.

Now that we've done this, let's see what cmds has to offer by listing its contents. Python offers a handy way to display the contents of any object via the `dir()` command. Let's use that to get a list of all the commands in `maya.cmds`:

```
commandList = dir(cmds)
for command in commandList:
    print(command)
```

Run the preceding code, and you'll see a long list of everything defined in the maya.cmds library. This will be an extensive list, indeed. Most of the commands you'll see are covered in the official docs, but it's good to know how to use dir to investigate a given library.

You can also use dir to investigate a specific command. For example, try the following code:

```
props = dir(cmds.polyCube)
for prop in props:
    print(prop)
```

Run the preceding code, and you'll see all of the properties for the polyCube command itself. However, the results will likely look a bit odd in that none of them have anything to do with generating a polygonal cube. That's because `maya.cmds.[commandName]` is a built-in function. So, if you use `dir()` to investigate it further, you'll just see the capabilities that are common to Python functions. For details on the specifics of a command, consult the built-in documentation for Maya's commands, which can be accessed by going to **Help | Maya Scripting Reference | Python Command Reference**.

How it works...

Like any other specific subdomain of Python functionality, the commands that expose Maya's toolset to Python are part of a library. In order to make use of them, you have to first import the library. Virtually, every script you write will require the "maya.cmds" library, and you will likely need to include additional libraries occasionally for additional capabilities, such as communicating with a webserver or reading in a particular file format.

Although you could just leave it at `import maya.cmds`, that would require a lot of additional typing. By using the `import [library] as [shortName]` syntax, you can tell Python to use a custom name as an alias for `maya.cmds`. You could use almost any name you want (`import maya.cmds as MyUncleFred` would work just fine), but in practice, you want to use something both short and descriptive. You'll also want to make sure that you don't overwrite any of Python's built-in libraries. For example, you *could* do the following:

```
import maya.cmds as math
```

This would rename `maya.cmds` as math and cause trouble if you wanted to use any of the functions defined in the math library. Don't do that.

For the sake of this book and consistency with Maya's documentation, we will be using "cmds" as the shorthand for "maya.cmds".

There's more...

The maya.cmds library is only one of several libraries that can be used to interface Maya with Python. One of the great things about Python support in Maya is that the old way of doing things, where there was both MEL (for day-to-day tasks) and the C++ API (for larger scale plugins), is unified under the banner of Python. The `maya.cmds` library handles the MEL component, but for functions previously accessed through the C++ API, you'll want to use maya.OpenMaya instead.

It (maya.cmds) is a lightweight wrapper around the MEL commands that many Maya users have grown accustomed to, and it has the benefit of being officially supported by Autodesk. However, it is not the only way to access MEL commands. There is also a third-party library, PyMEL (accessed by importing `pymel.core`). PyMEL has the benefit of being more "Pythonic" and offering nicer syntax, but is not directly supported by Autodesk. It also introduces additional layers of abstraction on top of the built-in functionality, which can lead to poorer performance.

Accessing documentation for a specific command

Maya is a complex tool, and it offers a wide range of functionality, all of it with corresponding commands that can be invoked via scripts. Each command has its own set of arguments, ranging from easily understood to quite cryptic.

When writing scripts for Maya (and as with any other kind of programming), it is vital to be able to find the appropriate documentation and to understand how to make sense of it.

How to do it...

Let's say that we want more information on a specific command, say the command to create a polygonal cube.

One way to view the help for the command is to use Maya's web-based command help, available by going to **Help | Python Command Reference** from within Maya. From there, you can either click on the "Polygons" subsection or use the search box.

There are a couple of other ways to get to the documentation for a command, though. You can also go directly to the documentation for a command from the Script Editor window. First, execute the corresponding action using Maya's interface, such as invoking the hotbox and choosing **Create | Polygon Primitives | Cube**.

That will cause the corresponding MEL command to be displayed in the output section of the **Script Editor**, in this case, "polyCube". From within the script editor, highlight the relevant line, and go to **Help | Help on Selected Command**. This will bring up a browser window with the documentation for that command. Note that it will default to the MEL version of the command; for the Python version, click on the "Python" link in the top-right corner of the window.

Finally, you can retrieve information about a command via Python directly using the help command. Try running the following:

```
print(cmds.help('polyCube'))
```

This will result in a list of the flags available for the given command, as well as the type of value that Maya expects for each, such as:

```
-sx -subdivisionsX        Int
```

This means that there is a flag named "sx" or "subdivisionsX" that expects an integer value.

How it works...

For the most part, you'll want just the Python command reference open in a browser window while you work on developing your scripts. Good reference documents are key to writing good software, and you should get used to just keeping the references close at hand.

There's more...

You can also use the help command to invoke the web-based documentation for a given command directly, such as:

```
cmds.help('polyCube', doc=True, language='python')
```

This would bring up the web page containing the documentation for the Python version of the polyCube command. That's definitely a clunky way to access the help, but might be useful if you wanted to give the users of your script an easy way to refer to relevant documentation directly from your script's user interface.

Understanding Create, Query, and Edit flags

One thing that is a bit strange about Maya scripting is that the same command can be used in up to three different ways—create, query, and edit modes—with the specifics varying for each of the command flags. This is a byproduct of the fact that the Python functionality is a wrapper around the older MEL-based scripting system, and it can seem a bit confusing when you're getting started. Nevertheless, it is important to understand the differences between the three modes and how to use them.

Getting ready

Open up the Python command reference by going to **Help** | **Python Command Reference** and navigate to the documentation for the polyCube command.

Also, be sure to have the script editor open in Maya and be in the Python tab. Alternatively, you can run the example commands Maya's command line; just make sure that you're running in Python mode rather than MEL (click on **MEL** to switch to Python and **Python** to switch back to MEL).

How to do it...

First off, take a look at the Properties column. You'll see that every flag has some combination of "C", "E", "Q", and "M" listed. Those refer to the different ways in which a command can be run and have the following meanings:

- ▶ **C**: "Create" flag is only relevant when first running the command, such as when you initially create a polygonal primitive
- ▶ **Q**: "Query" flag can be queried after the command has been run and can be used to retrieve information about something in the scene
- ▶ **E**: "Edit" flag can be edited after the fact
- ▶ **M**: "Multiple" flag can be used more than once in a single instance of the command (to create specify multiple points when creating a curve, for example)

For many flags, you'll see a full complement of create, query, and edit, but there are generally at least a few flags that aren't accessible for one or more of the modes.

Let's see how create, edit, and query play out in the case of the polyCube command.

First off, let's make a new cube and store the result in a variable, so we can make use of it later:

```
myCube = cmds.polyCube()
```

Now, let's change something about the cube, post-creation by using the edit mode:

```
cmds.polyCube(myCube, edit=True, subdivisionsX=5)
```

This will cause the cube that we created with the first command to be altered from the default (no subdivisions in the x axis) to having five.

Now, let's use the query mode to store the new number of divisions to a variable:

```
numberDivisions = cmds.polyCube(myCube, query=True,
subdivisionsX=True)
print(numberDivisions)
```

You should see "5.0" as the output. Note that even though the number of divisions of a polygonal cube must be an integer value, Maya is displaying it as "5.0".

How it works...

The important thing to note for the query and edit modes is that you run the command as you normally would (cmds.polyCube, for example), but with the following three key differences:

▸ The inclusion of the name of the object as the first argument. This can either be the name directly as a string ("pCube1", for example), or a variable.

▸ The inclusion of either edit=True or query=True as an argument.

▸ Additional arguments, with the specifics based on whether you're running the command in the query or edit mode.

For the edit mode, you'll want to specify the name of the property you want to change, along with the new value. For the query mode, you'll want to just include the name of the property and "=True". Think of this as saying that it is True that you want to know the value of the property. Note that you can only query a single flag at a time. If you need to query multiple values, run the command multiple times, changing the flag you pass in.

There's more...

Although many of the most-used properties can be used in all three modes, there are numerous examples of ones that cannot be, mainly because it wouldn't make sense to do so. For example, it's perfectly reasonable to set construction history on or off when creating a new object, and it's certainly reasonable to query that after the fact, but what would it mean to use the edit mode to enable construction history on an object that didn't already have it? That would require rebuilding the history of the object, which may have been manipulated in various ways since it was created. As a result, the "constructionHistory" (or "ch") flag only offers the Create and Query options.

You might think that this is all a bit clunky, and if all we wanted to do was set the number of subdivisions for a newly created cube, you would be correct. However, it's important to understand the different command modes, both to get information after the fact and because it's an important part of building user interface elements and getting information from them.

See also

We'll be making the extensive use of the Query mode to retrieve information from user interface elements throughout the rest of the book, starting in *Chapter 2, Creating User Interfaces*.

Adding custom folders to your script path

In order to write reusable scripts, you'll want to save your scripts to external files, and in order to do *that*, you'll need to make sure that Maya knows where they are.

How to do it...

Maya maintains a list of locations to search for scripts, used when you use the import (Python) or source (MEL) commands. If you want to see the full list, you can do so with the following code:

```
import sys

pathList = sys.path
for path in pathList:
    print(path)
```

This will provide you with a list of paths, including the following:

```
/Users/[username]/Library/Preferences/Autodesk/maya/[maya version]/
prefs/scripts
/Users/[username]/Library/Preferences/Autodesk/maya/[maya version]/
scripts
/Users/[username]/Library/Preferences/Autodesk/maya/scripts
```

Saving your scripts to any of those folders will allow Maya to find them. If you're fine with saving all of your scripts to one of those folders, that's totally fine.

However, you might want to add additional folders to the list. For example, you might want to save your scripts in a folder within the my Documents directory, maybe something like:

```
/Users/adrian/Documents/MayaScripting/examples/
```

Note that this is a typical example on Macintosh. On a Windows machine, it would look more like:

```
\Documents and Settings\[username]\MyDocuments\MayaScripting\examples
```

Either way, we'll need to tell Maya to look there to find scripts to execute. There are a few ways we could do it, but in keeping with the theme of the book, we'll do it using Python.

Run the following code in the script editor:

```
import sys
sys.path.append('/Users/adrian/Documents/MayaScripting/examples')
```

This is done by replacing /Users/adrian/Documents/MayaScripting/examples with whatever folder you want to use.

Once you've done this, you'll be able to import scripts stored in that directory as well. However, having to enter the preceding code every time you launch Maya would be quite frustrating. Luckily, Maya provides a way for us to execute custom Python code on a startup.

To make the code execute every time Maya opens, save it to a file named userSetup.py and save it to the following location for a Mac:

```
~/Library/Preferences/Autodesk/maya/<version>/scripts
```

Or for Windows, you can save it to:

```
<drive>:\Documents and Settings\<username>\My Documents\
maya\<version>\scripts
```

How it works...

All of the code contained in userSetup.py will be run every time Maya starts up.

While the base list of paths that Maya will search for scripts is not altered by the above, it will cause Maya to add your custom folder to the list every time it starts up, which in practice amounts to the same thing.

There's more...

You can also add to your paths by creating the Maya.env file and saving it to the following location (on a Mac machine):

```
/Users/<username>/Library/Preferences/Autodesk/maya/version
```

or

```
/Users/<username>/Library/Preferences/Autodesk/maya
```

On a Windows machine, save it to:

```
drive:\Documents and Settings\username\My Documents\maya\version
```

or

```
drive:\Documents and Settings\username\My Documents\maya
```

For the specifics of the `Maya.env` file syntax, consult Maya's documentation. However, editing `Maya.env` can lead to crashes and system instability if you're not careful, so I recommend relying on `userSetup.py` instead.

Writing and running an external script

In this recipe, we'll be writing and running our first actual script as an external Python file.

Getting ready

The Script Editor window is a bit of a misnomer. Although it's a great way to test out short snippets of code, it's awkward to use for any kind of real script development. For this, you'll want to have a programmer-friendly text editor setup. There are a ton of options out there, and if you're reading this book, you likely already have one that you like to use. Whatever it is, make sure that it's geared towards writing code, and it saves files in plain text.

How to do it...

First off, we'll need a script. Create a new file in your editor and add the following code:

```
import maya.cmds as cmds

print("Imported the script!")
def makeObject():
    cmds.polyCube()
    print("Made a cube!")
```

Now save the script as `myScript.py`. Once you've done that, switch back to Maya and run the following from either the script editor or the command line:

```
import myScript
```

This will cause Maya to read in the file, and you'll see the following in the script editor output:

```
Imported the script!
```

What you will not see, however, is a new cube. That's because the real functionality of our (simple) script is defined within a function named "makeObject".

Maya treats each Python file that you import as its own module, with the name of the file providing the name of the module. Once we've imported a file, we can invoke functions within it by calling [moduleName].[function name]. For the earlier-mentioned example, this would mean:

```
myScript.makeObject()
```

Run it, and you should see a newly minted cube show up, and "Made a cube!" in the output of the Script Editor.

Now, let's try changing our script. First, delete the cube we just made, then switch over to your text editor, and change the script to the following:

```
import maya.cmds as cmds

def makeObject():
    cmds.polySphere()
    print("Made a sphere!")
```

Switch back to Maya and run the script again with:

```
myScript.makeObject()
```

You'll see that rather than having a nice sphere, we still ended up with a cube. That's because when you ask Maya to execute a script that it has already executed, it will default to rerunning the same code that it ran previously. In order to ensure that we get the latest, greatest version of our script, we'll need to first run the following:

```
reload(myScript)
```

This will force Maya to reload the file. Note that the argument to reload isn't the file name itself (myScript.py in this case), but rather the name of the module that the file defines ("myScript").

Once you've done this, you can once again try:

```
myScript.makeObject()
```

This time, you'll see a proper polygonal sphere, just as we intended.

How it works...

It may seem like an unnecessary extra step to both import the script and call one of its functions, and you can indeed have the script automatically execute code (as demonstrated by the call to print("Imported Script!"). However, it's much better practice to wrap all of your functionality in functions, as it makes large scripts much easier to work with.

If you have functionality that you want to execute every time the script is run, it is best to define a function with a name like "main" and have the last line of your script invoke it. Take a look at the following example:

```
import maya.cmds as cmds

def makeObject():
    cmds.polyCube()
    print("Made a cube!")

makeObject()
```

This would define the `makeObject()` function, then (on the last line of the script) cause it to be executed.

When working on a script, it can get really tedious to reload, import, and run the script each time. An easy way to get around that is to enter the following into the script editor:

```
import myScript
reload(myScript)
myScript.myCommand()
```

Once you've done that, use **File | Save Script to Shelf...** to give yourself a button to easily rerun the latest version of your script. Note that the preceding code contains both import and reload. That's to make sure that the code will work both the first time you run it as well as successive times. The "import" command is there to ensure the module has been loaded at least once (necessary for a new script, or upon restarting Maya), and the "reload" command is there to ensure that what we're running is the latest version (necessary if we've made changes to the script with Maya still up).

There's more...

If you have a script that defines a lot of functionality, and you don't want to constantly type out the module name, you can use the same trick we used with `maya.cmds` to shorten things a bit. Namely, you can use the "as" syntax to provide a shorter name. For example, I could have done the following:

```
import myScript as ms
ms.makeObject()
```

This would have exactly the same effect.

Calling a MEL script with Python

Maya offers two different languages with which to create custom functionality via scripting—both Maya Embedded Language (MEL) scripts and Python. In practice, you'll only want to use one, and of the two, Python offers a much better and more flexible experience.

However, it is not uncommon to have legacy scripts that were written back before Maya added Python functionality. While the "right" solution would be to rewrite the scripts using Python, there's not always enough time to do so. In those cases, it can sometimes be helpful to be able to call out to legacy, MEL-based functionality from within your Python scripts.

Getting ready

Although Python is definitely the better way to create new functionality, it may sometimes be the case that you have older scripts that were written in MEL that you would like to incorporate.

The best option is to rewrite the script in Python, but if the script is complex or you don't have time, it may be easier to just invoke the MEL functionality from within a Python script. This way, you can incorporate legacy functionality without completely reinventing the wheel.

How to do it...

For this recipe, you'll need the MEL script. If you don't have one handy, open up a new file and enter the following:

```
global proc myMELScript()
{
    polyCube;
    print("Hello from MEL!");
}
```

Save this as `myMELScript.mel` in your `maya/scripts` directory. Although we won't be going into the details of MEL, do note that the file has the same name as the function that we're defining. Most MEL scripts will follow that convention. Also note the inclusion of semicolons after the end of each line. Although Python doesn't require them, MEL (and many other languages) does.

Once you have that, create a new file and name it `runMEL.py`. Enter the following:

```
import maya.cmds as cmds
import maya.mel as mel

def runMEL():
    print("Running MEL from Python")
    mel.eval("source myMELScript;")
    mel.eval("myMELScript;")

runMEL()
```

Save the script and run it with:

```
import runMEL
```

Because the last line of our script invokes the runMEL command, it will automatically take effect. You should see a new cube, as well as the following output in the Script Editor:

```
Running MEL from Python
Hello from MEL!
```

How it works...

In this example, we imported both maya.cmds and maya.mel. The maya.mel library provides support to interface Python with MEL, with one of its most useful commands being the eval function, which takes an arbitrary string and attempts to run it as an MEL command. In the earlier example, we do that twice, with the first command being:

```
source myMEL;
```

The source command does the same thing as reload, in that it ensures that Maya will reread the entire source file, rather than rerunning a potentially outdated version. This shouldn't matter because it's only necessary if you're making changes to the MEL script (and hopefully you're not doing that, use Python instead!) but it's a good thing to include just in case.

Once we've done this, we actually run the MEL script with:

```
myMEL;
```

2
Creating User Interfaces

In this chapter, we'll be taking a guided tour through Maya's collection of user interface elements and learning how to use them to create interfaces that you and your teammates will love to use. The following topics will be covered:

- ► Making a basic window
- ► Simple controls – making a button
- ► Retrieving input from controls
- ► Using classes to organize UI logic
- ► Using nested layouts
- ► Using tabs and scrolling
- ► Adding menu to your UIs

Introduction

While it is by no means required to create a graphical user interface (GUI) for your scripts, you're likely to want one in almost all cases. Very often, you'll find yourself creating scripts that are meant to be used by your teammates, some of whom may be less comfortable with command-line tools.

In this chapter, we'll be looking at how to create windows, fill them with interface elements, and link those elements up to other functionality within Maya.

Making a basic window

All great user interfaces start with window. In this example, we'll be creating a simple window and using the text label control to add a simple message.

We'll end up with something like the following:

How to do it...

Start by creating a new file in your scripts directory and naming it basic `Window.py`.

Add the following code:

```
import maya.cmds as cmds

def showUI():
    myWin = cmds.window(title="Simple Window", widthHeight=(300, 200))
    cmds.columnLayout()
    cmds.text(label="Hello, Maya!")

    cmds.showWindow(myWin)

showUI()
```

If you run the script, you should see a small window containing the text **Hello, Maya!**.

How it works...

To create a window, you'll need to use the window command.

```
myWin = cmds.window(title="Simple Window", widthHeight=(300, 200))
```

While all of the arguments are optional, there are a few that you'll generally want to include by default. Here, we're setting the title to "Simple Window" and the size of the window to 300 pixels wide by 200 pixels tall. Also note that we save the result of the command to a variable, myWin. This is necessary in order to use the showWindow command. More on that in a bit.

There is also one more requirement, that is, in order to add an element to a window, you must first specify a layout. Layouts are responsible for arranging items within a given area (either a window or another layout). If you fail to provide Maya with a layout, it won't be able to properly position any controls you add, and your script will error out. In this example, we're using a columnLayout, which will arrange all the controls we add in a single vertical column. We add a layout to the window with the following:

```
cmds.columnLayout()
```

Once we've created a window and specified a layout, we can start adding controls. In this case, we're using the text control that merely adds some text to the window. While you won't generally use text controls by themselves (it's far more common to use them next to other controls to provide labels or descriptive text), it serves as a good example of a typical, albeit simple, control.

```
cmds.text(label="Hello, Maya!")
```

At this point, we're done with our interface, but creating a window will not actually show anything in Maya. To have it shown up in Maya's interface, we'll also need to explicitly show it using the showWindow command. The reason for this is that you generally don't want to show a window until it has all of the controls and other UI elements you want it to have. However, in order to create a control, you must first have a window to add them to. Maya solves this by having you:

1. Create the window.
2. Add your controls.
3. Show the window once all of the controls have been added.

This is why, it was important to save the result of the window() command to a variable, so that we can tell Maya which window it should show to the user. Putting that together gives us the last line of our showUI function:

```
cmds.showWindow(myWin)
```

There's more...

Note that once a layout is created, it becomes the active context in order to add controls. You can certainly have multiple layouts in a single window (and even nest them within each other), but there is always exactly one current layout to which Maya will insert newly created controls.

One problem with this example is that running the script multiple times will result in multiple copies of the window, which is usually not what you want. For most purposes, you'll want to ensure that there is only ever a single instance of your UI open at any one time.

To do this, we'll need to:

  ▶ Choose a unique name for our window
  ▶ Before creating the window, check to see whether one already exists with that name
  ▶ If there's already a window by that name, delete it
  ▶ Create the window using the window command, passing in the name

When choosing a name, make sure that it's something that is unlikely to conflict with other scripts the user might be using. Generic names such as `"MyWindow"` or `"MainWindow"` are likely to cause conflicts; it is much better to have something unique like `"CharacterRigControl"`. To make it even better, add your initials, or the initials of your company to the start of the name (`"ahCharacterRig"`, for example). Note that the name (which is not shown to the user) is distinct from the title (which is), so it's perfectly fine to have a long or unwieldy name. Just make sure that it's unique.

Once you have a name, we'll want to start off by testing to see if a window by that name exists. We can do that with the window command and the `exists` flag. If we *do* find that a window of that name exists, we'll want to get rid of it with the `deleteUI` command:

```
if (cmds.window("ahExampleWindow", exists=True)):
    cmds.deleteUI("ahExampleWindow")
```

Finally, when we create a new window, we'll make sure to pass in our desired name as the first argument, which will give the window the desired name.

```
myWin = cmds.window("ahExampleWindow", title="Simple Window",
    widthHeight=(300, 200))
```

Alternatively, we could just stop the script if there's already a window with the given name, but the previously mentioned approach is more common. If the user invokes your script, they likely want to start with a fresh slate, so replacing the old window is often the best option.

Simple controls – making a button

Creating a window is only the beginning. In order to create a proper interface, we'll need to both add controls, and tie them to functionality. In this example, we'll be revisiting our good friend, the `polyCube` command, and tying it to a button press.

The resulting UI (and its output) will look similar to the following:

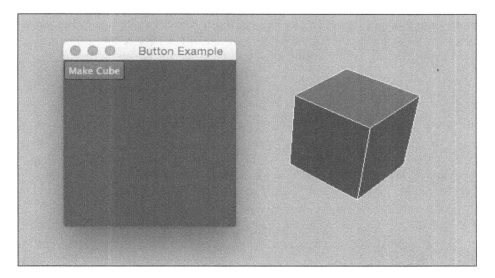

How to do it...

Create a new script and name it `buttonExample.py`. Add the following code:

```
import maya.cmds as cmds
def buttonFunction(args):
    cmds.polyCube()

def showUI():
    myWin = cmds.window(title="Button Example", widthHeight=(200,
200))
    cmds.columnLayout()
    cmds.button(label="Make Cube", command=buttonFunction)
    cmds.showWindow(myWin)
showUI()
```

Run the script, and you should see a 200 by 200 pixel window with a single button inside it. Pushing the button will create a polygonal cube with the default parameters.

How it works...

In order to trigger functionality from our UI, we'll first need to create a function to contain the functionality we want to trigger. We do that in our `buttonFunction` function:

```
def buttonFunction(*args):
    cmds.polyCube()
```

In this case, all we're doing is creating a polygonal cube. Note that the function accepts arguments, even though we aren't making use of them. That's actually necessary, since when Maya triggers a function from a control, it passes information to the respective function. Assume that we write the function without arguments, as follows:

```
def buttonFunction():
    cmds.polyCube()
```

We would get the following error when we attempted to run our script:

```
# Error: buttonFunction() takes no arguments (1 given)
```

There are situations where we'll want to make use of the information that gets passed in, but even if we fully intend to ignore it, we *must* write our UI-driven functions to accept arguments.

The `*args` syntax is a bit of handy Python that allows for a variable number of arguments to be passed in. Technically, all that really matters is the `*`; `*myEpicCollectionOfArguments` would work just as well, but `*args` is the general convention.

Once we have the function we want to trigger, we set up a window in the conventional way, creating it and adding a `columnLayout`:

```
def showUI():
    myWin = cmds.window(title="Button Example", widthHeight=(200,
200))
    cmds.columnLayout()
```

Next, we add the button itself with:

```
cmds.button(label="Make Cube", command=buttonFunction)
```

This is pretty straightforward—we set the text that appears within the button with the `label` argument, and we set the command to execute when it is pressed with the `command` (or "c") argument. Note that there are no parentheses after the name of the function. That's because we're not actually invoking the function; we're just passing the function itself in as the value for the command flag. We include parentheses, as in:

```
cmds.button(label="Make Cube", command=buttonFunction())     #
(usually) a bad idea
```

This would result in the function being invoked, and its return value (rather than the function itself) being used as the value of the flag. That's almost certainly not what you want. The only exception is if you happen to have a function that creates a function and returns it, which can be useful in some situations.

All that's left is to show our window in the normal way with:

```
cmds.showWindow(myWin)
```

There's more...

While this is the most common way to use buttons, there are a few other options that can be useful in specific circumstances.

For example, the `enable` flag can be a great way to prevent the user from taking action that they shouldn't be able to and to provide feedback. Let's say that we've created a button, but it shouldn't be active until the user takes some other action. If we set the enable flag to False, the button will appear grayed out and will not respond to the user input:

```
myButton = cmds.button(label="Not Yet", enable=False)
```

Later, you can make the button (or other control) active by using the edit mode to set the enable flag to True, as in the following:

```
cmds.button(myButton, edit=True, enable=True)
```

Keeping controls inactive, until it's appropriate to call them, can be a great way to make your scripts a bit more robust and easier to use.

Retrieving input from controls

While you will often need to add one-way controls (such as buttons) that trigger functions upon user input, you will also often need to retrieve information from the user before taking an action. In this example, we'll be looking at how to grab input from field controls, in both integer and float varieties.

The finished script will create a given number of polygonal spheres, each with a given radius. The resulting UI will look like the following:

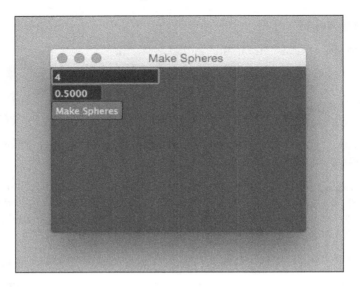

Pressing the **Make Spheres** button with the previously mentioned settings of 4 spheres at a radius of 0.5 units each will result in a line of spheres along the x-axis:

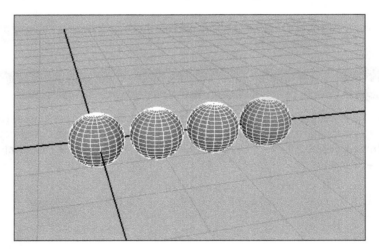

How to do it...

Create a new script and name it `makeSpheres.py`. Add the following code:

```python
import maya.cmds as cmds

global sphereCountField
global sphereRadiusField

def showUI():
    global sphereCountField
    global sphereRadiusField

    myWin = cmds.window(title="Make Spheres", widthHeight=(300, 200))
    cmds.columnLayout()
    sphereCountField = cmds.intField(minValue=1)
    sphereRadiusField = cmds.floatField(minValue=0.5)
    cmds.button(label="Make Spheres", command=makeSpheres)
    cmds.showWindow(myWin)

def makeSpheres(*args):
    global sphereCountField
    global sphereRadiusField

    numSpheres = cmds.intField(sphereCountField, query=True,
value=True)
    myRadius = cmds.floatField(sphereRadiusField, query=True,
value=True)

    for i in range(numSpheres):
        cmds.polySphere(radius=myRadius)
        cmds.move((i * myRadius * 2.2), 0, 0)

showUI()
```

Run the script, enter some values into the two fields, and click on the button. You should see a nice orderly line of polygonal spheres running along the x-axis.

How it works...

There are a few different things going on here, all of which are needed to grab information from the user. First, we create two variables to hold global references to our controls.

```
import maya.cmds as cmds

sphereCountField
sphereRadiusField
```

We need variables for the fields since we'll need to call the corresponding functions twice—once in the create mode (to make the control) and again in the query mode to determine what the current value is. We'll also want to make those variables global in scope so that we can have separate functions to create UI and actually perform the action.

The "scope" of a variable or a function refers to the context in which it is defined. If a variable is defined outside of any function, it is *global* in scope, meaning that it is always accessible. Variables defined within a function, however, are *local*, meaning that they only exist within the function in which they are defined. Since we need to refer to our controls from two different functions, we'll need to make sure that they are global in scope.

It isn't strictly necessary to have the variables declared at the top of the script as I've done here. We *could* just refer to them in the individual functions, and as long as we're careful to include the global keyword, it would still work.

However, I think that it makes things much easier to understand if we declare all our global variables at the start.

Next, we set up UI for the window. Note that we repeat the lines that we used to declare the global variables. This is necessary to tell Python that we want to use the global scope variables:

```
def showUI():
    global sphereCountField
    global sphereRadiusField
```

If we left out the `global sphereCountField`, we would still end up with a variable named `sphereCountField` set to the output of the intField command. However, that variable would be of local scope and only available from within the `showUI()` function.

In this case, `global sphereCountField` can almost be thought of as an import statement because it brings the global variable into the scope of the showUI function. We do the same thing in the `makeSpheres` function to make sure that we use the same variable.

Next, we set up a window as we've done in the past, with the `window()` and `columnLayout()` commands:

```
myWin = cmds.window(title="Make Spheres", widthHeight=(300, 200))
cmds.columnLayout()
```

Once we've done this, we can use two fields to collect input from the user. Since the number of spheres should always be a whole number value, and we should always make at least one sphere, we use an `intField` and set the minimum value to 1:

```
sphereCountField = cmds.intField(minValue=1)
```

For the radius of the spheres, we'll want to allow for non-integer values, but we likely want to ensure a reasonable minimum size. To do this, we create a `floatField` with a minimum value of 0.5. We have the following code:

```
sphereRadiusField = cmds.floatField(minValue=0.5)
```

Finally, we add a button to trigger the creation of the spheres and show the window with the `showWindow()` command.

Moving to the function to create the spheres, we start by (once again) telling Python that we want to make use of our two global variables, as follows:

```
def makeSpheres(*args):
    global sphereCountField
    global sphereRadiusField
```

Once we've done this, we retrieve the current values of the `intField` and `floatField`. In both cases, we do that by rerunning the same command that we used to create the control, but with the following differences:

1. We pass the name of the control (saved when we created it) as the first argument.
2. We set `query=True` to indicate to Maya that we want to retrieve information about the control.
3. We set `value=True` to indicate that the specific attribute that we want to retrieve is the control's value.

Putting that all together give us the following:

```
numSpheres = cmds.intField(sphereCountField, query=True, value=True)
myRadius = cmds.floatField(sphereRadiusField, query=True, value=True)
```

It may seem better to combine the two lines into the following:

```
global numSpheres = cmds.intField(sphereCountField, query=True,
value=True)
```

However, that doesn't actually work, owing to the way that Python works with global variables. Python requires that the declaration of a global variable remains separate from any commands that set the value of the variable.

Once we know how many spheres to create and how big to make each of them, we use a for loop to make and position them:

```
for i in range(numSpheres):
    cmds.polySphere(radius=myRadius)
    cmds.move((i * myRadius * 2.2), 0, 0)
```

For loops allow you to repeat the same code multiple times. Python implements them slightly differently than most other languages in which they always iterate over a list of some kind. This means that if we want to do something X times, we have to have a list of X items. For this, we'll want the built-in `range()` function. By passing `numSpheres` into `range()`, we are asking Python to create a list of numbers that starts at 0 and goes up to (numSpheres-1). We can then use that list with the for keyword to set our index variable (i) to each of the values in our list, which in this case means stepping from 0 to (numSpheres-1).

Note that we set the radius of each sphere with the radius flag. We also use the move function to separate each sphere from its neighbors by slightly more than their diameters (myRadius * 2.2). By default, the move command will affect the currently selected object (or objects). Since the `polySphere` command leaves the created sphere as the only selected object, that's what we'll move.

By default, the move command will accept three numbers for the amount by which to move the selected object(s)—one for each of the axes. There are a number of other ways that the move command can be used; be sure to check the documentation for details.

Using classes to organize UI logic

Using global variables is one way to allow the different parts of your script communicate with each other, but there's a better way. Instead of using globals, you can organize your script using custom class.

Creating a class for your script will not only allow you to easily access UI elements from various functions, but it will also make it easy to neatly contain other kinds of data, useful in more advanced scripts.

How to do it...

Create a new script and name it `SpheresClass.py`. Add the following code:

```python
import maya.cmds as cmds

class SpheresClass:

    def __init__(self):
        self.win = cmds.window(title="Make Spheres",
widthHeight=(300,200))
        cmds.columnLayout()
        self.numSpheres = cmds.intField(minValue=1)
        cmds.button(label="Make Spheres", command=self.makeSpheres)
        cmds.showWindow(self.win)

    def makeSpheres(self, *args):
        number = cmds.intField(self.numSpheres, query=True,
value=True)
        for i in range(0,number):
            cmds.polySphere()
            cmds.move(i*2.2, 0, 0)

SpheresClass()
```

Run the script, and you should get a window that allows you to create a line of polygonal spheres along the x-axis.

How it works...

The overall layout of the script is similar to what we've done before, in that we have one function to set up the interface and another function to actually perform the work. However, in this case, we wrap everything in a class, with:

```python
class SpheresClass:
```

Note that the name of the class has been capitalized, which may seem odd, given that all of our functions have been lowercase so far. Although that's by no means required, it's generally common practice to capitalize class names, as it helps to distinguish classes from functions. Otherwise, invoking a function can look very similar to instantiating a class, leading to confusion. We have the following code:

```python
myResult = myFunction()    # run a function and store the result in
myResult
myInstance = MyClass() #   create a new instance of the MyClass class
and name it
# myInstance
```

Instantiating a class means that you create a brand new copy of that class, and the new copy is referred to as an "instance" of the class. Defining a class and instantiating it are two separate actions. The entire block of code that starts with the "class" keyword makes up the class definition and defines all of the attributes and capabilities of a class. It can be thought of as the blueprint for that class. However, to actually make use of a class, we have to actually create one. Once you've defined a class, you can make as many instances as you want, each with their own properties. The class definition is like the CAD files for a product, whereas the instance is like the actual physical product that rolls off the assembly line.

Once we have a class, we can add functionality to it by adding functions. We have to at least create a function named __init__ that will be responsible for initializing each class instance. This function will be called automatically each time an instance of the class is called.

Note that the __init__ function takes one argument, which we've labeled "self". When Python instantiates a class, it always passes a reference to the instance itself to all of the member functions. We could call it anything we want, but "self" is the convention and one that we'll adhere to.

In the __init__ function, we'll do everything we need to do to set up out UI. In this case, we'll create one field and one button. We store references to the field in an instance variable as properties of the self-object (which remember, is just the class instance itself). Doing this will allow us to retrieve the values of the controls later in the script:

```
self.numSpheres = cmds.intField(minValue=1)
```

Similarly, when we want to tie our controls to actual functionality, we'll need to preface our functions with "self." to refer to the method of our class. We do this with the button code in the next line:

```
cmds.button(label="Make Spheres", command=self.makeSpheres)
```

Setting variables as properties of the class via self will make them accessible to other functions within the class. Note that we stored a reference to the field, but not to the button; this is because we're not likely to want to query anything about the button or to change anything about it after it's been created. In such cases, it's fine to just use local variables or to not store the results at all.

Once we have both our field and our button, we show the window. Now we're ready to add the makeSpheres function:

```
def makeSpheres(self, *args):
```

Note that the function signature includes "self" as the first argument and has "*args", our catch-all for any passed values as the second argument. This is another example of how Python passes the class instance into all of its member functions each time they are called.

The rest of the code for the `makeSpheres` function is very similar to what we wrote in the non-class-based example. We use the query mode to retrieve the number in the `intField`, then we make that many spheres, moving each one by the corresponding multiple of the radius to space them out nicely.

```
number = cmds.intField(self.numSpheres, query=True, value=True)
for i in range(0,number):
    cmds.polySphere()
    cmds.move(i*2.2, 0, 0)
```

And with this, we're done defining our class. However, we also need to actually create an instance of it in order to see anything happen. The last line of the script does exactly this:

```
SpheresClass()
```

This creates a new instance of our `SpheresClass` class and, in so doing, runs the __init__ function, which in turn, sets up our UI and shows it to the user.

There's more...

Object-oriented programming (OOP) is a huge topic, and a full treatment of all of the ins and outs is beyond the scope of this book. It's also something you're likely to be familiar with if you've been using Python (or any other object-oriented language) for any length of time.

If this is the first time you're seeing it, be sure to read through the Python documentation on classes. OOP practices may seem like a lot of unnecessary overhead at first, but they ultimately make it much easier to tackle complex problems.

Using nested layouts

Very often, the interfaces that you'll want to create cannot be implemented with a single layout. In those cases, you'll need to nest layouts inside each other.

In this example, we'll create `rowLayouts` within a single columnLayout. Each `rowLayout` will allow us to have two controls (in this case, some text and `intField`) next to each other horizontally, and the parent `columnLayout` will stack the combined text/field pairs on top of each other vertically.

The end result will be something like this:

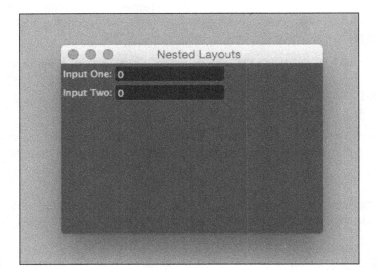

How to do it...

Make a new script and name it `nestedLayouts.py`. Add the following code:

```python
import maya.cmds as cmds

class NestedLayouts:

    def __init__(self):
        self.win = cmds.window(title="Nested Layouts",
widthHeight=(300,200))
        cmds.columnLayout()

        cmds.rowLayout(numberOfColumns=2)
        cmds.text(label="Input One:")
        self.inputOne = cmds.intField()
        cmds.setParent("..")

        cmds.rowLayout(numberOfColumns=2)
        cmds.text(label="Input Two:")
        self.inputTwo = cmds.intField()
        cmds.setParent("..")

        cmds.showWindow(self.win)

NestedLayouts()
```

Run the script, and you should see two rows, each with a bit of text and an `intField`.

How it works...

In this example, we start out by creating a `columnLayout`, just as we've done in other examples so far. Then, we immediately create another layout, and this time, it is a rowLayout:

```
cmds.columnLayout()

cmds.rowLayout(numberOfColumns=2)
```

When you create a layout, it immediately becomes the default parent for any other elements (either controls or other layouts) that you create. So, in this case, we have a columnLayout that contains a two-column rowLayout.

Once we've done this, we can add elements to our rowLayout, which we do with the following lines:

```
cmds.text(label="Input One:")
self.inputOne = cmds.intField()
```

At this point, our first rowLayout is filled because we created it with two columns and we've added two controls to it. If we attempt to add another control, we'll get an error similar to the following:

```
# Error: RuntimeError: file /nestedLayouts.py line 13: Too many
children in layout: rowLayout21
```

In order to continue to add elements to our UI, we'll need to jump up a level back to the `columnLayout`. At any given moment, there is exactly one and only one default parent to which Maya will add controls to. Every time you create a new layout, it becomes the default parent automatically. Sometimes, you'll need to change the default parent directly, which can be accomplished with the `setParent` command, as in the following:

```
cmds.setParent("..")
```

Using `setParent` and passing `".."` as the argument will move up a single level in the hierarchy of layouts. In this case, it means that we move up from the rowLayout back to the columnLayout. Once we've done this, we can create the second rowLayout, again with two columns. We are then free to add a second group of a text field and an int field:

```
cmds.setParent("..") # move one level up the UI hierarchy

cmds.rowLayout(numberOfColumns=2)   # add a second rowLayout
cmds.text(label="Input Two:")       # add a text control to the row
self.inputTwo = cmds.intField()     # add an intField to the row
```

There's more...

Jumping around the hierarchy can get a bit tedious. If you're going to have a number of controls that you want to add label text to, it might be best to create a helper function to your script's class to add a new control.

Here's an example of what that might look like:

```
def addLabeledIntField(self, labelText):
    cmds.rowLayout(numberOfColumns=2)
    cmds.text(label=labelText)
    newField = cmds.intField()
    cmds.setParent("..")
    return newField
```

Here, we take in the text to use for the label, and we return a reference to the newly created intField. Rewriting our example using the above would give us something like the following:

```
def __init__(self):
    self.win = cmds.window(title="Nested Layouts",
widthHeight=(300,200))
    cmds.columnLayout()

    self.inputThree = self.addLabeledIntField("Input Three")
    self.inputFour = self.addLabeledIntField("Input Four")

    cmds.showWindow(self.win)
```

This is quite a bit neater, indeed.

Note that our addLabeledIntField accepts two arguments, but we only pass a single one to it when we call it. This is due to the way that Python handles classes; every class method *always* receives a reference to the class itself. So, any arguments that we want to make use of start at the second one.

Using tabs and scrolling

In this example, we'll be looking at how to create UIs that contain tabs and how to provide scrollable containers.

Our UI will contain two tabs arranged horizontally, with each tab containing a scrollable column of 20 buttons. The final result will look something like this:

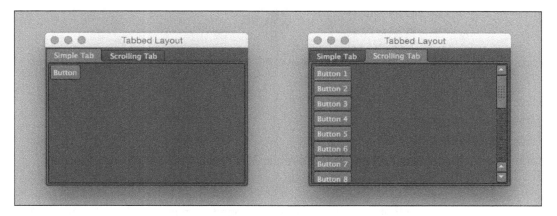

How to do it...

Create a new script, name it `tabExample.py` and add the following code:

```python
import maya.cmds as cmds

class TabExample:

    def __init__(self):
        self.win = cmds.window(title="Tabbed Layout",
widthHeight=(300, 300))

        self.tabs = cmds.tabLayout()

        # add first tab
        firstTab = cmds.columnLayout()
        cmds.tabLayout(self.tabs, edit=True, tabLabel=[firstTab,
'Simple Tab'])
        cmds.button(label="Button")
        cmds.setParent("..")

        # add second tab, and setup scrolling
        newLayout = cmds.scrollLayout()
        cmds.tabLayout(self.tabs, edit=True, tabLabel=[newLayout,
'Scrolling Tab'])
        cmds.columnLayout()

        for i in range(20):
            cmds.button(label="Button " + str(i+1))
```

```
                    cmds.setParent("..")
                    cmds.setParent("..")

                    cmds.showWindow(self.win)

            TabExample()
```

How it works...

Creating a tab layout is quite easy; all that's required is a call to the `tabLayout` function.

```
        self.tabs = cmds.tabLayout()
```

Note that we save the output of the `tabLayout` command to an instance variable, and we'll need that later. So now we have the tab layout, but we're still not ready to add any controls just yet. That's because the tab layout cannot actually contain controls directly; it is only meant to hold other layouts.

For the first tab, we'll keep it simple and just add a `columnLayout`:

```
        firstTab = cmds.columnLayout()
```

Note that we also store the output, which in this case is the name of the column layout (something like "columnLayout17" or similar). Now we can start adding controls if we want, but there's one more thing we'll want to do first.

By default, the text that is displayed in the actual tab of the tabbed layout will be the name of the child layout. This will almost never be what you want; you'll generally want to give your tabs nice, sensible labels instead of leaving them with names like "columnLayout23" and "scrollLayout19".

To do this, we'll need to edit our tab layout and use the `tabLabel` argument. The `tabLabel` argument expects a two-element array of strings, where the first string is the name of a child of the tab layout (in this case, our column layout), and the second is the text you want to display. Putting this all together gives us the following:

```
        cmds.tabLayout(self.tabs, edit=True, tabLabel=[firstTab, 'Simple
        Tab'])
```

We invoke the tabLayout command in the edit mode, direct it at our tab layout (which we stored in the `self.tabs` variable) and set the input to tabLabel such that we give our columnLayout the label of "Simple Tab".

Next, we add a single button, just so that we have something inside the tab:

```
        cmds.button(label="Button")
```

At this point, we're done with the first tab and ready to start on the second tab. But before we can do this, we need to jump up a level in the hierarchy so that we can add new content to the tab layout, rather than continuing to add to the column layout we created within it. We do this with the `setParent` command:

```
cmds.setParent("..")
```

Now we're ready to start on our second tab. This time, we'll add a scroll layout as follows:

```
newLayout = cmds.scrollLayout()
```

Once again, we'll edit the original tab layout so that the second tab has a proper name.

```
cmds.tabLayout(self.tabs, edit=True, tabLabel=[newLayout, 'Scrolling
Tab'])
```

To finish things off, we'll create a column layout within the scroll layout and add some buttons.

```
cmds.columnLayout()

for i in range(20):
    cmds.button(label="Button " + str(i+1))
```

Finally, we'll use setParent twice (once for the column layout and again for the scroll layout) to move back up the hierarchy to the tab layout:

```
cmds.setParent("..")
cmds.setParent("..")
```

We're now ready to add more tabs, if we want.

There's more...

If you ever need to know which tab is currently selected, you can find out via the `selectTabIndex` or sti flag. One gotcha to be aware of is that the number returned is indexed based on 1, rather than 0 as you might expect. If you *do* receive zero, it means that the tab layout in question doesn't have any children:

```
currTab = cmds.tabLayout(self.tabs, query=True, selectTabIndex=True)
```

You can also use the `selectTabIndex` to set which tab is currently active. For example, if we wanted to ensure that our example started out with the second tab selected, we could add the following line to our __init__ function:

```
cmds.tabLayout(self.tabs, edit=True, selectTabIndex=2)
```

When building complex UIs, having the ability to change behavior based on what part of the interface is currently active, or to start the script with a different part showing, can be a great way to make your scripts more responsive and easier to use.

Adding menus to your UIs

For more complex scripts, it can be helpful to add a drop-down menu to the top of your window. For example, you might want to have your script support custom configuration files and allow users to both save the current settings to disk, or to load previously saved settings. In that case, implementing the **File** menu with suboptions for **Save** and **Load** could be a very user-friendly option.

In this example, we'll be creating a window with its own menu, as well as looking at how to offer the user additional options via an option box, just like Maya's built-in menus.

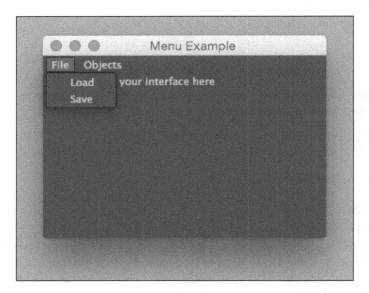

How to do it...

Create a new script and name it `customMenu.py`. Once again, we'll be creating a custom class to handle both our UI creation and functionality:

```
import maya.cmds as cmds

class CustomMenu:

    def __init__(self):
```

```
        self.win = cmds.window(title="Menu Example", menuBar=True,
widthHeight=(300,200))

        fileMenu = cmds.menu(label="File")
        loadOption = cmds.menuItem(label="Load")
        saveOption = cmds.menuItem(label="Save")
        cmds.setParent("..")

        objectsMenu = cmds.menu(label="Objects")
        sphereOption = cmds.menuItem(label="Make Sphere")
        cubeOption = cmds.menuItem(label="Make Cube")
        cmds.setParent("..")

        cmds.columnLayout()
        cmds.text(label="Put the rest of your interface here")

        cmds.showWindow(self.win)

CustomMenu()
```

If you run this code, you'll get a window with a two-item menu (**File** and **Objects**), each one of which provides two options.

To actually have something happen when the user selects an option, we'll need to provide a value for the command flag for one or more of our menuItem controls, as in the following (some of the preceding code has been removed to make the example shorter):

```
    def __init__(self):

        # set up the window and add any additional menu items
        # before the Objects menu

        objectsMenu = cmds.menu(label="Objects")
        sphereOption = cmds.menuItem(label="Make Sphere",
command=self.makeSphere)
        cubeOption = cmds.menuItem(label="Make Cube", command=self.
makeCube)
        cmds.setParent("..")

        # continue with the rest of the interface, and end with
        # cmds.showWindow()

    def makeSphere(self, *args):
        cmds.polySphere()

    def makeCube(self, *args):
        cmds.polyCube()
```

This would enable both of the **Make Sphere** and **Make Cube** menu items to create the respective polygonal geometry.

How it works...

Creating menus is pretty easy, and it is mainly just required that you:

1. Include the `menuBare=True` option when creating the initial window.
2. Add one or more menus with the `menu()` command.
3. For each menu, add one or more menuItem controls, providing a command for each.

There's more...

Many of Maya's commands offer the user two ways to trigger them—the default way and via the command's corresponding option box, which offers the user additional options for the command. You can do the same thing with your own menus by adding the second menuItem directly after the one to which you want to add an option box and setting the second menuItem's `optionBox` flag to true.

Let's say that we want to offer a command to create a polygonal sphere. We want the default radius to be 1 unit, but we also want to provide an option box, which when selected, will allow the user to specify a custom radius. To do this, we would want to add something like the following to our script:

```
        self.menu = cmds.menu(label="Objects")
        sphereCommandMI = cmds.menuItem(label="Make a Sphere",
command=self.myCommand)
        sphereCommandMIOption = cmds.menuItem(optionBox=True,
command=self.myCommandOptions)
```

Even though we're creating two menuItem controls, they would be presented to the user as a single entry in the `"Objects"` menu though one with an option box. When you add the `optionBox=True` flag to a menuItem control, Maya will add an option to the most recently created menuItem. Creating menuItem and setting `optionBox=True` without first creating a normal menuItem will leave Maya without anything to add the option box to and will result in an error.

This may seem a bit odd, but it makes a bit of sense since the default command and the option box are two separate clickable areas, so it's not totally unreasonable to implement them as separate controls.

Once we've set up the two controls, we'll want to make sure that they both do similar things, but one of them (the option box) provides additional input. An easy way to do it is with the `promptDialog` command, which provides an easy way to get a single value from the user. To ask the user to input a value for the sphere's radius, we could do the following:

```
promptInput = cmds.promptDialog(title="Sphere Radius",
message='Specify Radius:', button=['OK', 'CANCEL'],
defaultButton='OK', cancelButton='CANCEL', dismissString='CANCEL')
```

The preceding code would result in a new popup window with a single field and two buttons labeled **OK** and **CANCEL**. You'll note that we're storing the result of the promptDialog to a variable named promptInput.

You might think that this variable would hold the value that the user has entered, but that would be incorrect. Instead, it holds the value of the button that they pressed to dismiss the dialog. That probably seems strange, but it's necessary so that we can determine if the user has actually finalized the command or if they are decided to be canceled.

To actually make use of the input, we'll want to start by checking to see whether the user did, in fact, press the **OK** button. The promptDialog will return one of the two values:

1. If the user pressed one of the buttons, the return value will be the text associated with that button.

2. If the dialog was dismissed in some other way (like by clicking the X), whatever was provided as the dismissString will be returned.

In our example, if the user pressed one of the buttons, we will have either **OK** or **CANCEL** as the return value. Notice that we've also set the dismissString to **CANCEL** as well. So, all we have to do is to check to see whether **OK** was returned, as in:

```
if (promptInput == 'OK'):
```

Note that there are `two` equals signs, not one. This is a common source of error when people are new to Python. The key thing to remember is that a single equals sign always results in an `assignment`, and that you need to use two equals signs to perform a check for equality. This is true in many languages (not just Python) and stems from the fact that setting a variable to a given value is a very different operation than checking two values against each other. Since they are two different actions, Python (and most other languages) signifies each in a different way—one equals for assignment and two for comparison.

If that check passes, then we know that the user pressed **OK** and that we should grab the input value. We'll have to do that in a slightly different way than we have previously though. In the other examples, we've saved a reference to the created control and used that to specify the control when using the query mode to grab the value.

In this case, however, the promptDialog command returns the button pressed, rather than a reference to its field. So how are we to refer to the proper control?

As it turns out, we can just use the promptDialog command the second time, but in the query mode. Even though we don't specify the specific promptDialog to query, it will still work since Maya will default to the one that was most recently created. Since we're grabbing the value immediately after creating the dialog, this will work just fine. Putting that all together, gives us the following:

```
if (promptInput == 'OK'):
    radiusInput = cmds.promptDialog(query=True, text=True)
    self.makeSphere(radiusInput)
```

Note that we have to query "text" rather than "value". Also note that once we have the input, it gets passed to a separate function to actually do the work. This's important so that we can ensure that the exactly same code is triggered by both the default (non-option box) and option box versions of our menu item.

This may seem redundant here because we're just creating a sphere, but it's still a good idea. Don't duplicate code!

We would end up with three functions—first, to actually perform the work (in this case, creating a sphere), second, to call that function with default values (for the base menuItem), and third, to call that function after retrieving some additional information from the user. Putting all that together would give us something like this (the __init__ method omitted for brevity):

```
def myCommand(self, *args):
    self.makeSphere(1)

def myCommandOptions(self, *args):
    promptInput = cmds.promptDialog(title="Sphere
Radius", message='Specify Radius:', button=['OK', 'CANCEL'],
defaultButton='OK', cancelButton='CANCEL', dismissString='CANCEL')

    if (promptInput == 'OK'):
        radiusInput = cmds.promptDialog(query=True, text=True)
        self.makeSphere(radiusInput)

def makeSphere(self, sphereRadius):
    cmds.polySphere(radius=sphereRadius)
```

3

Working with Geometry

In this chapter, we'll be looking at ways to create and manipulate geometry with scripting. The following topics will be covered:

- ▶ Working with selected objects and checking node type
- ▶ Accessing geometric data in polygonal models
- ▶ Accessing geometric data in NURBS objects
- ▶ Creating curves
- ▶ Creating new polygonal faces
- ▶ Creating new modifiers (noise)
- ▶ Creating novel primitives (tetrahedron)

Introduction

In this chapter, we'll be looking at how to manipulate geometry within Maya via scripting. First off, we'll look at how to make sure that we have the right kind of object selected. From there, we'll look at how to retrieve information about particular kinds of geometry (both polygonal and NURBS).

We'll also be looking at how to create new geometry (both single faces and entire objects) and how to create per-vertex modifications to existing objects.

Working with selected objects and checking node type

Very often, you will want to make a script that only works on certain kinds of objects and the objects that already exist before the user invokes your script. In this case, you'll want to be able to not only determine what object(s) are currently selected but also to verify that the selected object(s) are of the appropriate type. In this example, we'll be creating a script that will verify that the currently selected object is, in fact, an instance of polygonal geometry and altering the user if it isn't.

How to do it...

Create a new script and add the following code:

```python
import maya.cmds as cmds

def currentSelectionPolygonal(obj):

    shapeNode = cmds.listRelatives(obj, shapes=True)
    nodeType = cmds.nodeType(shapeNode)

    if nodeType == "mesh":
        return True

    return False

def checkSelection():
    selectedObjs = cmds.ls(selection=True)

    if (len(selectedObjs) < 1):
        cmds.error('Please select an object')

    lastSelected = selectedObjs[-1]

    isPolygon = currentSelectionPolygonal(lastSelected)

    if (isPolygon):
        print('FOUND POLYGON')
    else:
        cmds.error('Please select a polygonal object')

checkSelection()
```

If you run the preceding script with nothing selected, you should get an error indicating that you should select something. If you run it with something other than a polygon object selected, you'll also get an error, but indicating this you should select a polygonal object.

If you run it with a polygonal object, however, the script will print **FOUND POLYGON**.

How it works...

The script consists of two functions—one (`currentSelectionPolygonal`) to test if a given object is polygonal geometry and another (`checkSelection`) to invoke that on the currently selected object. Because `checkSelection` is the entry point for the script, that's where we'll start.

The first thing that we have to do is to get a list of what object or objects are currently selected. To do this, we'll use the `ls` command. The `ls` command is short for *list* and another example of the bash scripting heritage of **Maya Embedded Language** (**MEL**) that carries over to the Python command list. The `ls` command can do a variety of things, but the most common way that you're likely to use it is with the `selection` flag to return a list of the currently selected nodes, as in:

```
selectedObjs = cmds.ls(selection=True)
```

Note that even though we're essentially asking Maya a question, it is not necessary to use the `query` flag. In fact, using the query mode for the `ls` command will generate an error. Note that we store the result of the `ls` command into a variable named `selectedObjects`. This will give us a collection of objects as a Python list, with objects appearing in the order in which they were selected. First, we want to make sure that at least one object is selected by checking the length of `selectedObjs`:

```
if (len(selectedObjs) < 1):
    cmds.error('Please select an object')
```

If the user hasn't selected anything, we use the `error` command to both notify the user and stop the execution of the script. Adding meaningful error messages is a great way to give your users quality feedback. You can also use the `warning()` command to present the user with feedback without stopping the script. In both cases, the error (or warning) will show to the user in the same way as built-in errors (or warnings), appearing in the bottom of Maya's interface and with a red (or yellow) background.

Once we know that we have at least one object selected, we want to make sure that the given object is a polygonal one. Using `-1` as the index into the list allows us to count backwards from the end. In this case, that will give us the most recently selected object.

```
lastSelected = selectedObjs[-1]
```

We then pass that object to our `currentSelectionPolygonal` function, which will determine if it is, in fact, a polygonal object. This function will handle the check and return either `True` or `False`, depending on whether or not the object in question is polygonal geometry.

```
isPolygon = currentSelectionPolygonal(lastSelected)
```

It's generally a good idea to break up your scripts into distinct parts, with each one responsible for one distinct task. This makes your scripts much easier to write and maintain. However, it also requires that the different parts be able to communicate with each other. The `return` statement is one of the most common ways to do this. It causes the current function to stop and *return* to the previous scope. If you give it a value, that value is brought back along, allowing information to be passed from one function to another.

We can check the type of given node by using the `nodeType()` command, but there's a bit more to it than that. If we check the type of the selected object itself, we'll almost always get *transform*. This is due to the fact that most things you interact with in Maya are composed of two nodes, not one. There is generally a shape node, which holds all of the specific data associated with a given object (faces, vertices, and so on), and a transform object that holds the position, rotation, and scale (along with a few other things) common to all objects that appear on screen and can be moved. The shape node is always a child of its corresponding transform node.

When you click on something in the interface, such as a polygonal object, you're actually clicking on the shape node, but Maya will automatically jump one step up the hierarchy to the transform node so that you can move it. That is often used to create controls for rigging by having the shape node for a curve be a child of some other transform, providing an easy way to grab bones inside a model by clicking on non-renderable curves (for example).

So, what we actually need in order to test the geometry type is the shape node associated with the transform. There are a couple of ways to go about this, but the best is to use the `listRelatives()` command with `shapes=True`. This will give us the shape node associated with the input node (if any):

```
def currentSelectionPolygonal(obj):
    shapeNode = cmds.listRelatives(obj, shapes=True)
```

Once we've done this, we can test its type with `nodeType` to see what kind of geometry we have. If we have a polygonal object, it will result in `mesh`. If the node type is, in fact `mesh`, we return a value of `True`. If it's anything other than `mesh`, we return `False` instead:

```
if nodeType == "mesh":
    return True


return False
```

Note that `return False` appears outside of an `else` block. This is mainly a stylistic choice. If you have a `return` statement inside a conditional (as we do here), it's a good idea to have a `return` statement that is outside the conditional that is guaranteed to be called, to ensure that there is no possible way that the function can fail to provide a return value.

Some people don't like to have multiple return values in a single function though, and if you're one of them, you could just as well create a variable and return that instead, as in:

```
isMesh = False
if (nodeType == "mesh"):
    isMesh = True


return isMesh
```

Or, for a more compact (but perhaps slightly less readable) approach, you could just return the result of the comparison itself:

```
return (nodeType == "mesh")
```

All of this would have the same result, in that the function would return `True` if and only if the object tested possessed a shape node of type `mesh`. At this point, we're done with the `currentSelectionPolygonal` function and can turn our attention back to `checkSelection`.

All that's left is to check the return value and notify the user of the result:

```
if (isPolygon):
    print('FOUND POLYGON')
else:
    cmds.error('Please select a polygonal object')
```

There's more...

We can use the same technique of grabbing the shape node with `listRelatives` and testing its type to identify other kinds of objects. Some of the more useful ones to be aware of are `nurbsCurve` for NURBS curves and `nurbsSurface` for NURBS objects.

Accessing geometric data in polygonal models

In this example, we'll be looking at how to get information about polygonal geometry, which will form the basis for more complex scripts.

Getting ready

Create a new scene and make sure that it contains one or more polygonal objects.

How to do it...

Create a new script, name it `polyStats.py`, and add the following code:

```python
import maya.cmds as cmds

# examine data for a currently-selected polygonal object
def getPolyData():
    selectedObjects = cmds.ls(selection=True)
    obj = selectedObjects[-1]

    vertNum = cmds.polyEvaluate(obj, vertex=True)
    print('Vertex Number: ',vertNum)

    edgeNum = cmds.polyEvaluate(obj, edge=True)
    print('Edge Number: ', edgeNum)

    faceNum = cmds.polyEvaluate(obj, face=True)
    print('Face Number: ',faceNum)

getPolyData()
```

Running the preceding code will result in information about the currently selected polygonal object being printed.

How it works...

The `polyEvaluate` command is pretty straightforward and can be used to determine various information about a polygonal object. In this case, we're just grabbing the number of vertices, edges, and faces that the object contains.

There's more...

Grabbing the number of components that an object contains isn't really all that useful, in and of itself. To perform the useful work, you'll likely want to access the components directly.

In order to do this, you'll want to be understand that each object has a collection of components stored as a Python list, which are named as follows:

Component	List name
Vertices	vtx
Edges	e
Faces	f

So, to select the first vertex for a given object (whose name is stored in a variable `obj`), you could do the following:

```
cmds.select(obj+'.vtx[0]', replace=True)
```

You could similarly grab the first edge with:

```
cmds.select(obj+'.e[0]', replace=True)
```

Or the first face with:

```
cmds.select(obj+'.f[0]', replace=True)
```

Since the lists of components are just ordinary Python lists, you can also refer to collections of components by using a colon along with a start or a stop index (or both). For example, if we wanted to select vertices from 5 to 12, we could do the following:

```
cmds.select(obj+'.vtx[5:12]', replace=True)
```

This would work, but could quickly get awkward if you wanted to have the starting and ending indices as variables as well, which would result in something like the following:

```
cmds.select(obj+'.vtx[' + str(startIndex) + ':' + str(endIndex) +
']', replace=True)
```

This would build up the proper value to pass to `cmds.select` (something like `polySurface5.vtx[5:12]`), but is a bit awkward to type. An easier way is to use Python's built-in string formatting capability, which can be used to fit variables into a specific string.

To do this, start with an example of the string you want to end up with, as in:

```
myObject.vtx[5:12]
```

Then, identify each portion of the string that will change. In this case, we want to pass in three things—the name of the object, the start index, and the end index. For each one, replace the specific value with a number wrapped in curly braces, as in:

```
{0}.vtx[{1}:{2}]
```

Once you've done this, you can call `format()` on the string, passing in values to replace the curly-bracketed numbers, as follows:

```
"{0}.vtx[{1}:{2}]".format("myObject", 5, 12)
```

The numbers inside the brackets serve as indices and tell Python which of the arguments passed into format should go where. In this case, we're saying that the first argument (the object name) should go at the start and that the next two should be placed inside the square brackets.

Here's an example of it all put together:

```
objectName = "myObject"
startIndex = 5
endIndex = 12
cmds.select("{0}.vtx[{1}:{2}]".format(objectName, startIndex,
endIndex), replace=True)
```

Accessing geometric data in NURBS objects

In this example, we'll be looking at how to retrieve information about NURBS surfaces, starting with the number of **control vertices** (**CVs**) they contain.

However, the number of CVs in a NURBS object isn't quite as straightforward as the number of vertices in a polygonal object. Although polygonal objects are relatively simple, with their shape determined directly by the position of the vertices, the curvature at any given point of a NURBS object is influenced by multiple points. The exact number of points that influence a given area depends on the degree of the surface.

To see how this works, we'll create a script that will determine the total number of CVs in each direction (U and V) of a NURBS surface, and we'll look at how to select a particular CV.

Getting ready

Make sure that you have a scene containing at least one NURBS surface.

How to do it...

Create a new file, name it `getNURBSinfo.py` (or similar), and add the following code:

```
import maya.cmds as cmds

def getNURBSInfo():
    selectedObjects = cmds.ls(selection=True)
    obj = selectedObjects[-1]
```

```
degU = cmds.getAttr(obj + '.degreeU')
spansU = cmds.getAttr(obj + '.spansU')
cvsU = degU + spansU
print('CVs (U): ', cvsU)

degV = cmds.getAttr(obj + '.degreeV')
spansV = cmds.getAttr(obj + '.spansV')
cvsV = degV + spansV
print('CVs (V): ', cvsV)
```

```
getNURBSInfo()
```

Select a NURBS surface and run the script. You'll see the number of CVs in each of the parametric directions (U and V) output to the script editor.

How it works...

In this example, we use the getAttr command to retrieve information about the selected object. The getAttr command is short for *get attribute* and can be used to retrieve the value of any attribute on a given node, making it useful in a wide range of circumstances.

In this particular situation, we're using it to get two things per direction along the surface—the number of spans and the degree, as follows:

```
degU = cmds.getAttr(obj + '.degreeU')
spansU = cmds.getAttr(obj + '.spansU')
```

The "degree" of a NURBS surface (or curve) is the number of points that influence each point along the geometry and ranges from 1 (linear) to 3. Curves and surfaces with degree of 1 are linear and resemble polygonal geometry. Curves and surfaces with degrees of greater than 1 interpolate multiple points to generate curvature. The total number of CVs in a curve or surface is always equal to the number of spans plus the degree.

One easy way to understand that is to think of the simplest possible curve—a straight line. That curve would have a single span (one segment) and would be of degree 1 (linear), and it would still require two points (the start and the end) in order to be defined. In that case, we would have:

(1 span) + (degree of 1) = 2 points

For more complex curves, more points would be needed, but it's the same principle—the minimum number will always be (degree of curve) plus one (since it's impossible to have a curve or a surface with zero spans).

So, to get the total number of CVs, we use `getAttr` twice, once to get the spans and again to get the degree, then we add the totals, as in the following:

```
degU = cmds.getAttr(obj + '.degreeU')
spansU = cmds.getAttr(obj + '.spansU')
cvsU = degU + spansU
print('CVs (U): ', cvsU)
```

Finally, to we'll finish off the script by selecting the first and last CVs. Selecting a CV on a NURBS surface is quite similar to selecting a vertex of a polygon, with the two following key differences:

▶ We use `.cv` instead of `.vtx`

▶ We need to specify two indices (one for `U` and one for `V`) instead of one

Selecting the first CV is pretty easy; we just use zero for both indices:

```
cmds.select(obj+'.cv[0][0]')
```

Selecting the last CV is a bit more involved and requires that we string together a few different parts to make sure that we end up with something like `myObj.cv[8][8]` in the case that the surface has nine CVs in each direction. We need to subtract one from the total CV number and wrap that in `str()` so that Python will allow us to combine it with the text. Putting this all together gives us:

```
cmds.select(obj+'.cv[' + str(cvsU-1) + '][' + str(cvsV-1) + ']',
add=True)
```

Alternatively, we could use string formatting to build up the input, as follows:

```
cmds.select("{0}.cv[{1}][{2}]".format(obj, (cvsU-1), (cvsV-1),
add=True)
```

There's more...

The previously mentioned discussion is based on having working with a NURBS surface. If we were working with a curve instead, things would be much the same, but we would use a single index to specify the CV rather than two, as in:

```
degree = cmds.getAttr(obj + '.degree')
spans = cmds.getAttr(obj + '.spans')
cvs = degree + spans
print('CVs: ', cvs)

cmds.select(obj+'.cv[0]')
cmds.select(obj+'.cv[' + str(cvs-1) + ']', add=True)
```

Also note that when we retrieve the values for degree and span, we do not specify U or V because curves have only one dimension rather than two.

Creating curves

In this example, we'll be looking at how to create curves with code. This can be used for a number of different purposes, such as forming the basis for further modeling operation or creating custom controls for complex rigs.

We'll actually be making two curves in this example—a simple one that we create directly and a more complex one that we create one point at a time.

Here's what we'll end up with as our output and moving both curves away from the origin.

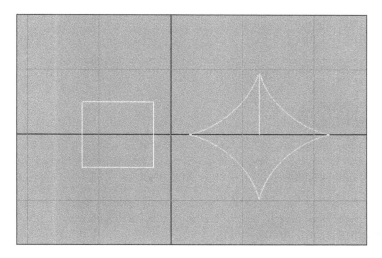

How to do it...

Create a new file and name it makeCurves.py or similar. Add the following code:

```
import maya.cmds as cmds
import math

def makeCurve():
    theCurve = cmds.curve(degree=1, p=[(-0.5,-0.5,0),(0.5,-
    0.5,0),(0.5,0.5,0), (-0.5,0.5,0), (-0.5, -0.5, 0)])

def curveFunction(i):
    x = math.sin(i)
    y = math.cos(i)
```

```
        x = math.pow(x, 3)
        y = math.pow(y, 3)
        return (x,y)

    def complexCurve():
        theCurve = cmds.curve(degree=3, p=[(0,0,0)])

        for i in range(0, 32):
            val = (math.pi * 2)/32 * i
            newPoint = curveFunction(val)
            cmds.curve(theCurve, append=True, p=[(newPoint[0],
            newPoint[1], 0)])


    makeCurve()
    complexCurve()
```

If you run the preceding code, you'll end up with two curves being created—a square and an astroid curve.

How it works...

To make a new curve, we'll want to first understand what we're trying to make. In the case of the square, it's easy enough. We just need to have four points—each half of the width away from the origin in each combination of positive and negative ((-,-), (-,+), (+,+), and (+,-)).

To actually make the curve, we'll use the `curve` command and specify a list of points. We'll also set the degree of our curve to `1`, that is, make it linear, which makes sense for a square. Putting that together gives us the following:

```
    theCurve = cmds.curve(degree=1, p=[(-0.5,-0.5,0),(0.5,-
    0.5,0),(0.5,0.5,0), (-0.5,0.5,0), (-0.5, -0.5, 0)])
```

Note that we specify five points rather than four. If we leave it at only four points, we would end up with three spans rather than four, leaving one of the sides of our square missing. One way to address this is to simply repeat the first point at the end of the point list to close the curve.

For a more complex example, we'll create an **astroid curve** using some fun math. To make this easier, we'll create a function that will accept a parameterized input and output a two-element tuple with the *X* and *Y* coordinates of the curve for that input. We'll also append points to the curve as we go, as it is sometimes an easier way to approach things for more complex curves.

The parameterized equations for the curve can be written as:

Here, theta ranges from 0 to 2pi. Putting the value in terms of Python gives us the following:

```
def curveFunction(i):
    x = math.sin(i)
    y = math.cos(i)
    x = math.pow(x, 3)
    y = math.pow(y, 3)
    return (x,y)
```

Now that we have a function that will give us the curve we want, we'll create a new curve and add points to it one at a time. First, we make the curve and set it to have a degree of three (cubic) so that it's nice and smooth, as follows:

```
theCurve = cmds.curve(degree=3, p=[(0,0,0)])
```

Now, we'll step through our range of zero to (2 * pi) and add a new point to the existing curve:

```
for i in range(0, 32):
    val = (math.pi * 2)/32 * i
    newPoint = curveFunction(val)
    cmds.curve(theCurve, append=True, p=[(newPoint[0],
    newPoint[1], 0)])
```

We start by calculating our input as 1/32nd of (2 * pi) times our index and passing it into our curve function. We then use the `curve` command again, but with a couple of changes, namely:

- ▸ We specify the curve we're working on by passing it as the first argument
- ▸ We use the `append=True` flag to let Maya know that the points should be added to the existing curve instead of creating a new one
- ▸ We specify a single point using the output of our `curveFunction` for the *X* and *Y* coordinates and 0 for the *Z* coordinate

There's more...

Although you likely won't have a need for astroid curves in your own projects, there are plenty of situations where you may want to create curves in a step-by-step fashion. For example, you might want to create a curve based on an animation sequence, by adding a point for the position of a given object each frame. We'll see how to grab positions on a frame-by-frame basis when we look at scripting for animation.

See also

For more information on the astroid curve, have a look at its entry on the Wolfram MathWorld website, `http://mathworld.wolfram.com/Astroid.html`. That's just one of the fun curves that the site explains, along with all sorts of other mathematical resources that you might find useful.

Creating new polygonal faces

In this example, we'll be looking at how to create new polygonal faces with code, both a simple quad and a more complex example that incorporates an internal hole.

How to do it...

Create a new file, name it `polyCreate.py` (or similar), and add the following code:

```python
import maya.cmds as cmds
import math

def makeFace():

    newFace = cmds.polyCreateFacet(p=[(-1,-1,0),(1,-1,0),(1,1,0),(-1,1,0)])

def makeFaceWithHole():
    points = []

    # create the inital square
    points.append((-5, -5, 0))
    points.append(( 5, -5, 0))
    points.append(( 5,  5, 0))
    points.append((-5,  5, 0))

    # add empty point to start a hole
    points.append(())

    for i in range(32):
        theta = (math.pi * 2) / 32 * i
        x = math.cos(theta) * 2
        y = math.sin(theta) * 2
        points.append((x, y, 0))

    newFace = cmds.polyCreateFacet(p=points)

makeFace()
makeFaceWithHole()
```

If you run the preceding script, you'll see two new objects created, both in the *XY* plane—one is a simple square and the other is a square with a hole in the center.

How it works...

The `polyCreateFacet` command is fairly straightforward and expects to receive an array of point positions. Each point should be stored in a tuple of three values, each one for the *X*, *Y*, and *Z* position of the vertex.

In the first example, we merely call the `polyCreateFacet` command directly and provide the four points that make up the corners of a 2-unit square centered at the origin and aligned in the *XY* plane. We have the following code:

```
newFace = cmds.polyCreateFacet(p=[(-1,-1,0),(1,-1,0),(1,1,0),(-1,1,0)])
```

You can also create polygons with internal holes, but in order to do that, you'll need to signal to Maya that you're starting a hole. To do this, you'll need to feed the `polyCreateFacet` command a blank point as an empty tuple.

When creating more complex faces, it can be easier to create an array to hold the various points and push them onto it one at a time, rather than trying to have a single long argument to the `polyCreateFacet` command.

We start, once again, with four points to define a square in the *XY* plane, as follows:

```
points = []

# create the inital square
points.append((-5, -5, 0))
points.append(( 5, -5, 0))
points.append(( 5, 5, 0))
points.append((-5, 5, 0))
```

In order to get Maya to start creating a hole in the face we're making, we next add an empty tuple:

```
points.append(())
```

Now we can start adding the points for the hole. In this case, we'll add points to make a circular hole with 32 points. This's done easily enough with a little bit of trigonometry. Because we're making a hole with 32 segments, we divide one full rotation (in radians, so `math.pi * 2`) by `32` and multiply by our index to get the value we feed to the trigonometric functions.

Putting that all together give us the following:

```
for i in range(32):
        theta = (math.pi * 2) / 32 * i
        x = math.cos(theta) * 2
        y = math.sin(theta) * 2
        points.append((x, y, 0))
```

Then, we'll have an array of 37 tuples representing 36 points plus one blank entry to indicate the start of a cutout region. Passing that into the `polyCreateFacet` command gives us the final result. We use the following code:

```
newFace = cmds.polyCreateFacet(p=points)
```

There's more...

When creating polygonal faces, the order in which the vertices are specified is important. It's likely obvious that adding vertices out of order would cause the resulting faces to be bent in unintended ways, but the order also affects the direction that the face or faces **normals** will point. Always be sure to specify your points around the outer edge of the face that you're creating, and in the counter-clockwise direction, which will cause the normals to point out of the screen.

If you want the normals to point in the other direction, either specify them in the opposite order or explicitly reverse the normals on the created faces using the `polyNormal` command as follows:

```
# with a polygonal object selected
cmds.polyNormal(normalMode=4)
```

The 4 variable likely seems cryptic, but the `polyNormal` command can perform a few different specific functions (including a few deprecated options), and the `normalMode` flag is how to tell Maya which one you want. For details, be sure to consult the Python command documentation.

If you find yourself creating complex faces, such as our second example with the hole, you might want to ensure that you are left with faces of no more than four sides. You can certainly do it by creating the faces one at a time and joining them (which we will do in the custom primitive example, mentioned later), or you can create the shape as a single face, then triangulate it.

To triangulate the resulting face, run the `polyTriangulate` command after creating it, as in the following:

```
cmds.polyCreateFacet(p=myPoints)
cmds.polyTriangulate()
```

You can also have Maya attempt to combine the resulting triangles into quads by running the `polyQuad` command as follows:

```
# attempt to form quads from a recently-triangulated poly mesh
cmds.polyQuad()
```

Quadrangulation doesn't always work, but it also generally doesn't hurt anything. Leaving **ngons** in your meshes, on the other hand, can lead to all sorts of problems down the road and is best avoided.

Creating new modifiers (noise)

Many 3D modeling and animation packages provide a way to add a bit of random noise to the vertices of an object, but Maya does not. This may seem like an oversight, but it also provides us with a great example project.

In this example, we'll write a script to step through all of the vertices of a polygonal object and move each of them slightly. Here's an example of what a simple polygonal sphere looks like both before and after applying the script that we'll be developing:

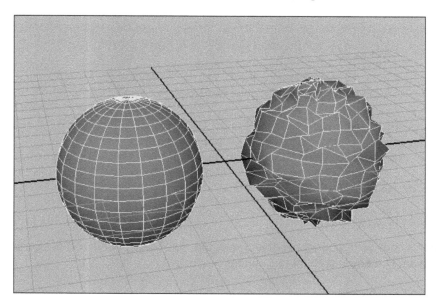

How to do it...

Create a new script, name it `addNoise.py`, and add the following code:

```python
import maya.cmds as cmds
import random

def addNoise(amt):

    selectedObjs = cmds.ls(selection=True)
    obj = selectedObjs[-1]

    shapeNode = cmds.listRelatives(obj, shapes=True)

    if (cmds.nodeType(shapeNode) != 'mesh'):
        cmds.error('Select a mesh')
        return

    numVerts = cmds.polyEvaluate(obj, vertex=True)

    randAmt = [0, 0, 0]
    for i in range(0, numVerts):

        for j in range(0, 3):
            randAmt[j] = random.random() * (amt*2) - amt

        vertexStr = "{0}.vtx[{1}]".format(obj, i)
        cmds.select(vertexStr, replace=True)
        cmds.move(randAmt[0], randAmt[1], randAmt[2], relative=True)

    cmds.select(obj, replace=True)

addNoise(0.2)
```

If you run this code with a polygonal object selected, you'll see that each of the vertices is moved by a small random amount (0.2 units).

How it works...

First off, we'll want to make sure that we have a polygonal object selected by:

- ▸ Grabbing the currently selected objects
- ▸ Determining the shape node (if any) attached to the most recently selected object
- ▸ Testing the shape node to make sure that it's a polygonal object

Take a look at the following code:

```
selectedObjs = cmds.ls(selection=True)
obj = selectedObjs[-1]

shapeNode = cmds.listRelatives(obj, shapes=True)
```

Once we've done that, we'll want to loop through each of the vertices of the object, but first we'll need to know how many vertices it contains. So, we use the `polyEvaluate` command as follows:

```
numVerts = cmds.polyEvaluate(obj, vertex=True)
```

Now we're ready to loop through the vertices and move each one. Because we'll want each axis to be independent, we'll start by creating a variable to hold the offsets for each:

```
randAmt = [0, 0, 0]
```

Now we're ready to loop through the object. For each pass, we'll want to set the `randAmt` array to random variables, then apply those to the position of the vertex:

```
for j in range(0, 3):
    randAmt[j] = random.random() * (amt*2) - amt
```

 A note on how we're setting the random amount—we want to make sure that the values produced range between the input value (as the maximum) and its negative equivalent (as the minimum).

The `random.random()` function will produce a random number between 0 and 1. Multiplying it by doubling the input will give us a value between 0 and (amt * 2), and subtracting the input value will give us the proper range.

Now we'll actually move the vertices by first selecting the individual vertex and moving it using the `move` command:

```
vertexStr = "{0}.vtx[{1}]".format(obj, i)
cmds.select(vertexStr, replace=True)
cmds.move(randAmt[0], randAmt[1], randAmt[2],
relative=True)
```

Note that Maya does also offer a `polyMoveVertex` command, which might seem like a better way to go about tweaking the position of each vertex. While that will absolutely work, it will run much slower due to the additional overhead of creating another **database availability group** (**DAG**) node for each moved vertex. If you would like to see for yourself, try commenting out the lines that select and move the vertices and adding the following:

```
cmds.polyMoveVertex(vertexStr, t=randAmt)
```

Try running this and see how long it takes, then comment out this, re-enable the select and move lines and rerun the script. You'll likely see that the `polyMoveVertex` version takes a significantly longer time.

Once we've run through all of the vertices and moved each one slightly, we'll want to make sure that we finish up by selecting the original object, thereby setting the user up to take further actions on the object. Take a look at the following code:

```
cmds.select(obj, replace=True)
```

There's more...

This example would only work on polygonal objects, but it would be easy to extend it to work with NURBS surface or even curves as well. To do this, we would need to do the following two things:

- ▶ Test for the type of geometry (`nurbsSurface` or `nurbsCurve`)
- ▶ Alter the point selection code to reference the appropriate type of point

One further complication is that CVs of a NURBS surface have to be accessed in a two-dimensional array, rather than the flat array of the polygonal surfaces `vtx` list.

Creating novel primitives (tetrahedron)

In this example, we'll be creating a brand new (to Maya) geometric primitive—a tetrahedron. Tetrahedrons are simple in principle, but would require numerous steps to create using Maya's interface. As such, they make a great candidate for scripting.

We'll be creating a script that will create a tetrahedron of a given edge width as a polygonal mesh.

Getting ready

Before we start writing code, we'll want to make sure that we have a good grasp on the math behind tetrahedrons. A tetrahedron is the simplest regular polyhedron that consists of four faces, each of which is an equilateral triangle.

Each tetrahedron consists of only four points. For convenience, we'll name the three around the base **A**, **B**, and **C**, and the point at the tip **D**, as in the following illustration:

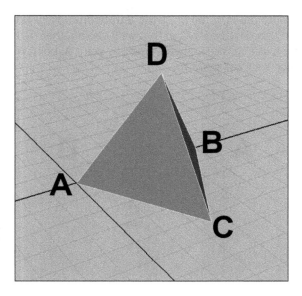

To make the math easier, we'll set point **A** to the origin ([0,0,0]). Because every side of the base is of the same length, we can find point **B** by simply moving along the x axis by the desired edge length, giving us [length, 0, 0] for **B**.

Point **C** is only slightly more involved. First, we note that every equilateral triangle can be split into two similar right triangles as follows:

Finding the X coordinate of point **C** is easy; all we have to do is halve the edge length. The Z coordinate is in turn equal to the height of each of the half triangles in the previously mentioned illustration, which we don't yet know. However, we *do* know the length of the other two sides, that is, the shorter side is half of our edge length, and the hypotenuse is just the full edge length itself.

Therefore, by the Pythagorean theorem, we know that:

$$\left(\frac{side}{2}\right)^2 + Cz^2 = side^2$$

Or, rewriting it a bit, we have the following:

$$Cz = \sqrt{side^2 - \left(\frac{side}{2}\right)^2}$$

Finally, we'll need the coordinates of the tip of the tetrahedron. We'll get those in a way similar to how we arrived at the coordinates for **C**, in that we'll use another right triangle, but this one will be slightly different; it will be the triangle formed by point **A**, point **D**, and the point in the center of the base (which we'll call point **E**).

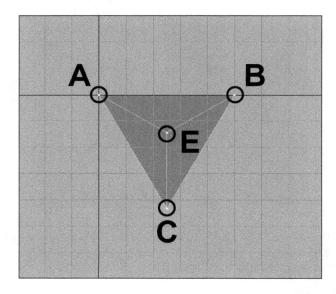

First, let's find point **E**. Because it's the center of the base, we can just average the X and Z coordinates of **A**, **B**, and **C**, and we'll have **E**'s location. Then, we can construct a triangle that will allow us to determine the vertical position of point **D**.

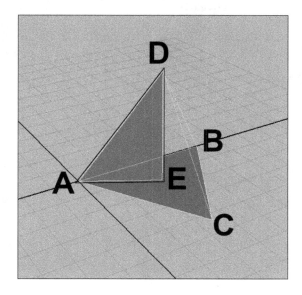

Point **D** will have the same *X* and *Z* coordinates as **E**, but needs to be raised by the proper amount along the *y* axis to create a proper tetrahedron. To find that distance, we'll use the triangle formed by **A**, **E**, and **D**. The hypotenuse is, once again, a full side of the tetrahedron, so that's easy. The shorter base (**A-E**) is the distance from **A** to the center of the base. To find that, we can use the distance formula, making the calculation simpler by choosing point **A** as the origin.

$$distanceAE = \sqrt{\left(Ex - Ax\right)^2 + \left(Ez - Az\right)^2}$$

Because both the *X* and *Z* coordinates of point **A** are zero, we get the following:

$$distanceAE = \sqrt{Ex^2 + Ez^2}$$

Once we've done that, we know the lengths of two of the sides of the triangle, and we can calculate the third by using the Pythagorean theorem once again, as follows:

$$Dy = \sqrt{side^2 - distanceAE^2}$$

Now that we have a good handle on how to create a tetrahedron, we're ready to actually write the script.

How to do it...

Create a new script and name it `makeTetrahedron.py`. Add the following code:

```python
import maya.cmds as cmds
import math

def makeTetra(size):

    pointA = [0, 0, 0]
    pointB = [size, 0, 0]

    pointC = [size/2.0, 0, 0]
    # set the Z position for C
    pointC[2] = math.sqrt((size*size) - (size/2.0 * size/2.0))

    pointE = [0,0,0]
    # average the A, B, and C to get E
    # first add all the values
    for i in range(0,3):
```

```
            pointE[i] += pointA[i]
            pointE[i] += pointB[i]
            pointE[i] += pointC[i]
        # now divide by 3
        for i in range(0,3):
            pointE[i] = pointE[i] / 3.0

        # start point D with the X and Z coordinates of point E
        pointD = [0,0,0]
        pointD[0] = pointE[0]
        pointD[2] = pointE[2]

        distanceAE = math.sqrt((pointE[0] * pointE[0]) + (pointE[2] *
        pointE[2]))

        # set the Y coordinate of point D
        pointD[1] = math.sqrt((size * size) - (distanceAE *
        distanceAE))

        faces = []
        faces.append(cmds.polyCreateFacet(p=[pointA, pointB, pointC],
        texture=1))
        faces.append(cmds.polyCreateFacet(p=[pointA, pointD, pointB],
        texture=1))
        faces.append(cmds.polyCreateFacet(p=[pointB, pointD, pointC],
        texture=1))
        faces.append(cmds.polyCreateFacet(p=[pointC, pointD, pointA],
        texture=1))

        cmds.select(faces[0], replace=True)
        for i in range(1, len(faces)):
            cmds.select(faces[i], add=True)

        obj = cmds.polyUnite()

        cmds.select(obj[0] + ".vtx[:]")
        cmds.polyMergeVertex(distance=0.0001)

        cmds.select(obj[0])

        cmds.move(-pointE[0], 0, -pointE[2])
        cmds.xform(pivots=(pointE[0], 0, pointE[2]))
        cmds.makeIdentity(apply=True)
        cmds.delete(ch=True)

    makeTetra(5)
```

Run this code, and you should end up with a tetrahedron with a side length of 5 units, with the base centered at the origin.

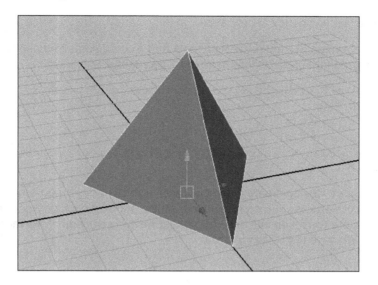

How it works...

First off, we calculate all the points that we'll need, as outlined in the preceding *Getting ready* section. Each point is a three-element array of *X*, *Y*, and *Z* coordinates.

The first two points are easy:

```
pointA = [0, 0, 0]
pointB = [size, 0, 0]
```

pointC is a bit more complex and requires us to use the Pythagorean theorem:

```
pointC = [size/2.0, 0, 0]
# set the Z position for C
pointC[2] = math.sqrt((size*size) - (size/2.0 * size/2.0))
```

In order to calculate the position for pointD, we first determine the center of the base, which we'll call pointE. Use the following code:

```
pointE = [0,0,0]
# average the A, B, and C to get E
# first add all the values
for i in range(0,3):
    pointE[i] += pointA[i]
    pointE[i] += pointB[i]
```

```
        pointE[i] += pointC[i]
# now divide by 3
for i in range(0,3):
        pointE[i] = pointE[i] / 3.0
```

Finally, we can determine `pointD` by setting the *X* and *Z* coordinates to those of `pointE` and using the Pythagorean theorem to determine the *Y* coordinate as follows:

```
# start point D with the X and Z coordinates of point E
pointD = [0,0,0]
pointD[0] = pointE[0]
pointD[2] = pointE[2]
distanceAE = math.sqrt((pointE[0] * pointE[0]) + (pointE[2] *
pointE[2]))
```

Once we've done that, we can create individual faces with the `polyCreateFacet` command. We'll use the `polyCreateFacet` command four times, once for each of the tetrahedron's faces. We'll also store the result into an array so that we can select all of the faces for final processing later. We have the following code:

```
faces = []
faces.append(cmds.polyCreateFacet(p=[pointA, pointB, pointC],
texture=1))
faces.append(cmds.polyCreateFacet(p=[pointA, pointD, pointB],
texture=1))
faces.append(cmds.polyCreateFacet(p=[pointB, pointD, pointC],
texture=1))
faces.append(cmds.polyCreateFacet(p=[pointC, pointD, pointA],
texture=1))
```

At this point, we have all of our geometry created, but we'll want to do a few things to finish off the object, namely:

1. Combine all the faces into a single object.
2. Move the object so that the base is centered at the origin.
3. Set the object's pivot point so that it is also centered at the base.
4. Freeze the transformations.

First off, let's combine the faces into a single object by selecting them. We start by replacing the current selection by the first face, then adding each of the additional three faces to the selection by using `add=True` in our call to `cmds.select()`. We have the following code:

```
cmds.select(faces[0], replace=True)
for i in range(1, len(faces)):
        cmds.select(faces[i], add=True)
```

Once we have all the faces selected, we can combine them with `polyUnite`:

```
obj = cmds.polyUnite()
```

It will cause all of the faces to be combined into a single polygonal object, but it's only the start. If we leave things at that, we'll end up with disconnected faces and multiple vertices at each of the tetrahedron's four points. To finish off, we'll want to make sure that vertices that are on top of each other are merged.

To do this, we'll start by selecting all of the vertices in our model:

```
cmds.select(obj[0] + ".vtx[:]")
```

Note that we use the `vtx` list to select vertices, but we leave out both the start and end indices, having just a colon. That's an easy shorthand way to refer to the entire contents of a list and will cause all of the vertices in our model to be selected. Once we've done it, we tell Maya to merge nearby vertices with the `polyMergeVertex` command, passing in a small threshold distance.

```
cmds.polyMergeVertex(distance=0.0001)
```

This tells Maya that any vertices that are less than 0.0001 units apart should be merged into a single vertex. At this point, we have a proper tetrahedron with four faces and four vertices. Because the rest of the operations we want to perform deal with the object as a whole (rather than its vertices), we switch back to the object mode by reselecting the object.

```
cmds.select(obj[0])
```

Now we have a single object, but we want to center it. Luckily, we still have `pointE`, which contains the *X* and *Z* coordinates of the base's center, relative to the origin. So, we'll start by moving the combined object in the negative direction on *X* and *Z* by the same amount:

```
cmds.move(-pointE[0], 0, -pointE[2])
```

Now we have the object where we want it, but its pivot point is still located at what used to be the origin (`pointA`). To fix it, we'll use the `xform` command to move the pivot point, as follows:

```
cmds.xform(pivots=(pointE[0], 0, pointE[2]))
```

The `pivots` flag will move the object's pivot to the specified location. In this case, we're moving it by the same amount (but in the opposite direction) that we moved the object, resulting in the pivot remaining at the origin, even though the object itself has been moved.

Finally, we'll finish off by freezing the transformations so that our object starts off with 0,0,0 for its position, and we will delete the construction history.

```
cmds.makeIdentity(apply=True)
cmds.delete(ch=True)
```

Then, we're left with a fully-formed tetrahedron, centered at the origin and with a clean construction history and ready for further use.

There's more...

A tetrahedron is a fairly simple object, but all of the principles we used to create it can easily be extended to more complex shapes with more inputs.

4
Giving Things a Coat of Paint – UVs and Materials

In this chapter, we will be looking at topics related to the UV layout and shader creation:

- ▸ Querying UV data
- ▸ Laying out UVs with Python
- ▸ Creating shading networks with code
- ▸ Applying shaders to objects
- ▸ Using shading nodes for non-rendering tasks

Introduction

In the previous chapter, we looked at how to manipulate geometry with script. However, for most projects, creating the models is only the first step. Unless you want everything to look like boring gray plastic, you'll need to layout UVs, then create and apply shading networks.

In this chapter, we will be looking at how to do just that.

Querying UV data

In this example, we will be looking at how to get information about UVs on a polygonal object. We will look at examining how many UV sets the object contains, getting the UVs for a given part of the object, and grabbing the position of a given UV point.

We will also look at how to convert one kind of selection to another and use that to determine if a given edge can be split or not.

Getting ready

Make sure that you have a scene that contains at least one polygonal object that has UVs—either an object that you have unwrapped or any of the built-in primitive shapes, which have UVs by default.

How to do it...

Create a new file, name it uvInfo.py (or similar), and add the following code:

```
import maya.cmds as cmds

def uvInfo():

    sel = cmds.ls(selection=True)
    obj = sel[0]

    uvs = cmds.polyEvaluate(obj, uvComponent=True)
    uvPos = cmds.polyEditUV(obj + '.map[0]', query=True)
        isFirstEdgeSplit = isSplitEdge(obj, 0)

    print('Num UVs: ' + str(uvs))
    print("Position of first UV: ", uvPos)
     print("First edge is split: ", isFirstEdgeSplit))

    cmds.select(obj, replace=True)

def isSplitEdge(obj, index):

    result = cmds.polyListComponentConversion(obj + '.e[' + str(index)
+ ']', fromEdge=True, toUV=True)
    cmds.select(result, replace=True)
    vertNum = cmds.polyEvaluate(vertexComponent=True)

    result = cmds.polyListComponentConversion(obj + '.e[' + str(index)
+ ']', fromEdge=True, toVertex=True)
    cmds.select(result, replace=True)
    uvNum = cmds.polyEvaluate(uvComponent=True)

    if (uvNum == vertNum):
        return False

    return True

uvInfo()
```

If you run the preceding script with a polygonal object selected, you will get some information about the object's UVs, specifically:

► How many UVs the object has.

► The location (in UV space) of the first UV point

► Whether or not the first edge lies on the border between two separate UV shells.

How it works...

We start by grabbing the currently selected object and storing it into our `obj` variable. Once we have done this, we use the `polyEvaluate` command to determine the total number of UVs the object has. This is similar to what we did in the previous chapter to find the number of geometric components, but this time around, we use the `uvComponent/uvc` flag.

```
uvs = cmds.polyEvaluate(obj, uvComponent=True)
```

Next up, we will find the specific position of the first UV point. UVs can be accessed in much the same way other polygonal components, but using the "map" list instead of the "f" (faces), "e" (edges), or "vtx" (vertices). Therefore, if we want to refer to the first UV of an object named `myObject`, we would use the following:

```
myObject.map[0]
```

Here, 0 indicates the first entry in the list and therefore the first UV of the object.

To actually find the specific U and V coordinates of a given UV, we can use the `polyEditUV` command in a query mode, as in the following:

```
uvPos = cmds.polyEditUV(obj + '.map[0]', query=True)
```

Next up is determining whether a given edge is internal to a UV shell or if it is on the border between two different shells. To do this, we create a function that accepts the name of an object and the index of an edge to check:

```
isFirstEdgeSplit = isSplitEdge(obj, 0)
```

The key thing that we are doing is to see how many vertices and how many UVs correspond to the given edge. If the number of vertices is not equal to the number of UVs, then that edge must be straddling the border of two different UV shells.

To determine how many vertices/UVs correspond to a given edge, we'll convert the edge to the desired component type using the `polyListComponentConversion` command. For that to work properly, we will need to specify both what we are converting from (in this case, edges), and what we're converting to (either vertices or UVs). The way that we do that is a bit odd; instead of specifying the types of each, we have to set two Boolean flags to true, one for the source type and one for the destination.

For example, if we were to convert the first edge of an object named `myObject` to vertices, we would need to do the following:

```
cmds.polyListComponentConversion('myObject.e[0]', fromEdge=True,
toVertex=True)
```

Adding in the proper variables to set the name of the object and the index of the edge gives us:

```
result = cmds.polyListComponentConversion(obj + '.e[' + str(index) +
']', fromEdge=True, toVertex=True)
```

Note that we store the output of the command to a variable named "result". This is important because getting an accurate count of the number of points requires that we first select the components we want to count. This is easily done in the following way:

```
cmds.select(result, replace=True)
```

Once we've done this, we can use the `polyEvaluate` command with the proper flag to give us the number of *currently selected* components. For vertices and UVs, we will want to use `vertexComponent` and `uvComponent`, respectively. In both cases, we store the result to another variable, as follows:

```
vertNum = cmds.polyEvaluate(vertexComponent=True)
```

At this point, we have the number of vertices that correspond to the given edge. We then do the same operation (but with slightly different flags) to determine the number of UVs:

```
result = cmds.polyListComponentConversion(obj + '.e[' + str(index) +
']', fromEdge=True, toUV=True)
cmds.select(result, replace=True)
uvNum = cmds.polyEvaluate(uvComponent=True)
```

Finally, we compare the number of UVs to the number of vertices. If they are not the same, then the edge in question must exist on more than one UV shell and, as such, represents a border:

```
if (uvNum == vertNum):
        return False

    return True
```

Back in our main function, we output the results of our various queries with a few print statements:

```
        print('Num UVs: ' + str(uvs))
        print("Position of first UV: ", uvPos)
        print("First edge is split: ", isFirstEdgeSplit)
```

Finally, we will be sure to select the original object once again because we selected subcomponents during the `isSplitEdge` function:

```
cmds.select(obj, replace=True)
```

Laying out UVs with Python

In this example, we will look at how to actually lay out UVs using Python. We will be applying planar, cylindrical, and spherical projections, each to a different subset of the faces of the selected object.

Getting ready

Make sure that you have a scene containing a polygonal object. We will be applying three different mappings to different parts of the object (selected by dividing the total number of faces by three), so it is best to have an object with at least a few dozen faces. If you do not have a model handy, make a polygonal sphere of at least 10 or so divisions along both height and axis.

How to do it...

Create a new script and add the following code:

```
import maya.cmds as cmds

def layoutUVs():

    selected = cmds.ls(selection=True)
    obj = selected[0]

    totalFaces = cmds.polyEvaluate(obj, face=True)

    oneThird = totalFaces/3

    startFace = 0
    endFace = oneThird - 1
    cmds.polyProjection(obj + '.f[' + str(startFace) + ':' +
str(endFace) + ']', type="planar")

    startFace = oneThird
    endFace = (oneThird * 2) - 1
    cmds.polyProjection(obj + '.f[' + str(startFace) + ':' +
str(endFace) + ']', type="cylindrical")
```

```
        startFace = (oneThird * 2)
        endFace = totalFaces - 1
        cmds.polyProjection(obj + '.f[' + str(startFace) + ':' +
str(endFace) + ']', type="spherical")

    layoutUVs()
```

Run this script with a polygonal object selected and then switch to the UV Texture Editor panel to see the results.

How it works...

The main thing that we are doing here is to apply a new UV layout to a subset of the object's faces. This is a somewhat artificial example because we are selecting faces by just splitting the total number into thirds.

First off, we grab the currently selected object and determine the total number of faces it has using polyEvaluate:

```
    selected = cmds.ls(selection=True)
    obj = selected[0]
    totalFaces = cmds.polyEvaluate(obj, face=True)
```

Then, we determine what one-third of that number is. Note that Python will default to integer division because both totalFaces and 3 are whole integer values. That happens to be exactly what we need for this application, but can easily lead to errors if you are not expecting it:

```
    oneThird = totalFaces/3
```

If you ever want to ensure that you get a proper decimal value as a result, just be sure to divide by a floating-point value, as in:

```
    oneThirdAsDecimal = totalFaces/3.0
```

We also create a couple of helper variables to hold the start and end indices for each of the three sets of faces:

```
    startFace = 0
    endFace = oneThird - 1
```

There is nothing particularly hard about what we are doing here though some care is needed to ensure that we include the entire range of faces. The values that we use are as follows:

	Start index	**End index**	**Example indices (based on a 100-face object)**
1st (planar) mapping	0	oneThird - 1	0-32
2nd (cylindrical) mapping	oneThird	(oneThird * 2) - 1	33-65
3rd (spherical) mapping	oneThird * 2	totalFaces - 1	66-99

Now we are ready for the meat of the script—actually, applying mappings. All three mapping types (planar, cylindrical, and spherical) are applied using the same command, `polyProjection`.

A brief aside on UV mapping—it might seem strange that the three types of mapping are planar, cylindrical, and spherical; why those particular shapes and no others? The reason for this is that if you think of the surface of the model as a two-dimensional skin, then any given part of the model can be classified as belonging to one of only three groups:

▶ The region doesn't have any significant curvature.
▶ The region has significant curvature in a single direction (horizontal or vertical).
▶ The region has significant curvature in both directions.

That maps neatly onto the three options of planar (no curve), cylindrical (single-direction curve), and spherical (curvature in both directions). While the part you are trying to map may be very different from a perfect plane, cylinder, or sphere, start by asking yourself how many directions it curves in and select your mapping accordingly.

There are two things we need to supply to the `polyProjection` command for it to work—the specific faces that should receive the mapping and the type of mapping to apply. To specify the range of faces, we will want to index into the faces or "f" array of the object. We can specify more than one face at a time using two indices with a colon in between. For example, if our object was named `mySphere`, and we wanted to refer to the first six faces, we could do that with:

```
mySphere.f[0:5]
```

In this case, we'll want to use the name of the selected object, and the `startFace` and `endFace` variables for the indices. Doing this gives us the following:

```
obj + '.f[' + str(startFace) + ':' + str(endFace) + ']'
```

Now that we have a way to specify the range of faces, we can apply the mappings, using the `type` flag to specify which kind of mapping to apply:

```
cmds.polyProjection(obj + '.f[' + str(startFace) + ':' + str(endFace)
+ ']', type="planar")
```

From here, we just repeat the process with different values for `startFace` and `endFace`, and different options for the type flag.

There's more...

If you want to apply a mapping to the entire object, you might think that you just have the name of the object and leave out the face indices. This doesn't work, but there is an easy way to tell Maya that you want to refer to all of the faces. To do this, just leave out both indices, but keep the colon, as in:

```
myObject.f[:]
```

If the starter index is missing, Maya will substitute 0, and if the ending index is missing, Maya will substitute the maximum index. Leaving *both* out will result in the mapping being applied to the entire object.

So far, we've only looked at selecting contiguous sequences of faces, but there are lots of situations where you might want to select faces that aren't consecutive indices. You can do that by having multiple selections separated by commas as first argument(s) to a function.

For example, let us say that we wanted to select the first 5 faces *and* faces 32 through 76 of `myObject`. We could use the following:

```
cmds.select('myObject.f[0:4]', 'myObject.f[32:76]', replace=True)
```

Applying this to UV mapping would give us something like the following:

```
cmds.polyProjection('myObject.f[0:4]', 'myObject.f[32:76]',
type="planar")
```

When working with ranges of faces, it's very common that you'll determine the specific indices at runtime, either through some kind of calculation or based on a user input. It's easy enough to do, but can lead to overly complex sequences of stick together string literals and variables, such as the following:

```
obj + '.f[' + str(startFace) + ':' + str(endFace) + ']'
```

It's also very easy to forget to convert numerical values to strings with the `str()` command, which can lead to errors. Luckily enough, Python provides an alternative way to deal with building formatted strings from variables in the form of the `format` command.

To use the format command, you create a string with sections you want to replace with variables. Each replaceable section is represented with curly brackets containing a number such as `{0}`. You can then call the format command on that string and pass in variables that will replace the `{}` clauses. The numbers are used to specify which variables should go where ("{0}" means "replace with the first variable", for example).

So, as a really simple example, we could wish someone happy birthday with the following:

```
personAge = 21
personName = "Alice"
"Congratulations on turning {0}, {1}!".format(personAge, personName)
# results in "Congratulations on turning 21, Alice!"
```

Turning back to Maya, let's say that we wanted to have a generic way to select a range of faces. We would want to pass in the name of the object, the start index, and the ending index as variables. We could do this with:

```
cmds.select(myObject + '.f[' + str(startFace) + ':' + str(endFace) +
']', replace=True)
```

This would work just fine, but is a bit hard to read and is an easy way to introduce errors. If we were to rewrite that using the format command, we would have something like this:

```
cmds.select("{0}.f[{1}:{2}]".format(myObj, startFace, endFace),
replace=True)
```

This tends to be a lot easier to think through because it allows you to separate the structure (the string) from the variables that should be slotted into it. You certainly don't have to use format, but as Maya scripting very often requires building up strings from variables in this way, using it will likely save you a lot of headaches. It also makes your code a lot more readable.

See also

The official Python documentation for the format command is a bit hard to wade through and presents the information in an overly opaque way. Instead, I highly recommend having a look at `https://pyformat.info/`, for a detailed, yet highly readable explanation of the intricacies of the format command.

Creating shading networks with code

In this example, we'll be looking at how to create shading networks with code. We'll be creating a simple toon shader, with a solid color in the interior and a different color at the edges of the object. There are a few different ways to do this, including by creating a rampShader, but we'll be doing it in the somewhat old-fashioned way using a samplerInfo node, as it provides a great example of a relatively simple yet somewhat novel shading network.

First off, let's have a look at what our shader will do and how it will do it. The key characteristic of a toon shader is that the object has an outline around its edges that changes as the object moves. So, the first thing we'll need is some way of knowing what the angle is between a given part of the model and the camera. Luckily, Maya provides a utility node that does just that in the form of samplerInfo. SamplerInfo nodes provide us with a `facingRatio` attribute that ranges from 0 (when a surface is perpendicular to the camera) to 1 (when a surface is facing directly at the camera).

Once we have the facing ratio, we'll need to tie it to a color change somehow. The easiest and most flexible way to do this is to use a ramp texture with linear interpolation to provide a sharp cutoff between the border and interior colors.

Putting all that together gives us a relatively simple, three-node shading network similar to the following:

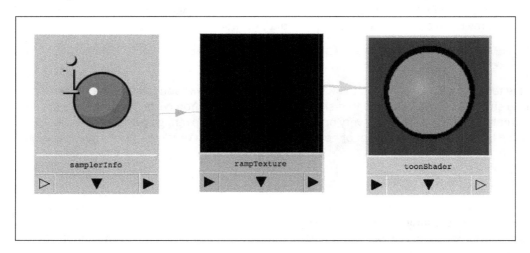

How to do it...

Create a new script and add the following code:

```
import maya.cmds as cmds

def createNodes():

    shaderNode = cmds.shadingNode('blinn', asShader=True)
    rampTexture = cmds.shadingNode('ramp', asTexture=True)
    samplerNode = cmds.shadingNode('samplerInfo', asUtility=True)

    cmds.setAttr(rampTexture + '.interpolation', 0)
    cmds.setAttr(rampTexture + '.colorEntryList[0].position', 0)
    cmds.setAttr(rampTexture + '.colorEntryList[1].position', 0.45)
    cmds.setAttr(rampTexture + '.colorEntryList[0].color', 0, 0, 0,
    type="float3")
    cmds.setAttr(rampTexture + '.colorEntryList[1].color', 1, 0, 0,
    type="float3")

    cmds.connectAttr(samplerNode + '.facingRatio', rampTexture +
    '.vCoord')
    cmds.connectAttr(rampTexture + '.outColor', shaderNode + '.color')

createNodes()
```

If you run the script, you should see a new shader appear in the hypershade, consisting of a red interior and a black exterior edge.

How it works...

There are three parts of the script—creating the nodes, setting their attributes, and connecting them to each other.

First off, we create the three nodes we need with the `shadingNode` command:

```
shaderNode = cmds.shadingNode('blinn', asShader=True)
rampTexture = cmds.shadingNode('ramp', asTexture=True)
samplerNode = cmds.shadingNode('samplerInfo', asUtility=True)
```

The first thing to note is that the shadingNode command is used for all three nodes we create even though they're three different types (one shader, one texture, and one utility). In all cases, you get the results you want by specifying the specific kind of node that you want to create (`'blinn'`, for example) and also including one of the following flags set to True: asShader, asTexture, asUtility, asPosProcess, asRendering, asLight.

Leaving out those flags will result in an error. If you include the wrong flag (asTexture=True when creating a Blinn shader, for example), the command will still work, but I don't recommend it.

Creating the nodes is pretty straightforward—just make sure that you also save the output to a variable (as we've done here) so that you can later set their attributes and connect them.

Once we have all of our nodes created, we need to set their attributes. In this case, we need to do the following few different things that are applied to the ramp texture:

- ▸ Ensure that the color interpolation is set to linear to give us nice sharp transitions between colors, rather than smooth gradients.
- ▸ Make sure that the color swatches are positioned correctly along the length of the ramp.
- ▸ Set both the colors to have the edge color and the interior color that we want.

For all of the above, we'll use the setAttr command. The setAttr command expects the name of the attribute to set as the first argument, followed by the value to which it should be set. For single value, numeric values, that's pretty straightforward. For example, the following sets the ramp's interpolation to none:

```
cmds.setAttr(rampTexture + '.interpolation', 0)
```

Although the type of interpolation isn't actually a numerical value, it's a common practice in Maya (and other places) to use integers to represent various options. When setting attribute values that are represented in the interface by a drop-down menu, you'll generally want to use an integer, with the specific value corresponding to the position of the option in the list (with 0 being the first one).

Next, we'll want to set the colors of the ramp texture to have the correct positions and colors. The first thing to understand is that ramp textures maintain an array of nodes, contained in their colorEntryList attribute. Each entry in that list represents a stop in the ramp texture and has both a position and a color.

We'll want to make sure that the first entry is at the very beginning of the ramp, and the second entry is slightly less than halfway along it, as it gives us a good default edge thickness for the shader. We do this using setAttr to set the position of the first two entries in the colorEntryList array, as follows:

```
cmds.setAttr(rampTexture + '.colorEntryList[0].position', 0)
cmds.setAttr(rampTexture + '.colorEntryList[1].position', 0.45)
```

Next, we'll want to set the colors. That's a bit different, in that we need to feed three separate values into the setAttr command (one each for red, green, and blue). To do this, we'll need to provide all three numbers, and we'll also need to tell Maya to expect multiple inputs to the setAttr command by using the type flag.

The `setAttr` command is one of the most powerful and most flexible commands that Maya offers. It can be used to alter any value of any node. All that power requires the command be able to accept various kinds of inputs, all specified with the type flag. In this case, we need a format that supports decimal values (since colors are represented as number from 0 to 1), and that supports three separate values. Either `float3` or `double3` will work. Putting that all together gives us the following:

```
cmds.setAttr(rampTexture + '.colorEntryList[0].color', 0, 0, 0,
type="float3")
cmds.setAttr(rampTexture + '.colorEntryList[1].color', 1, 0, 0,
type="float3")
```

At this point, we've set all of the attribute values that we need for the shader. All that's left is to connect the nodes to each other. We do it with the `connectAttr` command. That's fairly straightforward and just requires that we specify first the source attribute, then the destination.

In this case, we want to make two connections:

- ▶ The `facingRatio` attribute of the samplerInfo to the V coordinate of the ramp
- ▶ The `outColor` of the ramp texture to the color of the shader

Doing this ends up looking like:

```
cmds.connectAttr(samplerNode + '.facingRatio', rampTexture +
'.vCoord')
cmds.connectAttr(rampTexture + '.outColor', shaderNode + '.color')
```

There's more...

Creating nodes and connecting their attributes is a great way to approach a wide range of tasks in Maya, but it can sometimes be tedious. For example, if we wanted to create a `place2dTexture` utility node and connect it to a texture node, we would have to make over a dozen connections, which is tedious, to say the least. Luckily, Maya provides an easy shortcut to create nodes with the default behavior in the form of the `defaultNavigation` command.

Here's what that would look like:

```
fileTex = cmds.shadingNode('file', asTexture=True)
placeTex = cmds.shadingNode('place2dTexture', asUtility=True)
cmds.defaultNavigation(connectToExisting=True, source=placeTex,
destination=fileTex)
```

Note the inclusion of the `connectToExisting=True` to indicate that the nodes being connected are already present in the scene. Much nicer than 18 separate calls to `connectAttr`, indeed.

You can also break connections between nodes with Python with the `disconnectAttr` command. For example, if we wanted the previously mentioned two-node network of a place2dTexture and a file texture to share everything `except` the offset attribute, we could do the following:

```
cmds.disconnectAttr(placeTex + '.offset', fileTex + '.offset')
```

Sometimes, it might be faster to connect two nodes with the default connections (with defaultNavigation) and break a few specific connections you don't want, instead of manually creating all the connections you do want.

See also

Be sure to refer to the built-in documentation for the `setAttr` command for a complete list of the types of inputs it can accept. The documentation is a bit dense, but it's definitely worth a look.

Applying shaders to objects

Once you have a shading network created, you'll generally want to apply it to one or more objects. In this example, we'll be looking at how to do it. Along the way, we'll create a script that can be used to apply a shader to all of the objects in the scene that are without one.

Getting ready

Make sure that you have a scene with a few different objects in it. Select a few objects and apply a shader to them in the normal way, using the hypershade's interface. Delete the shader, leaving at least one object without any shader of any kind.

How to do it...

Create a new script and add the following code:

```
import maya.cmds as cmds

def shadersFromObject(obj):
    cmds.select(obj, replace=True)
    cmds.hyperShade(obj, shaderNetworksSelectMaterialNodes=True)
    shaders = cmds.ls(selection=True)
    return shaders

def isGeometry(obj):
    shapes = cmds.listRelatives(obj, shapes=True)
```

```
        shapeType = cmds.nodeType(shapes[0])
        geometryTypes = ['mesh', 'nurbsSurface', 'subdiv']

        if shapeType in geometryTypes:
            return True

        return False

    def findUnattachedObjects():

        objects = cmds.ls(type="transform")

        unShaded = []

        for i in range(0, len(objects)):
            if (isGeometry(objects[i])):
                shaders = shadersFromObject(objects[i])
                if (len(shaders) < 1):
                    unShaded.append(objects[i])

        newShader = cmds.shadingNode('blinn', asShader=True)
        cmds.setAttr(newShader + '.color', 0, 1, 1, type="double3")

        cmds.select(unShaded, replace=True)
        cmds.hyperShade(assign=newShader)

    findUnattachedObjects()
```

Run the script, and you should see any and all of the objects that were previously without a shader sporting a brand new, cyan-colored blinn shader.

How it works...

The script works by:

▶ Getting a list of all the objects in the scene.

▶ Running through the list and checking whether a given node is geometry.

▶ For any geometric node, find the shaders applied to it.

▶ If a given object has no shaders, add it to a list of non-shaded objects.

▶ Create a new shader to apply.

▶ Apply the shader to the shader-less objects.

This script makes use of the `hyperShade` command in a couple of different ways—to find the shaders attached to an object, the objects attached to a shader, and to apply a shader.

First, let's look at how to grab the shaders for a given object. To make things easier on ourselves later, we'll create a function to do it. We have the following code:

```
def shadersFromObject(obj):
    cmds.select(obj, replace=True)
    cmds.hyperShade(shaderNetworksSelectMaterialNodes=True)
    shaders = cmds.ls(selection=True)
    return shaders
```

The main thing that we're doing is to use the hyperShade command with the `shaderNetworksSelectMaterialNodes` (or just `smn`) flag set to true. That will select the shader (or shaders) of the currently selected objects. Because the command works on selections, we have to make sure that the object (or objects) we want to know about are selected before we run it. Once we've run it, we'll need to examine the currently selected nodes to get the list of shaders.

Next, we create a function to easily tell if a given transform node corresponds to actual geometry. We need it because we're going to iterate over all the transforms in the scene, and there are many things (lights, cameras, and so on) that have transforms but that aren't geometry. We accept the name of the node as an input and find the corresponding shape node:

```
def isGeometry(obj):
    shapes = cmds.listRelatives(obj, shapes=True)
```

Then, we examine the shape node to find what kind of object it is:

```
    shapeType = cmds.nodeType(shapes[0])
```

Note that the `listRelatives` command returns an array, so we need to index into that and grab the first element. It's unlikely that an object would have multiple shape nodes, but `listRelatives` can also be used to find an object's children, which will often be multiple nodes. Since it can sometimes result in multiples, the command therefore always returns an array even if there's only a single item.

Each of the three types of geometry in Maya (polygon, NURBS, and subdivision surfaces) has its own corresponding shape node. For the sake of convenience and code readability, we'll create an array of those types and check the current shape node's type against it:

```
    geometryTypes = ['mesh', 'nurbsSurface', 'subdiv']

    if shapeType in geometryTypes:
        return True
```

At this point, we're ready to jump into the real meat of the script. We start by grabbing a list of all of the transforms in the scene using the `ls` command. So far, we've mainly used that to find what's currently selected, but it can also be used to grab all the nodes of a specific type (selected or not):

```
objects = cmds.ls(type="transform")
```

Then, we create an empty list to which we'll add any object that we find to be lacking a shader and start running through the list of transforms. First, we check to make sure that the node in question is geometry of some kind. If that's the case, we use our `shadersFromObject` function to find the shader(s) applied to the object. Once we've done this, we check the length of the returned list- if it's zero, then the object had no shaders, and we add it to our list:

```
unShaded = []

for i in range(0, len(objects)):
    if (isGeometry(objects[i])):
        shaders = shadersFromObject(objects[i])
        if (len(shaders) < 1):
            unShaded.append(objects[i])
```

At this point, the `unShaded` list contains all of the objects in the scene that lack shaders. We create a new shader, a simple blinn, and set its color to cyan:

```
newShader = cmds.shadingNode('blinn', asShader=True)
cmds.setAttr(newShader + '.color', 0, 1, 1, type="double3")
```

Finally, we select the contents of the `unShaded` list and apply the shader we just made. For that, we'll use the `hyperShade` command again, but this time with the assign flag to apply the specified shader to the currently selected objects. We have the following code:

```
cmds.select(unShaded, replace=True)
cmds.hyperShade(assign=newShader)
```

There's more...

The `hyperShade` command can be used to do most of the tasks one would normally accomplish in the hypershade panel interface. In the previous example, we grabbed shaders from objects, but the command can also be used to find the objects associated with a given shader with the `objects` flag. Wrapping that up in a nice function to return the objects for a given shader would look something like the following:

```
def objectsFromShader(shader):
    cmds.hyperShade(objects=shader)
    objects = cmds.ls(selection=True)
    return objects
```

Once again, the `hyperShade` changes the current selection, and we use the `ls` command to retrieve the selection as an array.

Using shading nodes for non-shading tasks

One of the really great things about the various nodes that Maya provides is that there are very few limits on how you use them. To Maya, all nodes are just collections of functionality with certain inputs and outputs, and as long as the type of data lines up, it doesn't really care how you connect them.

This means that it's completely possible (and often very useful) to use hypershade nodes for tasks that aren't related to creating shading networks. In this example, we'll be doing just that using a plus/minus/average utility node to set the position of a given object to the average position of a number of others. This could be used, for example, to ensure that the pelvis of a character always stays centered in between the IK handles controlling its feet.

Using utility nodes can be used for tasks where you might otherwise write an expression, but with the added benefit that they update constantly, not just while the playback head is moving.

Getting ready

Be sure that you have a scene with at least three objects in it.

How to do it...

Create a new script and add the following code:

```
import maya.cmds as cmds

def keepCentered():

    objects = cmds.ls(selection=True)

    if (len(objects) < 3):
        cmds.error('Please select at least three objects')

    avgNode = cmds.shadingNode('plusMinusAverage', asUtility=True)
    cmds.setAttr(avgNode + '.operation', 3)

    for i in range(0, len(objects) - 1):
```

```
        cmds.connectAttr(objects[i] + '.translateX', avgNode +
'.input3D[{0}].input3Dx'.format(i))
        cmds.connectAttr(objects[i] + '.translateZ', avgNode +
'.input3D[{0}].input3Dz'.format(i))

    controlledObjIndex = len(objects) - 1

    cmds.connectAttr(avgNode + '.output3D.output3Dx',
objects[controlledObjIndex] + '.translateX')
    cmds.connectAttr(avgNode + '.output3D.output3Dz',
objects[controlledObjIndex] + '.translateZ')

keepCentered()
```

Select at least three objects, making sure that the object you want to be controlled is the last one selected, and run the script. Once you've done that, try moving the objects around, and you'll see that the X and Z position of the controlled object is always an average of the X and Z positions of all the other objects.

How it works...

First off, we check to make sure that there are at least three objects selected and error out if there isn't:

```
objects = cmds.ls(selection=True)

if (len(objects) < 3):
    cmds.error('Please select at least three objects')
```

If we have at least three objects, we proceed to create a brand new utility node, in this case a plus/minus/average node. Since the plus/minus/average node can perform three completely separate actions, we also need to set its "operation" attribute to average (which happens to be the fourth option in the corresponding dropdown, so has a value of 3), as follows:

```
avgNode = cmds.shadingNode('plusMinusAverage', asUtility=True)
cmds.setAttr(avgNode + '.operation', 3)
```

Once we've done this, we run through the list of selected objects and connect all but the last one to the utility node as inputs. PlusMinusAverage nodes can have one-dimensional, two-dimensional, or three-dimensional inputs. In this case, we'll use 3D inputs.

We're only using two inputs (X and Z), so we certainly could get by with 2D inputs instead. However, since we're dealing with position data, I think it's better to use full 3D inputs and just leave the Y inputs empty. This way, it's easier to later modify the script to allow the user to select any combination of X, Y, and Z that they want.

Of course, the "X", "Y", and "Z" of the plusMinusAverage node don't have any intrinsic meaning; they're just three separate pathways for the calculation, and we could certainly use them for things that have nothing to do with position.

The plusMinusAverage node holds an array for each type of input (one-dimensional, two-dimensional, and three-dimensional). So to do anything with it, we'll need to first access the proper array. If we had a plusMinusAverage node named `avgNode` and wanted to do something with the second one-dimensional input, we would use the following:

```
avgNode.input1D[1]
```

For two- and three-dimensional inputs, we need to specify not only the proper array but also the proper entry. For two-dimensional inputs, the array is specified as:

```
avgNode.input2D[0].input2Dy
```

For three-dimensional inputs, the array is specified as:

```
avgNode.input3D[0].input3Dx
```

We don't need to explicitly add inputs to the utility node; we can just use connectAttr to connect inputs to successive indices of the node's input 3D array.

In this case, we want to run through all of the selected objects except for the last one and connect their X and Z positions, which is easy enough:

```
for i in range(0, len(objects) - 1):
    cmds.connectAttr(objects[i] + '.translateX', avgNode +
'.input3D[{0}].input3Dx'.format(i))
    cmds.connectAttr(objects[i] + '.translateZ', avgNode +
'.input3D[{0}].input3Dz'.format(i))
```

At that point, we're mainly done. All that's left is to connect the outputs of the plusMinusAverage node to the controlled object. Storing the index of the controlled object as a variable isn't necessary, but does make the code a bit more readable:

```
controlledObjIndex = len(objects) - 1

cmds.connectAttr(avgNode + '.output3D.output3Dx',
objects[controlledObjIndex] + '.translateX')
cmds.connectAttr(avgNode + '.output3D.output3Dz',
objects[controlledObjIndex] + '.translateZ')
```

There's more...

In the discussed example, we created a very simple network, but it's certainly possible to create more complex networks. One important thing to bear in mind is that, while all the nodes have certain uses that they were created for, in no way this limits the kind of use to which they can be put. To Maya, numbers are just numbers, and there's nothing to stop you from using color channels to control position or rotation to control transparency.

5
Adding Controls – Scripting for Rigging

This chapter will cover how to use Python to build rigs by:

- ► Creating skeletons with script
- ► Setting up set-driven key relationships with script
- ► Adding custom attributes and locking and hiding attributes
- ► Setting up inverse kinematics (IK) with script

Introduction

Once you've created your model, laid out the UVs, and set up the shading networks, you'll still need to build controls into it if you want it to move. In this chapter, we'll be looking at how to do that with scripts.

We'll be looking at how to use Python to automate tasks related to rigging. Rigging is already one of the more technical aspects of 3D animation, and as such lends itself quite well to a script-based approach.

Creating skeletons with script

In this example, we'll be looking at how to create skeletons with script. We'll create two examples, one simple chain of bones and one branching set, similar to what you might want for a creature's hand.

How to do it...

Create a new file and add the following code:

```
def createSimpleSkeleton(joints):
    '''
    Creates a simple skeleton as a single chain of bones
    ARGS:
        joints- the number of bones to create
    '''


    cmds.select(clear=True)

    bones = []
    pos = [0, 0, 0]

    for i in range(0, joints):
        pos[1] = i * 5
        bones.append(cmds.joint(p=pos))

    cmds.select(bones[0], replace=True)


def createHand(fingers, joints):
    '''
    Creates a set of 'fingers', each with a set number of joints
    ARGS:
        fingers- the number of joint chains to create
        joints- the number of bones per finger
    '''


    cmds.select(clear=True)

    baseJoint = cmds.joint(name='wrist', p=(0,0,0))

    fingerSpacing = 2
    palmLen = 4
    jointLen = 2
```

```
    for i in range(0, fingers):
        cmds.select(baseJoint, replace=True)
        pos = [0, palmLen, 0]

        pos[0] = (i * fingerSpacing) - ((fingers-1) * fingerSpacing)/2

        cmds.joint(name='finger{0}base'.format(i+1), p=pos)

        for j in range(0, joints):
            cmds.joint(name='finger{0}joint{1}'.format((i+1),(j+1)),
relative=True, p=(0,jointLen, 0))

    cmds.select(baseJoint, replace=True)


createSimpleSkeleton(5)
createHand(5, 3)
```

Run this code, and you'll see two separate networks of bones, both centered at the origin—one that is a straight vertical chain of five bones and one that approximates a hand (five fingers with three joints each).

The end result should look something like the following (shown after moving the two skeletons apart).

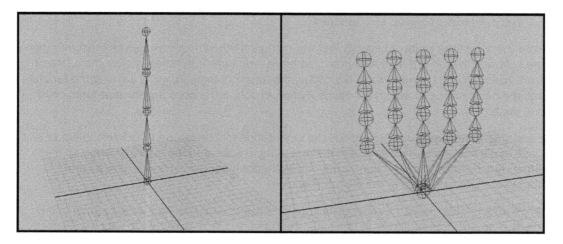

How it works...

We'll start with the `createSimpleSkeleton` command. Note that we start the function with a triple-quoted comment:

```
def createSimpleSkeleton(joints):
    '''
    Creates a simple skeleton as a single chain of bones
    ARGS:
        joints- the number of bones to create
    '''
```

By placing a comment as the very first thing in the function definition, Python will recognize it as a *docstring*.

Docstrings are a great way to provide documentation to the end user about what your code does and how it should be used. If you've added docstrings to your functions, the user will be able to view them with the help command. For example, let's say we have a file named `myFunctions.py` with a handful of functions, and we start the first one in the following manner:

```
def functionOne():
    """Description of function one"""
```

The user could use the following command to view our description for functionOne:

```
help(myFunctions.functionOne)
```

Note the use of dot syntax to specify first the module (Python treats all files as modules) then the specific function within it. Also note that there aren't any parentheses after the name of the function; that's because we're not calling the function. Instead, we're passing the function into the help command, which will cause Python to output the docstring for that function, if one exists.

Docstrings can also be used to provide documentation for classes and modules. In either case, make sure that the docstring is the first thing to appear in the class, function, or file, either directly after "def [functionName]", as we've done here, after "class [className]:" (for classes), or at the top of the file (for modules).

When adding docstrings, it's generally a good practice to describe each of the inputs to the function and what they signify. In this case, our function has a single input, which will specify the number of bones to create.

Now that we've properly documented our code, it's time to actually make some bones. The bulk of the work is done using the joint tool to create a new bone using the position/p flag to specify where it should go, as follows:

```
cmds.joint(position=(1, 1, 1))
```

In our first example, we make things slightly easier on ourselves by creating an array to hold the position of the bones and passing that in to each successive call to the joint command. This way, we can easily just modify the Y position of the joints that we create, while keeping the X and Z coordinates the same to produce a vertical chain of bones:

```
pos = [0, 0, 0]
```

We also create an array to hold the output of the joint command after each bone is created in order to allow us to take further actions on the bones once they've been created:

```
bones = []
```

Once we have both of those, we simply run through a loop, changing the second element of our pos array to alter the Y-value and creating a new joint:

```
for i in range(0, joints):
    pos[1] = i * 5
    bones.append(cmds.joint(p=pos))
```

The most notable thing about the this is what we're *not* doing. Note that this code merely creates bones; it does nothing to explicitly create any sort of hierarchy between them. Nevertheless, the preceding code will result in a proper chain of bones, with each one a child of the previous bone.

This is due to the fact that, when creating bones, Maya will automatically make any newly created joint a child of the currently selected object, if that object happens to be a joint. That, combined with the fact that all of Maya's commands that result in the creation of a new object leave that new object selected means that, as we build up the chain of joints, Maya automatically connects them into the proper hierarchy. This also explains why the first line of the function was:

```
cmds.select(clear=True)
```

This ensured that nothing was selected. When creating new joint networks, it is always good to make sure that your selection is clear before starting; otherwise, you may end up with connections that you don't want.

Now that we've looked at making a simple chain of bones, we'll move on to a slightly more complex example in the createHand function. Once again, we'll add a docstring at the start of the function to properly document the inputs to the function and the effects of each:

```
def createHand(fingers, joints):
    '''
    Creates a set of 'fingers', each with a set number of joints
    ARGS:
        fingers- the number of joint chains to create
        joints- the number of bones per finger
    '''
```

We start by creating a single joint to be the root bone and saving it in the `baseJoint` variable, so we can easily refer to it again later.

```
baseJoint = cmds.joint(name='wrist', p=(0,0,0))
```

We'll also make sure to give our new bone a sensible name. In this case, we'll use "wrist" since it will be serving as the parent bone for all of our fingers. You might be wondering why we're setting the name *and* storing the result into a variable. That is necessary in order to avoid problems if there is already something named "wrist" in our scene. If there *is* something named "wrist", then Maya would append a number onto the name of the newly created bone, resulting in something like "wrist1". If we later tried to do something to "wrist", we would end up affecting a different object. So, we have to do two things; we'll store the output of the joint command into a variable so that we can refer to it later *and* we give it a name so that it's nicer to work with.

Having all of the bones in your rig named "jointX" is a great way to make things unnecessarily confusing, so always be sure to give your bones proper names; just don't trust those names to always be unique.

Now that we have our base bone, we create a few variables to control the layout of the "hand"—one for the length of the palm, one for the length of each finger joint, and one for the gap between each finger.

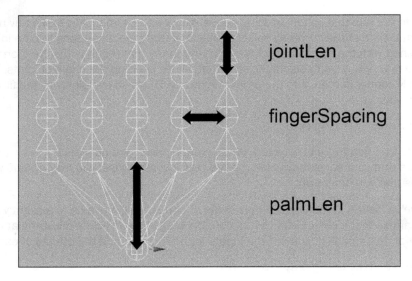

Now we're ready to create each finger. We start each pass through the loop by first selecting the baseJoint bone. That's all we need to do in order to make sure that we have the proper hierarchy, with each finger having a separate chain and each chain being parented to the base joint.

We start each finger with a joint that is palmLen units above the base joint. The horizontal spacing is a little more involved and requires some explanation. We have the following code:

```
pos[0] = (i * fingerSpacing) - ((fingers-1) * fingerSpacing)/2
```

There are two parts to the preceding code:

```
(i * fingerSpacing)
```

This will ensure that the fingers are spaced out horizontally by the proper amount, but if we left it at that, we would have all of the fingers to the right of the wrist. To fix this, we need to move all of our positions to the left by one half of the total width. The total width is equal to our fingerSpacing variable multiplied by the number of gaps between the fingers. Since the number of gaps is equal to the number of fingers, minus one, we have:

```
((fingers-1) * fingerSpacing)/2
```

Subtracting the second part from the first will keep the finger-to-finger spacing the same, but will move everything such that the fingers are centered over the based joint.

Now that we have the proper position for the base of our "finger", we create the first joint, as follows:

```
cmds.joint(name='finger{0}base'.format(i+1), p=pos)
```

Note that we use the string format command to build up the name of the joint from some literals and the number of the finger we're on at the moment (adding one so that the first finger is a more readable "1" instead of "0"). This will give us joints named along the lines of "finger1base", "finger2base", and so on. We'll do something similar with the successive joints to name them with both the name of the finger and the name of the joint ("finger1joint1", for example).

Once we've started the finger, we run through another loop to create each of the finger joints:

```
for j in range(0, joints):
    cmds.joint(name='finger{0}joint{1}'.format((i+1),(j+1)),
relative=True, p=(0,jointLen, 0))
```

Note that there's one small difference with this, in that we're passing what appears to be the same position in to the joint command. That still works because we're also using the `relative` command, which will cause Maya to position the new bone relative to its immediate parent. In this case, this means that each new bone will be created `jointLen` units above the previous one.

There's more...

In order to create branching skeletons, it is necessary to change the currently selected bone before creating child bones. In the preceding example, we did that directly, by explicitly selecting our base joint again before starting each new branch.

That's not the only way though you can also use the `pickWalk` command. The `pickWalk` command operates on the current selection and allows you to move around its hierarchy. To use the command, you have to specify a direction—up, down, left, or right. The most useful options are up, which will change the selection to be the parent of the currently selected node, and down, which will change the selection to a child of the currently selected node (assuming it has children). So, another option to create a branching network of joints would be

to import maya.cmds as cmds, as follows:

```
cmds.joint(p=(0,0,0))
cmds.joint(p=(-5, 5, 0))
cmds.pickWalk(direction="Up")
cmds.joint(p=(5, 5, 0))
```

The first two lines create a base bone and add a child bone one unit up and to the left. Then, the `pickWalk` command is used to move the selection back to the base joint before creating a third bone.

The results of creating three bones in sequence. The left image indicates what happens if pickWalk is used to move back up the hierarchy after creating the second, and the right image indicates what happens if pickWalk is omitted.

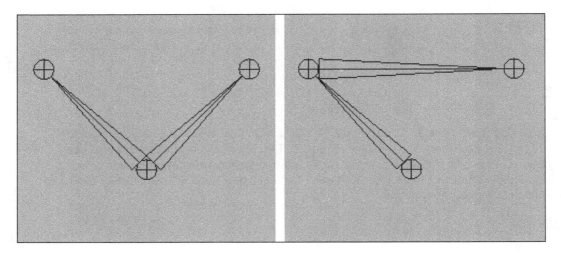

Setting up set-driven key relationships with script

A great deal of rigging is nothing more than setting up connections between attributes. Sometimes, those connections can be very direct, such as making sure that two joints are always in exactly the same position in world space, but in other times, something other than a direct one-to-one mapping is called for.

There are a few different ways to connect attributes in non-linear ways, including using Maya's set-driven key capability to map one arbitrary range of an attribute onto a different arbitrary range of another. In this example, we'll be looking at how to set that up with scripting.

Our example will set up the "Hello World" equivalent for using a set-driven key, a finger that curls all of its joints smoothly at the same time, allowing the animator to keyframe a single attribute per finger instead of three (or possibly even more).

Getting ready

For this example, you'll want to have a simple chain of at least three bones. The output of the script will cause all of the bones downstream from the selected bone to rotate when the parent bone (the knuckle) is rotated. Either create a simple chain of bones, or use the output from this chapter's example on bone creation.

How to do it...

Create a new script and enter the following code:

```python
import maya.cmds as cmds


def setDrivenKeys():
    objs = cmds.ls(selection=True)
    baseJoint = objs[0]

    driver = baseJoint + ".rotateZ"

    children = cmds. listRelatives(children=True, allDescendents=True)

    for bone in children:
        driven = bone + ".rotateZ"
```

```
        cmds.setAttr(driver, 0)
        cmds.setDrivenKeyframe(driven, cd=driver, value=0,
    driverValue=0)

        cmds.setAttr(driver, 30)
        cmds.setDrivenKeyframe(driven, cd=driver, value=30,
    driverValue=30)


    cmds.setAttr(driver, 0)


setDrivenKeys()
```

Once you have the script ready, select the "knuckle" bone and run it. Then, try rotating the knuckle bone around the *z* axis. You should see all of the bones downstream from the knuckle rotate as well:

[fig setDrivenKey_1]

How it works...

There are two main aspects to the script—the actual set-driven key setup and some code to walk down the chain of bones.

First off, we start by grabbing the currently selected object, as we've done in the past.

```
objs = cmds.ls(selection=True)
baseJoint = objs[0]
```

We store the selected object to a variable (baseJoint) so that we can easily refer to it later. We'll also want an easy way to refer to the driver attribute, in this case, the Z-rotation of the base bone, so we store that to a variable as well.

```
driver = baseJoint + ".rotateZ"
```

Now we're ready to start stepping through our chain of bones. To do this, we'll need to first grab a list of all of the downstream bones from the selected joint. We can do that using the `listRelatives` command with the children flag. Normally, that would only use the direct children of the given node, but if we also set the `allDescendents` flag to True, we will be given the full list of children, grandchildren, and so on down the entire hierarchy:

```
children = cmds.listRelatives(children=True, allDescendents=True)
```

Now that we have a list of all of the nodes that are children of the selected node (in this case, our base joint), we're ready to step through the list and set up a set-driven key relationship on each. To do this, we'll use the `setDrivenKeyframe` command.

In each iteration through our loop, we'll:

1. Set our `driven` variable to the proper attribute (bone + ".rotateZ").
2. Set the value of our driven attribute using setAttr to its minimum value.
3. Use the `setDrivenKeyframe` command to link the two attributes.
4. Repeat steps 2 and 3 to set the maximum values.

The `setDrivenKeyframe` command is fairly straightforward, requiring that we pass in the driver attribute, the driven attribute, and the values for each. In both cases, the attributes in question need to be the full name (node name, ".", and attribute name). So, to set it up so that our driven attribute is at 0 when our driver attribute is at -10, we could use the following:

```
cmds.setDrivenKeyframe(driven, cd=driver, value=-10, driverValue=0)
```

This should be enough to get the results we want, but the command can often fail unless the driver value is explicitly set beforehand. That's why, we use `setAttr` before calling `setDrivenKeyframe`.

The `setAttr` command is a real workhorse, and it is the one that you're likely to use in a great deal of different scenarios. Luckily, it's also very easy to use; just call it and pass in first the attribute you're setting, then the value to which you want to set it, as in:

```
cmds.setAttr(driver, 30)
```

Once we've set at least two keys on each bone, we'll have a proper set-driven key relationship. Putting this all together gives us the following loop:

```
for bone in children:
    driven = bone + ".rotateZ"

    cmds.setAttr(driver, 0)
    cmds.setDrivenKeyframe(driven, cd=driver, value=0,
driverValue=0)

    cmds.setAttr(driver, 30)
    cmds.setDrivenKeyframe(driven, cd=driver, value=30,
driverValue=30)
```

Finally, we'll finish off the script with a little bit of cleanup to ensure that we leave things as we found them. In this case, it means setting the driver value back to zero.

```
cmds.setAttr(driver, 0)
```

There's more...

In the preceding example, we used only two keyframes, but you can certainly have more than two points on the graph relating the driven variable to the driver if you wanted to have a more non-linear relationship between the attributes. For example, if we wanted to have the driven variable change at a greater rate during the last third of the range, we could do something like the following:

```
cmds.setAttr(driver, 0)
cmds.setDrivenKeyframe(driven, cd=driver, v=0, dr=0)

cmds.setAttr(driver, 20)
cmds.setDrivenKeyframe(driven, cd=driver, v=20, dr=10)

cmds.setAttr(driver, 30)
cmds.setDrivenKeyframe(driven, cd=driver, v=30, dr=30)
```

In this code, the first twenty units of change in the driver (0–20) would result in only 10 units of change in the driven (0–10), but the last 10 units of change in the driver (20–30) would drive a 20-unit change in the driven attribute.

Another thing you might want to consider is what kind of curve you want to create. Each of the keyframes added with `setDrivenKeyframe` can be given its own tangent types, for both the input and output. To do it, set either the `inTangentType` or `outTangentType` when calling the function. In either case, you'll want to give it a string representing the tangent type you want.

So, if we wanted to have linear tangents for both the input and output of a new driven keyframe, we could do the following:

```
cmds.setDrivenKeyframe(driven, cd=driver, v=30, dr=30,
inTangentType="linear", outTangentType="linear")
```

For a full list of the allowed options, consult the documentation for the `setDrivenKeyframe` command.

Adding custom attributes and locking and hiding attributes

As you build up the rig for a model, it is often helpful to create custom attributes so that you can link things to `forefingerRight.curl` (for example), instead of `forefingerRight.rotateZ`. Not only will that make your rigs a great deal easier to understand, but it also allows you to tie actions of the rig to values that are completely independent of any built-in affects such as rotation or translation.

Just as there are sometimes attributes that you will want to add to a given node, there are often attributes on a node that you know you'll never want to animate. Locking such attributes and hiding them in the channel box is another way to make your rigs easier to work with.

In this example, we'll be looking at how to do both things—adding new, custom attributes to a node and hiding undesirable or unimportant attributes from view. More specifically, we'll be hiding the rotation and scale attributes and adding some attributes of the sort that you might want in order to animate a facial rig.

Here's a screenshot of the channel box both before and after the example script is run:

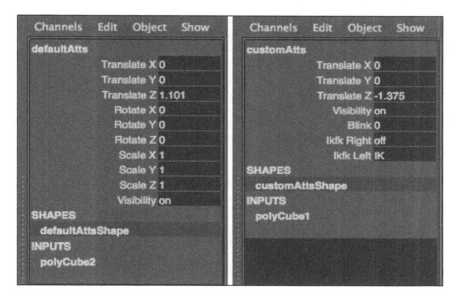

Getting ready

Before adding to or altering the attributes on a node, it's important to determine exactly what you need. In this case, we'll be setting things up in a way similar to what we might want for control of a facial rig. This means for the node itself, we'll likely want to be able to change its position, but not the rotation or scale.

We'll also want to add several different attributes to control the parts of our rig. These will naturally vary from rig to rig, but in all cases, it's necessary to think about what kind of data we need for each. For the sake of the example, let's say that we want the following controls:

- A "blink" attribute, which will cause both eyelids to close and open.
- An "IK/FK" switch control for each of the legs that can switch between IK and FK controls

For each of these, we'll need to think about what kind of data we need. For the blink attribute, we want a number that can vary smoothly from one value (representing fully open) to another (representing fully closed). For that, we'll need a decimal number.

For the IK/FK switch, we could approach it in two different ways. We could have a value that represents whether IK is on, with "off" meaning that FK is currently being used. For that, we would want to use a simple on/off value. Alternatively, we could implement our IK/FK switch as a dropdown of options. That would likely be a better and more user-friendly way to go. In this example, we'll be implementing both approaches for the sake of completeness.

How to do it...

Create a new file and add the following code:

```
def addCustomAttributes():

    objs = cmds.ls(selection=True)
    cmds.addAttr(objs[0], shortName="blink", longName="blink",
defaultValue=0, minValue=-1, maxValue=1, keyable=True)

    cmds.addAttr(objs[0], shortName="ikfkR", longName="ikfkRight",
attributeType="bool", keyable=True)
    cmds.addAttr(objs[0], shortName="ikfkL", longName="ikfkLeft",
attributeType="enum", enumName="IK:FK", keyable=True)

    cmds.setAttr(objs[0]+".rotateX", edit=True, lock=True,
keyable=False, channelBox=False)

    for att in ['rotateY','rotateZ','scaleX','scaleY','scaleZ']:
        lockAndHide(objs[0], att)

def lockAndHide(obj, att):

    fullAttributeName = obj + '.' + att

    cmds.setAttr(fullAttributeName, edit=True, lock=True,
keyable=False, channelBox=False)


setup()
addCustomAttributes()
```

Select an object and run the preceding script, making sure that you have the channel box visible when you do so. You should see the rotation and scale attributes disappear and the new attributes appear.

How it works...

First off, we grab the currently selected object, just as we've done in the past. Once we've done that, we start by adding the blink attribute with the following:

```
cmds.addAttr(objs[0], shortName="blink", longName="blink",
defaultValue=0, minValue=-1, maxValue=1, keyable=True)
```

This is a fairly involved command, but the general idea is that we specify the following for each attribute we want to add:

- ► The name
- ► The type of attribute
- ► Any additional information that the specific type of attribute requires

The names of attributes come in two flavors—the short name and the long name. You have to specify at least one of those to have the command work, but it's generally a good idea to specify both. In this case, "blink" is sufficiently short to use it for both the short and long versions.

If we don't directly specify the type of attribute we're creating, Maya will default to a numerical type, which happens to be exactly what we want for the blink attribute. Since a "blink" attribute has a natural upper and lower bound (since eyelids open by a finite amount), it also makes sense to give our attribute minimum and maximum values, with the default being in between. Here, we're using -1 and 1 for the minimum and maximum, which is fairly standard.

Finally, in order to ensure that our new attribute shows up in the channel box, we need to make sure that we set the `keyable` flag to true.

Next up is our simple on/off version of the IK/FK switch. For this, we'll be using a Boolean type. For non-numeric types, we'll need to use the `attributeType` flag with the appropriate value (in this case, "bool"). We still specify the short and long names, and use the `keyable` flag to make it appear in the channel box:

```
cmds.addAttr(objs[0], shortName="ikfkR", longName="ikfkRight",
attributeType="bool", keyable=True)
```

The resulting attribute will accept values of either 0 or 1, but will display them as "off" or "on" (respectfully) in the channel box.

For our final attribute, we'll create one with two possible states, either "IK" or "FK", presented to the user as a drop-down list. For that, we'll create an attribute of type "enum" (short for "enumerated list"). We'll also need to specify the specific options that we want with the `enumName` flag. The `enumName` flag expects a string containing one or more options, all separated with colons.

So, in order to have "IK" and "FK" options, we'll want the value of our `enumName` flag to be "IK:FK". Putting this all together gives us:

```
cmds.addAttr(objs[0], shortName="ikfkL", longName="ikfkLeft",
attributeType="enum", enumName="IK:FK", keyable=True)
```

Note that, in order to actually hook our new attribute up to anything, it's important to know what the actual values of each option are. By default, the first option will have a value of 0, with each successive option increasing by one. So, in this case, "IK" will correspond to 0 and "FK" will correspond to 1. If you want to have specific numerical values for specific options, that's also possible. For example, if we wanted "IK" to correspond to 5 and "FK" to 23, we could do that with the following:

```
cmds.addAttr(objs[0], longName="ikCustomVals", attributeType="enum",
enumName="IK=5:FK=23", keyable=True)
```

At this point, we're all done adding attributes and can move on to hiding the ones we don't want—the rotation and scale attributes. We'll want to do three separate things to properly hide each attribute, namely:

1. Lock the attribute so that its value cannot be changed.
2. Set the attribute to not be keyable.
3. Set the attribute to not appear in the channel box.

All of these can be accomplished with the `setAttr` command, used in the edit mode, as in:

```
cmds.setAttr(objs[0]+".rotateX", edit=True, lock=True, keyable=False,
channelBox=False)
```

Note that the first thing we pass in to setAttr is the full name of the attribute (object name and attribute name, joined by a "."). That can be a little tedious to do each time though, so we create a function that accepts the object and attribute name, and locks and hides it.

```
def lockAndHide(obj, att):

    fullAttributeName = obj + '.' + att
    cmds.setAttr(fullAttributeName, edit=True, lock=True,
keyable=False, channelBox=False)
```

We can then use a bit of Python's built-in functionality to make it even easier to lock a list of attributes by iterating over a list of attribute names and passing them to our `lockAndHide` function, as follows:

```
for att in ['rotateY','rotateZ','scaleX','scaleY','scaleZ']:
    lockAndHide(objs[0], att)
```

In this case, Python's approach to for loops (iterating over a list) makes things very straightforward, indeed.

There's more...

If you look at the documentation for the addAttr command, you'll see that there is an extensive list of attribute types. Don't let the length of that list scare you; the vast majority of attributes you're likely to want to add can be implemented as the default (double) type with the appropriate minimum and maximum values. "Double" in this context is short for "double precision" meaning a decimal value that uses twice the number of bytes as a typical float.

While the several different flavors of integer and floating-point numeric values aren't likely to make much of a difference in your scripts, a few of the more esoteric types may come in handy.

One thing you might find useful is the ability to add a color attribute to a node. Adding a color requires adding a compound attribute, which is a little bit more involved than what we've seen so far. First, you need to add an attribute to serve as the parent, then you'll need to add successive child attributes, of the same type and of the right number as the parent attribute's type.

For a color, we'll need to use an attribute type with three values for the parent, such as "float3". We'll also want to set the usedAsColor flag to true so that it is properly recognized as a color by Maya.

```
cmds.addAttr(objs[0], longName='colorTest', attributeType='float3',
usedAsColor=True)
```

Once we've done that, we can add attributes for each component of the parent attribute (in this case, values for the red, green, and blue components). Note the use of the parent flag to properly tie the new attributes to our "colorTest" group:

```
    cmds.addAttr(objs[0], longName='colorR', attributeType='float',
parent='colorTest' )
    cmds.addAttr(objs[0], longName='colorG', attributeType='float',
parent='colorTest' )
    cmds.addAttr(objs[0], longName='colorB', attributeType='float',
parent='colorTest' )
```

Note that some types of attributes won't display in the channel box. To see such attributes, select the node they've been added to, open the attribute editor, and expand the "extra attributes" tab.

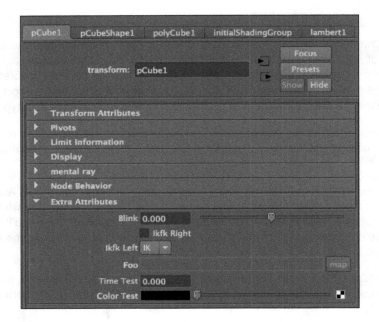

Setting up inverse kinematics (IK) with script

While it is very likely that any given model will require at least some custom rigging work, it can often be helpful to automate the setup of common subcomponents that occur frequently in many different rigs. In this example, we'll be doing just that and setting up a simple inverse kinematics (IK) system with code.

Although our example will be simple, it will still demonstrate a common issue—the need to accurately position joints to match the specific proportions of a model. As such, the script will have the following two distinct parts:

- ▶ A preliminary step, where we create locators representing where the various joints will be created.

- ▶ A secondary step, where we build a skeleton and set up its attributes based on the position of the locators.

By breaking the script into two parts, we allow the user to alter the positions of the locators after they've been created, but before the actual skeleton has been set up. This tends to be a much more effective way to match rigs to characters, and there can also be a great way to solicit input from the user for other kinds of tasks as well.

Getting ready

While you running the example script doesn't require having a suitable model, you might enjoy it more if you have a bipedal model to fit the joints we'll be creating to.

How to do it...

Create a new script and add the following code:

```
import maya.cmds as cmds

def showUI():
    myWin = cmds.window(title="IK Rig", widthHeight=(200, 200))
    cmds.columnLayout()
    cmds.button(label="Make Locators", command=makeLocators,
width=200)
    cmds.button(label="Setup IK", command=setupIK, width=200)

    cmds.showWindow(myWin)


def makeLocators(args):
    global hipLoc
    global kneeLoc
    global ankleLoc
    global footLoc

    hipLoc = cmds.spaceLocator(name="HipLoc")
    kneeLoc = cmds.spaceLocator(name="KneeLoc")
    ankleLoc = cmds.spaceLocator(name="AnkleLoc")
    footLoc = cmds.spaceLocator(name="FootLoc")

    cmds.xform(kneeLoc, absolute=True, translation=(0, 5, 0))
    cmds.xform(hipLoc, absolute=True, translation=(0, 10, 0))
    cmds.xform(footLoc, absolute=True, translation=(2, 0, 0))
```

```
def setupIK(args):
    global hipLoc
    global kneeLoc
    global ankleLoc
    global footLoc

    cmds.select(clear=True)

    pos = cmds.xform(hipLoc, query=True, translation=True,
worldSpace=True)
    hipJoint = cmds.joint(position=pos)

    pos = cmds.xform(kneeLoc, query=True, translation=True,
worldSpace=True)
    kneeJoint = cmds.joint(position=pos)

    pos = cmds.xform(ankleLoc, query=True, translation=True,
worldSpace=True)
    ankleJoint = cmds.joint(position=pos)

    pos = cmds.xform(footLoc, query=True, translation=True,
worldSpace=True)
    footJoint = cmds.joint(position=pos)

    cmds.ikHandle(startJoint=hipJoint, endEffector=ankleJoint)

showUI()
```

How it works...

Since this script requires two separate parts, we'll need to implement a simple UI in order to allow the user to run the first part, alter the positions of the locators, and invoke the second. The UI isn't anything complicated, but just two buttons, and should look familiar if you've worked through any of the examples in *Chapter 2, Creating User Interfaces*. We simply create a window, add a layout, and add one button for each of the steps of our script. We have the following code:

```
def showUI():
    myWin = cmds.window(title="IK Rig", widthHeight=(200, 200))
    cmds.columnLayout()
    cmds.button(label="Make Locators", command=makeLocators,
width=200)
    cmds.button(label="Setup IK", command=setupIK, width=200)

    cmds.showWindow(myWin)
```

The things start to get interesting in the `makeLocators` function, which will create four locator objects in a default layout. Before creating the locators, we'll create four global variables so that we can store references to them for later use. The `global` keyword tells Python that these variables should be treated as global in scope, meaning that they will be available beyond the immediate, local scope (in this case, the `makeLocators` function). Later on, we'll invoke the global variables again from within our second function (the `setupIK` function) in order to refer to the locators we're about to create:

```
global hipLoc
global kneeLoc
global ankleLoc
global footLoc
```

Now we're ready to create the locators. Locators are especially useful for rigging because they provide a bare-bones transform node that is nonrenderable, but easily selectable in Maya's interface.

To make a locator, we can use the `spaceLocator` command. We'll use the name flag to set the name of created locator, but this is mainly just to make things nice for the end user.

Although it is sometimes nice to give created nodes names, you should never rely on those names for later reference, as there's no guarantee that the name you specify is the name that the object will end up with. If you name something `myObject`, but there's already a node in your scene by that name, Maya will force the newly created object to be named `myObject1`, and any code that you wrote referencing `myObject` would be pointed at the wrong thing. Never, ever, trust names in Maya; instead store the output of commands that create nodes to variables and use those variables to refer to the created objects.

We'll create four locators in total, one each for the hip, knee, ankle, and toe of a simple leg. The output of each of our calls to the `spaceLocator` command is saved to one of our global variables:

```
hipLoc = cmds.spaceLocator(name="HipLoc")
kneeLoc = cmds.spaceLocator(name="KneeLoc")
ankleLoc = cmds.spaceLocator(name="AnkleLoc")
footLoc = cmds.spaceLocator(name="FootLoc")
```

If you look at the documentation for the `spaceLocator` command, you'll see that there is a `position` flag that can be used to set the position of the created locator. However, note that we're not using that flag in the previous code. This's because while the locator will appear to be at the specified position, the pivot point for the locator will remain at the origin. Since we're creating the locators specifically to use them to grab positions in world space, which makes things difficult for us.

There's an easy workaround, though we'll just leave the position unspecified, which will cause both the locator and its pivot to be at the origin, then use the xform (short for "transform") command to set the position of each locator to a reasonable starting position. This ends up looking like the following:

```
cmds.xform(kneeLoc, absolute=True, translation=(0, 5, 0))
cmds.xform(hipLoc, absolute=True, translation=(0, 10, 0))
cmds.xform(footLoc, absolute=True, translation=(2, 0, 0))
```

The xform command can be used in several different ways, all related to querying or altering the transform (position, rotation, and scale) values of nodes. In this case, we're using it to set the translation of the locators to set values. We also set the absolute flag to true to indicate that the values represent where the locator should be moved to in absolute coordinates (as opposed to a relative displacement from its current position).

We move the hip joint up a bit, the knee joint up half as far, and the foot (toe) joint forward a bit on the *x* axis. The ankle joint is left at the origin.

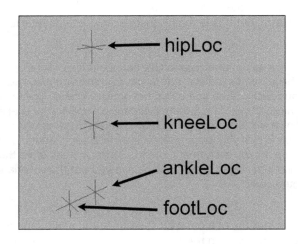

Once we've set up the necessary locators, the user can then adjust their position to better match the specifics of the model to which the joints will be applied. Once that's been done, we can move on to creating joints and setting up the IK system, which we handle in the setupIK function.

First off, we need to invoke our global variables so that we can grab the positions of the locators and create bones at the positions of each one. We also clear out our selection, just to be on the safe side. We're about to create bones and we don't want our newly created joints to be children of any joints that might be selected when the user runs this part of the script. Once again, we use the global keyword to specify that we mean the variables that are in global scope instead of local variables:

```
global hipLoc
global kneeLoc
global ankleLoc
global footLoc

cmds.select(clear=True)
```

Once we've done all this, we're ready to make the bones. For each bone, we'll need to first determine the world-space position of each of our locators, which we can do with the xform command. By calling xform in the query mode, we'll retrieve, rather than set, the position of our locators. We'll also make sure to set the worldSpace flag to true to get the true (world space) position of the locators, rather than their local position.

We'll start with the hip locator and work our way down our list of locators, grabbing each one's location and feeding it into the joint command to create the bone:

```
    pos = cmds.xform(hipLoc, query=True, translation=True,
worldSpace=True)
    hipJoint = cmds.joint(name="hipBone", position=pos)

    pos = cmds.xform(kneeLoc, query=True, translation=True,
worldSpace=True)
    kneeJoint = cmds.joint(name="kneeBone",position=pos)

    pos = cmds.xform(ankleLoc, query=True, translation=True,
worldSpace=True)
    ankleJoint = cmds.joint(name="akleBone", position=pos)

    pos = cmds.xform(footLoc, query=True, translation=True,
worldSpace=True)
    footJoint = cmds.joint(name="footBone", position=pos)
```

Once again, we rely on Maya's default behavior of automatically connecting joints to build the skeleton. Once all the joints have been created, we can finally create the IK system.

Setting up IK is actually really straightforward; all we have to do it to call the `ikHandle` command and specify the appropriate start and end joints with the `startJoint` and `endEffector` flags. In our case, we'll want the IK system to run from the hip to the ankle. Translating that into code ends up looking like the following:

```
cmds.ikHandle(startJoint=hipJoint, endEffector=ankleJoint)
```

Once we've done this, we'll be left with a brand new IK system.

There's more...

Although this example covers the basics of creating a joint chain from locators and adding an IK handle, there are a number of additional things needed to finish it off. To set up a real IK system, you'll likely want to constrain the behavior of each of the joints in the chain (knee joints, for example, should only rotate around a single axis).

Properly constraining the joints in an IK system generally involves at least two things—locking attributes that shouldn't rotate at all and setting limits on the axes that *should* rotate so that a joint that should be a knee doesn't bend in the wrong direction.

To prevent a joint from rotating at all around a given axis, we can set the relevant `jointType` attribute to 0 to completely disable rotation around that axis. For example, if we wanted to make sure that our knee joint is prevented from rotating around either the *x* or *y* axes, we could do the following:

```
cmds.setAttr(kneeJoint + ".jointTypeX", 0)
cmds.setAttr(kneeJoint + ".jointTypeY", 0)
```

This will completely prevent any rotation around the *x* and *y* axes. For the remaining axis (*z*, in this case), we would likely want to limit the rotation to a specific range. For this, we could use the `transformLimits` command, which will allow us to set minimum and maximum values for rotation.

To make use of the `transformLimits` command, we'll need to not only specify the specific minimum and maximums, but we'll also need to enable the limits. This is similar to what one sees when setting joint limits in the attribute editor, that is, the values for the minimums and maximums don't actually apply unless you've *also* clicked the checkboxes to enable limits.

Let's say that we wanted the knee to only rotate from -90 to 0 degrees. We could set that up with the following line of code:

```
cmds.transformLimits(kneeJoint, rotationZ=(-90, 0),
enableRotationZ=(1,1))
```

The `rotationZ` flag in the preceding code is used to set the minimum and maximum values for the given node. The `enableRotationZ` is somewhat confusingly named, in that it really controls the setting of rotation *limits*. So, passing (1, 1) into `enableRotationZ` means that we're enabling limits for both the minimum and maximum values. If we wanted to only have a minimum (but no maximum) value, we could do the following instead:

```
cmds.transformLimits(kneeJoint, rotationZ=(-90, 0),
enableRotationZ=(1,0))
```

In the preceding code, the (1,0) passed to `enableRotationZ` would both enable a minimum limit and disable the maximum.

6
Making Things Move – Scripting for Animation

This chapter will cover various recipes related to animating objects with scripting:

- ▶ Querying animation data
- ▶ Working with animation layers
- ▶ Copying animation from one object to another
- ▶ Setting keyframes
- ▶ Creating expressions via script

Introduction

In this chapter, we'll be looking at how to use scripting to create animation and set **keyframes**. We'll also see how to work with animation layers and create expressions from code.

Querying animation data

In this example, we'll be looking at how to retrieve information about animated objects, including which attributes are animated and both the location and value of keyframes. Although this script is unlikely to be useful by itself, knowing the number, time, and values of keyframes is sometimes a prerequisite for more complex animation tasks.

Getting ready

To make get the most out of this script, you'll need to have an object with some animation curves defined. Either load up a scene with animation or skip ahead to the recipe on setting keyframes.

How to do it...

Create a new file and add the following code:

```
import maya.cmds as cmds

def getAnimationData():
    objs = cmds.ls(selection=True)
    obj = objs[0]

    animAttributes = cmds.listAnimatable(obj);

    for attribute in animAttributes:

        numKeyframes = cmds.keyframe(attribute, query=True,
        keyframeCount=True)

        if (numKeyframes > 0):
            print("--------------------------")
            print("Found ", numKeyframes, " keyframes on ",
            attribute)

            times = cmds.keyframe(attribute, query=True,
            index=(0,numKeyframes), timeChange=True)
            values = cmds.keyframe(attribute, query=True,
            index=(0,numKeyframes), valueChange=True)

            print('frame#, time, value')
            for i in range(0, numKeyframes):
                print(i, times[i], values[i])

            print("--------------------------")

getAnimationData()
```

If you select an object with animation curves and run the script, you should see a readout of the time and value for each keyframe on each animated attribute. For example, if we had a simple bouncing ball animation with the following curves:

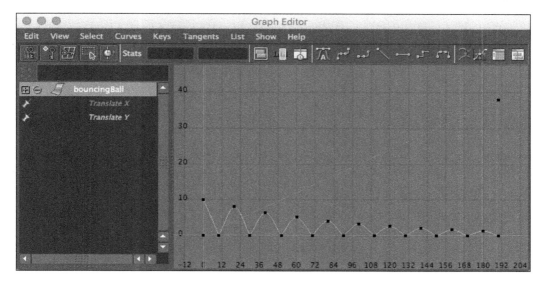

We would see something like the following output in the script editor:

```
---------------------------
('Found ', 2, ' keyframes on ', u'|bouncingBall.translateX')
frame#, time, value
(0, 0.0, 0.0)
(1, 190.0, 38.0)
---------------------------
---------------------------
('Found ', 20, ' keyframes on ', u'|bouncingBall.translateY')
frame#, time, value
(0, 0.0, 10.0)
(1, 10.0, 0.0)
(2, 20.0, 8.0)
(3, 30.0, 0.0)
(4, 40.0, 6.400000000000004)
(5, 50.0, 0.0)
(6, 60.0, 5.120000000000001)
(7, 70.0, 0.0)
(8, 80.0, 4.096000000000001)
(9, 90.0, 0.0)
(10, 100.0, 3.276800000000001)
(11, 110.0, 0.0)
(12, 120.0, 2.6214400000000011)
(13, 130.0, 0.0)
(14, 140.0, 2.0971520000000008)
(15, 150.0, 0.0)
```

```
(16,  160.0,  1.6777216000000008)
(17,  170.0,  0.0)
(18,  180.0,  1.3421772800000007)
(19,  190.0,  0.0)
---------------------------
```

How it works...

We start out by grabbing the selected object, as usual. Once we've done that, we'll iterate over all the `keyframeable` attributes, determine if they have any keyframes and, if they do, run through the times and values. To get the list of `keyframeable` attributes, we use the `listAnimateable` command:

```
objs = cmds.ls(selection=True)
obj = objs[0]

animAttributes = cmds.listAnimatable(obj)
```

This will give us a list of all the attributes on the selected object that can be animated, including any custom attributes that have been added to it.

If you were to print out the contents of the `animAttributes` array, you would likely see something like the following:

```
|bouncingBall.rotateX
|bouncingBall.rotateY
|bouncingBall.rotateZ
```

Although the `bouncingBall.rotateX` part likely makes sense, you may be wondering about the | symbol. This symbol is used by Maya to indicate hierarchical relationships between nodes in order to provide fully qualified node and attribute names. If the `bouncingBall` object was a child of a group named `ballGroup`, we would see this instead:

```
|ballGroup|bouncingBall.rotateX
```

Every such fully qualified name will contain at least one pipe (|) symbol, as we see in the first, nongrouped example, but there can be many more—one for each additional layer of hierarchy. While this can lead to long strings for attribute names, it allows Maya to make use of objects that may have the same name, but under different parts of a larger hierarchy (to have control objects named `handControl` for each hand of a character, for example).

Now that we have a list of all of the possibly animated attributes for the object, we'll next want to determine if there are any keyframes set on it. To do this, we can use the `keyframe` command in the query mode.

```
for attribute in animAttributes:
    numKeyframes = cmds.keyframe(attribute, query=True,
    keyframeCount=True)
```

At this point, we have a variable (`numKeyframes`) that will be greater than zero for any attribute with at least one keyframe. Getting the total number of keyframes on an attribute is only one of the things that the `keyframe` command can do; we'll also use it to grab the time and value for each of the keyframes.

To do this, we'll call it two more times, both in the query mode—once to get the times and once to get the values:

```
times = cmds.keyframe(attribute, query=True,
index=(0,numKeyframes), timeChange=True)
values = cmds.keyframe(attribute, query=True,
index=(0,numKeyframes), valueChange=True)
```

These two lines are identical in everything except what type of information we're asking for. The important thing to note here is the index flag, which is used to tell Maya which keyframes we're interested in. The command requires a two-element argument representing the first (inclusive) and last (exclusive) index of keyframes to examine. So, if we had a total 20 keyframes, we would pass in (0,20), which would examine the keys with indices from 0 to 19.

The flags we're using to get the values likely look a bit odd—both `valueChange` and `timeChange` might lead you to believe that we would be getting relative values, rather than absolute. However, when used in the previously mentioned manner, the command will give us what we want—the actual time and value for each keyframe, as they appear in the graph editor.

If you want to query information on a single keyframe, you still have to pass in a pair of values—just use the index that you're interested in twice—to get the fourth frame, for example, use (3,3).

At this point, we have two arrays—the `times` array, which contains the time value for each keyframe, and the `values` array that contains the actual attribute value. All that's left is to print out the information that we've found:

```
print('frame#, time, value')
for i in range(0, numKeyframes):
    print(i, times[i], values[i])
```

There's more...

Using the indices to get data on keyframes is an easy way to run through all of the data for a curve, but it's not the only way to specify a range. The `keyframe` command can also accept time values. If we wanted to know how many keyframes existed on a given attribute between frame 1 and frame 100, for example, we could do the following:

```
numKeyframes = cmds.keyframe(attributeName, query=True,
time=(1,100) keyframeCount=True)
```

Also, if you find yourself with highly nested objects and need to extract just the object and attribute names, you may find Python's built-in split function helpful. You can call split on a string to have Python break it up into a list of parts. By default, Python will break up the input string by spaces, but you can specify a particular string or character to split on. Assume that you have a string like the following:

```
|group4|group3|group2|group1|ball.rotateZ
```

Then, you could use split to break it apart based on the | symbol. It would give you a list, and using -1 as an index would give you just `ball.rotateZ`. Putting that into a function that can be used to extract the object/attribute names from a full string would be easy, and it would look something like the following:

```
def getObjectAttributeFromFull(fullString):
    parts = fullString.split("|")
    return parts[-1]
```

Using it would look something like this:

```
inputString = "|group4|group3|group2|group1|ball.rotateZ"
result = getObjectAttributeFromFull(inputString)
print(result) # outputs "ball.rotateZ"
```

Working with animation layers

Maya offers the ability to create multiple layers of animation in a scene, which can be a good way to build up complex animation. The layers can then be independently enabled or disabled, or blended together, granting the user a great deal of control over the end result.

In this example, we'll be looking at how to examine the layers that exist in a scene, and building a script will ensure that we have a layer of a given name. For example, we might want to create a script that would add additional randomized motion to the rotations of selected objects without overriding their existing motion. To do this, we would want to make sure that we had an animation layer named `randomMotion`, which we could then add keyframes to.

How to do it...

Create a new script and add the following code:

```
import maya.cmds as cmds

def makeAnimLayer(layerName):

    baseAnimationLayer = cmds.animLayer(query=True, root=True)
```

```
        foundLayer = False

    if (baseAnimationLayer != None):
        childLayers = cmds.animLayer(baseAnimationLayer,
        query=True, children=True)

        if (childLayers != None) and (len(childLayers) > 0):
            if layerName in childLayers:
                foundLayer = True

    if not foundLayer:
        cmds.animLayer(layerName)
    else:
        print('Layer ' + layerName + ' already exists')

    makeAnimLayer("myLayer")
```

Run the script, and you should see an animation layer named `myLayer` appear in the **Anim** tab of the channel box.

How it works...

The first thing that we want to do is to find out if there is already an animation layer with the given name present in the scene. To do this, we start by grabbing the name of the root animation layer:

```
baseAnimationLayer = cmds.animLayer(query=True, root=True)
```

In almost all cases, this should return one of two possible values—either `BaseAnimation` or (if there aren't any animation layers yet) Python's built-in `None` value.

We'll want to create a new layer in either of the following two possible cases:

- There are no animation layers yet
- There are animation layers, but none with the target name

In order to make the testing for the above a bit easier, we first create a variable to hold whether or not we've found an animation layer and set it to `False`:

```
foundLayer = False
```

Now we need to check to see whether it's true that *both* animation layers exist and one of them has the given name. First off, we check that there was, in fact, a base animation layer:

```
if (baseAnimationLayer != None):
```

If this is the case, we want to grab all the children of the base animation layer and check to see whether any of them have the name we're looking for. To grab the children animation layers, we'll use the `animLayer` command again, again in the query mode:

```
childLayers = cmds.animLayer(baseAnimationLayer, query=True,
children=True)
```

Once we've done that, we'll want to see if any of the child layers match the one we're looking for. We'll also need to account for the possibility that there were no child layers (which could happen if animation layers were created then later deleted, leaving only the base layer):

```
if (childLayers != None) and (len(childLayers) > 0):
    if layerName in childLayers:
        foundLayer = True
```

If there were child layers and the name we're looking for was found, we set our `foundLayer` variable to `True`.

If the layer wasn't found, we create it. This's easily done by using the `animLayer` command one more time, with the name of the layer we're trying to create:

```
if not foundLayer:
    cmds.animLayer(layerName)
```

Finally, we finish off by printing a message, if the layer was found, to let the user know.

There's more...

Having animation layers is great, in that we can make use of them when creating or modifying keyframes. However, we can't actually add animation to layers without first adding the objects in question to the animation layer.

Let's say that we had an object named `bouncingBall`, and we wanted to set some keyframes on its `translateY` attribute, in the `bounceLayer` animation layer. The actual command to set the keyframe(s) would look something like this:

```
cmds.setKeyframe("bouncingBall.translateY", value=yVal,
time=frame, animLayer="bounceLayer")
```

However, this would only work as expected if we had first added the `bouncingBall` object to the `bounceLayer` animation layer. To do it, we could use the `animLayer` command in the edit mode, with the `addSelectedObjects` flag. Note that because the flag operates on the currently selected objects, we would need to first select the object we want to add:

```
cmds.select("bouncingBall", replace=True)
cmds.animLayer("bounceLayer", edit=True, addSelectedObjects=True)
```

Adding the object will, by default, add all of its animatable attributes. You can also add specific attributes, rather than entire objects. For example, if we only wanted to add the `translateY` attribute to our animation layer, we could do the following:

```
cmds.animLayer("bounceLayer", edit=True,
attribute="bouncingBall.translateY")
```

Copying animation from one object to another

In this example, we'll create a script that will copy all of the animation data on one object to one or more additional objects, which could be useful to duplicate motion across a range of objects.

Getting ready

For the script to work, you'll need an object with some keyframes set. Either create some simple animation or skip ahead to the example on creating keyframes with script, later in this chapter.

How to do it...

Create a new script and add the following code:

```
import maya.cmds as cmds

def getAttName(fullname):
    parts = fullname.split('.')
    return parts[-1]

def copyKeyframes():
    objs = cmds.ls(selection=True)

    if (len(objs) < 2):
        cmds.error("Please select at least two objects")

    sourceObj = objs[0]

    animAttributes = cmds.listAnimatable(sourceObj);

    for attribute in animAttributes:
```

```
numKeyframes = cmds.keyframe(attribute, query=True,
keyframeCount=True)

if (numKeyframes > 0):

    cmds.copyKey(attribute)

    for obj in objs[1:]:
        cmds.pasteKey(obj,
        attribute=getAttName(attribute), option="replace")

copyKeyframes()
```

Select the animated object, shift-select at least one other object, and run the script. You'll see that all of the objects have the same motion.

How it works...

The very first part of our script is a helper function that we'll be using to strip the attribute name off a full object name/attribute name string. More on it will be given later.

Now on to the bulk of the script. First off, we run a check to make sure that the user has selected at least two objects. If not, we'll display a friendly error message to let the user know what they need to do:

```
objs = cmds.ls(selection=True)

if (len(objs) < 2):
    cmds.error("Please select at least two objects")
```

The `error` command will also stop the script from running, so if we're still going, we know that we had at least two objects selected. We'll set the first one to be selected to be our source object. We could just as easily use the second-selected object, but that would mean using the first selected object as the destination, limiting us to a single target:

```
sourceObj = objs[0]
```

Now we're ready to start copying animation, but first, we'll need to determine which attributes are currently animated, through a combination of finding all the attributes that *can* be animated, and checking each one to see whether there are any keyframes on it:

```
animAttributes = cmds.listAnimatable(sourceObj);

for attribute in animAttributes:
    numKeyframes = cmds.keyframe(attribute, query=True,
    keyframeCount=True)
```

If we have at least one keyframe for the given attribute, we move forward with the copying:

```
if (numKeyframes > 0):
    cmds.copyKey(attribute)
```

The `copyKey` command will cause the keyframes for a given object to be temporarily held in memory. If used without any additional flags, it will grab all of the keyframes for the specified attribute, exactly what we want in this case. If we wanted only a subset of the keyframes, we could use the time flag to specify a range.

We're passing in each of the values that were returned by the `listAnimatable` function. These will be full names (both object name and attribute). That's fine for the `copyKey` command, but will require a bit of additional work for the paste operation.

Since we're copying the keys onto a different object than the one that we copied them from, we'll need to separate out the object and attribute names. For example, our `attribute` value might be something like this:

```
|group1|bouncingBall.rotateX
```

From this, we'll want to trim off just the attribute name (`rotateX`) since we're getting the object name from the selection list. To do this, we created a simple helper function that takes a full-length object/attribute name and returns just the attribute name. That's easy enough to do by just breaking the name/attribute string apart on the `.` and returning the last element, which in this case is the attribute:

```
def getAttName(fullname):
    parts = fullname.split('.')
    return parts[-1]
```

Python's `split` function breaks apart the string into an array of strings, and using a negative index will count back from the end, with `-1` giving us the last element.

Now we can actually paste our keys. We'll run through all the remaining selected objects, starting with the second, and paste our copied keyframes:

```
for obj in objs[1:]:
    cmds.pasteKey(obj, attribute=getAttName(attribute),
    option="replace")
```

Note that we're using the nature of Python's for loops to make the code a bit more readable. Rather than using an index, as would be the case in most other languages, we can just use the `for x in y` construction. In this case, `obj` will be a temporary variable, scoped to the for loop, that takes on the value of each item in the list. Also note that instead of passing in the entire list, we use `objs[1:]` to indicate the entire list, starting at index 1 (the second element). The colon allows us to specify a subrange of the `objs` list, and leaving the right-hand side blank will cause Python to include all the items to the end of the list.

We pass in the name of the object (from our original selection), the attribute (stripped from full name/attribute string via our helper function), and we use `option="replace"` to ensure that the keyframes we're pasting in replace anything that's already there.

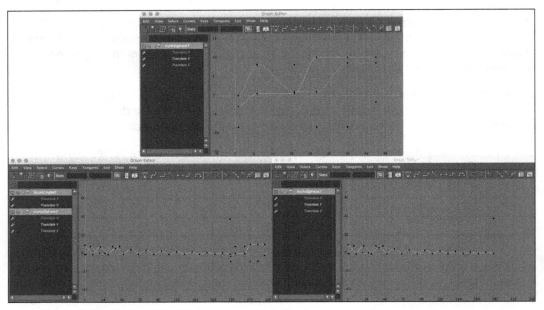

Original animation (top). Here, we see the result of pasting keys with the default settings (left) and with the replace option (right). Note that the default results still contain the original curves, just pushed to later frames

If we didn't include the `option` flag, Maya would default to inserting the pasted keyframes while moving any keyframes already present forward in the timeline.

There's more...

There are a lot of other options for the option flag, each of which handles possible conflicts with the keys you're pasting and the ones that may already exist in a slightly different way. Be sure to have a look at the built-in documentation for the `pasteKeys` command for more information.

Another, and perhaps better option to control how pasted keys interact with existing one is to paste the new keys into a separate animation layer. For example, if we wanted to make sure that our pasted keys end up in an animation layer named `extraAnimation`, we could modify the call to `pasteKeys` as follows:

```
cmds.pasteKey(objs[i], attribute=getAttName(attribute),
option="replace", animLayer="extraAnimation")
```

Note that if there was no animation layer named `extraAnimation` present, Maya would fail to copy the keys. See the section on working with animation layers for more information on how to query existing layers and create new ones.

Setting keyframes

While there are certainly a variety of ways to get things to move in Maya, the vast majority of motion is driven by keyframes. In this example, we'll be looking at how to create keyframes with code by making that old animation standby—a bouncing ball.

Getting ready

The script we'll be creating will animate the currently selected object, so make sure that you have an object—either the traditional sphere or something else you'd like to make bounce.

How to do it...

Create a new file and add the following code:

```python
import maya.cmds as cmds

def setKeyframes():
    objs = cmds.ls(selection=True)
    obj = objs[0]

    yVal = 0
    xVal = 0
    frame = 0

    maxVal = 10

    for i in range(0, 20):
        frame = i * 10
        xVal = i * 2

        if i % 2 == 1:
            yVal = 0
        else:
            yVal = maxVal
            maxVal *= 0.8
```

```
cmds.setKeyframe(obj + '.translateY', value=yVal,
time=frame)
cmds.setKeyframe(obj + '.translateX', value=xVal,
time=frame)

setKeyframes()
```

Run the preceding script with an object selected and trigger playback. You should see the object move up and down.

How it works...

In order to get our object to bounce, we'll need to set keyframes such that the object alternates between a *Y*-value of zero and an ever-decreasing maximum so that the animation mimics the way a falling object loses velocity with each bounce. We'll also make it move forward along the x-axis as it bounces.

We start by grabbing the currently selected object and setting a few variables to make things easier to read as we run through our loop. Our $yVal$ and $xVal$ variables will hold the current value that we want to set the position of the object to. We also have a frame variable to hold the current frame and a $maxVal$ variable, which will be used to hold the *Y*-value of the object's current height.

 This example is sufficiently simple that we don't really need separate variables for frame and the attribute values, but setting things up this way makes it easier to swap in more complex math or logic to control where keyframes get set and to what value.

This gives us the following:

```
yVal = 0
xVal = 0
frame = 0

maxVal = 10
```

The bulk of the script is a single loop, in which we set keyframes on both the *X* and *Y* positions.

For the $xVal$ variable, we'll just be multiplying a constant value (in this case, 2 units). We'll do the same thing for our frame. For the $yVal$ variable, we'll want to alternate between an ever-decreasing value (for the successive peaks) and zero (for when the ball hits the ground).

To alternate between zero and non-zero, we'll check to see whether our loop variable is divisible by two. One easy way to do this is to take the value *modulo* (%) 2. This will give us the remainder when the value is divided by two, which will be zero in the case of even numbers and one in the case of odd numbers.

For odd values, we'll set yVal to zero, and for even ones, we'll set it to maxVal. To make sure that the ball bounces a little less each time, we set maxVal to 80% of its current value each time we make use of it.

Putting all of that together gives us the following loop:

```
for i in range(0, 20):
    frame = i * 10
    xVal = i * 2

    if (i % 2) == 1:
        yVal = 0
    else:
        yVal = maxVal
        maxVal *= 0.8
```

Now we're finally ready to actually set keyframes on our object. This is easily done with the setKeyframe command. We'll need to specify the following three things:

- ▶ The attribute to keyframe (object name and attribute)
- ▶ The time at which to set the keyframe
- ▶ The actual value to set the attribute to

In this case, this ends up looking like the following:

```
cmds.setKeyframe(obj + '.translateY', value=yVal, time=frame)
cmds.setKeyframe(obj + '.translateX', value=xVal, time=frame)
```

And that's it! A proper bouncing ball (or other object) animated with pure code.

There's more...

By default, the setKeyframe command will create keyframes with both in tangent and out tangent being set to spline. That's fine for a lot of things, but will result in overly smooth animation for something that's supposed to be striking a hard surface.

We can improve our bounce animation by keeping smooth tangents for the keyframes when the object reaches its maximum height, but setting the tangents at its minimum to be linear. This will give us a nice sharp change every time the ball strikes the ground.

To do this, all we need to do is to set both the `inTangentType` and `outTangentType` flags to `linear`, as follows:

```
cmds.setKeyframe(obj + ".translateY", value=animVal, time=frame,
inTangentType="linear", outTangentType="linear")
```

To make sure that we only have linear tangents when the ball hits the ground, we could set up a variable to hold the tangent type, and set it to one of two values in much the same way that we set the `yVal` variable.

This would end up looking like this:

```
tangentType = "auto"

for i in range(0, 20):
    frame =  i * 10
    if i % 2 == 1:
        yVal = 0
        tangentType = "linear"
    else:
        yVal = maxVal
        tangentType = "spline"
        maxVal *= 0.8

    cmds.setKeyframe(obj + '.translateY', value=yVal, time=frame,
    inTangentType=tangentType, outTangentType=tangentType)
```

Creating expressions via script

While most animation in Maya is created manually, it can often be useful to drive attributes directly via script, especially for mechanical objects or background items. One way to approach this is through Maya's expression editor.

In addition to creating expressions via the expression editor, it is also possible to create expressions with scripting, in a beautiful example of code-driven code. In this example, we'll be creating a script that can be used to create a sine wave-based expression to smoothly alter a given attribute between two values. Note that expressions cannot actually use Python code directly; they require the code to be written in the MEL syntax. But this doesn't mean that we can't use Python to *create* expressions, which is what we'll do in this example.

Getting ready

Before we dive into the script, we'll first need to have a good handle on the kind of expression we'll be creating. There are a lot of different ways to approach expressions, but in this instance, we'll keep things relatively simple and tie the attribute to a sine wave based on the current time.

Why a sine wave? Sine waves are great because they alter smoothly between two values, with a nice easing into and out of both the minimum and maximums. While the minimum and maximum values range from −1 to 1, it's easy enough to alter the output to move between any two numbers we want. We'll also make things a bit more flexible by setting up the expression to rely on a custom `speed` attribute that can be used to control the rate at which the attribute animates.

The end result will be a value that varies smoothly between any two numbers at a user-specified (and keyframeable) rate.

How to do it...

Create a new script and add the following code:

```
import maya.cmds as cmds

def createExpression(att, minVal, maxVal, speed):
    objs = cmds.ls(selection=True)
    obj = objs[0]

    cmds.addAttr(obj, longName="speed", shortName="speed", min=0,
    keyable=True)

    amplitude = (maxVal - minVal)/2.0
    offset = minVal + amplitude

    baseString =  "{0}.{1} = ".format(obj, att)
    sineClause = '(sin(time * ' + obj + '.speed)'
    valueClause = ' * ' + str(amplitude) + ' + ' + str(offset) +
    ')'

    expressionString = baseString + sineClause + valueClause

    cmds.expression(string=expressionString)

createExpression('translateY', 5, 10, 1)
```

How it works...

The first that we do is to add a `speed` attribute to our object, as in the custom attribute recipe in *Chapter 5, Adding Controls – Scripting for Rigging*. We'll be sure to make it keyable for later animation:

```
cmds.addAttr(obj, longName="speed", shortName="speed", min=0,
keyable=True)
```

It's generally a good idea to include at least one keyframeable attribute when creating expressions. While math-driven animation is certainly a powerful technique, you'll likely still want to be able to alter the specifics. Giving yourself one or more keyframeable attributes is an easy way to do just that.

Now we're ready to build up our expression. But first, we'll need to understand exactly what we want; in this case, a value that smoothly varies between two extremes, with the ability to control its speed. We can easily build an expression to do that using the sine function, with the current time as the input. Here's what it looks like in a general form:

```
animatedValue = (sin(time * S) * M) + O;
```

Where:

▸ S is a value that will either speed up (if greater than 1) or slow down (if less) the rate at which the input to the sine function changes

▸ M is a multiplier to alter the overall range through which the value changes

▸ O is an offset to ensure that the minimum and maximum values are correct

You can also think about it visually—S will cause our wave to stretch or shrink along the horizontal (time) axis, M will expand or contract it vertically, and O will move the entire shape of the curve either up or down.

S is already taken care of; it's our newly created "speed" attribute. M and O will need to be calculated, based on the fact that sine functions always produce values ranging from -1 to 1.

The overall range of values should be from our `minVal` to our `maxVal`, so you might think that M should be equal to *(maxVal – minVal)*. However, since it gets applied to both -1 and 1, this would leave us with double the desired change. So, the final value we want is instead *(maxVal – minVal)/2*. We store that into our amplitude variable as follows:

```
amplitude = (maxVal - minVal)/2.0
```

Next up is the offset value O. We want to move our graph such that the minimum and maximum values are where they should be. It might seem like that would mean just adding our `minVal`, but if we left it at that, our output would dip below the minimum for 50% of the time (anytime the sine function is producing negative output). To fix it, we set O to *(minVal + M)* or in the case of our script:

```
offset = minVal + amplitude
```

This way, we move the O position of the wave to be midway between our `minVal` and `maxVal`, which is exactly what we want.

To make things clearer, let's look at the different parts we're tacking onto `sin()`, and the way they effect the minimum and maximum values the expression will output. We'll assume that the end result we're looking for is a range from 0 to 4.

Expression	Additional component	Minimum	Maximum
sin(time)	None- raw sin function	−1	1
*sin(time * speed)*	Multiply input by "speed"	−1 (faster)	1 (faster)
*sin(time * speed) * 2*	Multiply output by 2	−2	2
*(sin(time * speed) * 2) + 2*	Add 2 to output	0	4

Note that *2 = (4-0)/2* and *2 = 0 + 2*.

Here's what the preceding progression looks like when graphed:

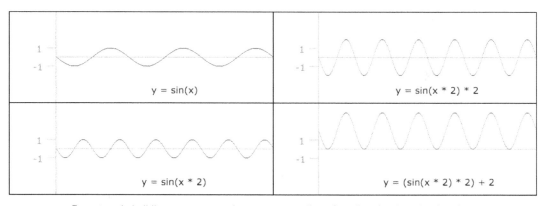

Four steps in building up an expression to var an attribute from 0 to 4 with a sine function.

Okay, now that we have the math locked down, we're ready to translate that into Maya's expression syntax. If we wanted an object named `myBall` to animate along *Y* with the previous values, we would want to end up with:

```
myBall.translateY = (sin(time * myBall.speed) * 5) + 12;
```

This would work as expected if entered into Maya's expression editor, but we want to make sure that we have a more general-purpose solution that can be used with any object and any values. That's straightforward enough and just requires building up the preceding string from various literals and variables, which is what we do in the next few lines:

```
baseString = "{0}.{1} = ".format(obj, att)
sineClause = '(sin(time * ' + obj + '.speed)'
valueClause = ' * ' + str(amplitude) + ' + ' + str(offset) + ')'

expressionString = baseString + sineClause + valueClause
```

I've broken up the string creation into a few different lines to make things clearer, but it's by no means necessary. The key idea here is that we're switching back and forth between literals (`sin(time *`, `.speed`, and so on) and variables (`obj`, `att`, `amplitude`, and `offset`) to build the overall string. Note that we have to wrap numbers in the `str()` function to keep Python from complaining when we combine them with strings.

At this point, we have our expression string ready to go. All that's left is to actually add it to the scene as an expression, which is easily done with the `expression` command:

```
cmds.expression(string=expressionString)
```

And that's it! We will now have an attribute that varies smoothly between any two values.

There's more...

There are tons of other ways to use expressions to drive animation, and all sorts of simple mathematical tricks that can be employed.

For example, you can easily get a value to move smoothly to a target value with a nice easing-in to the target by running this every frame:

```
animatedAttribute = animatedAttribute + (targetValue -
animatedAttribute) * 0.2;
```

This will add 20% of the current difference between the target and the current value to the attribute, which will move it towards the target. Since the amount that is added is always a percentage of the current difference, the per-frame effect reduces as the value approaches the target, providing an ease-in effect.

If we were to combine this with some code to randomly choose a new target value, we would end up with an easy way to, say, animate the heads of background characters to randomly look in different positions (maybe to provide a stadium crowd).

Assume that we had added custom attributes for `targetX`, `targetY`, and `targetZ` to our object that would end up looking something like the following:

```
if (frame % 20 == 0)
{
    myCone.targetX = rand(time) * 360;
    myCone.targetY = rand(time) * 360;
    myCone.targetZ = rand(time) * 360;
}


myObject.rotateX += (myObject.targetX - myCone.rotateX) * 0.2;
myObject.rotateY += (myObject.targetY - myCone.rotateY) * 0.2;
myObject.rotateZ += (myObject.targetZ - myCone.rotateZ) * 0.2;
```

Note that we're using the modulo (%) operator to do something (setting the target) only when the frame is an even multiple of 20. We're also using the current time as the seed value for the `rand()` function to ensure that we get different results as the animation progresses.

The previously mentioned example is how the code would look if we entered it directly into Maya's expression editor; note the MEL-style (rather than Python) syntax. Generating this code via Python would be a bit more involved than our sine wave example, but would use all the same principles—building up a string from literals and variables, then passing that string to the `expression` command.

7

Scripting for Rendering

In this chapter, we'll be looking at the following topics:

- ▸ Creating and editing lights
- ▸ Creating GUI to control all lights
- ▸ Creating cameras from code
- ▸ Rendering a sprite sheet

Introduction

So far, we've looked at ways scripting can help with modeling, texturing, rigging, and animation. Once all of that is done, all that's left is to actually render out your scene. In this chapter, we'll be looking at how to set up lights and cameras, as well as how to render out scenes.

Creating and editing lights

In this example, we'll be building a script to quickly and easily set up a simple three-point lighting setup via script.

This will end up providing us with a nice overview of creating different types of lights with script, as well as leaving us with a handy tool.

The result of running the script-key, fill, and back lights all pointed at the origin

Getting ready

For best results, make sure that you have an object with a decent level of detail in your scene before running the script.

How to do it...

Create a new file and add the following code:

```
import maya.cmds as cmds

def createLightRig():

    offsetAmount = 10
    lightRotation = 30
```

```
newLight = cmds.spotLight(rgb=(1, 1, 1), name="KeyLight")
lightTransform = cmds.listRelatives(newLight, parent=True)
keyLight = lightTransform[0]

newLight = cmds.spotLight(rgb=(0.8, 0.8, 0.8),
name="FillLight")
lightTransform = cmds.listRelatives(newLight, parent=True)
fillLight = lightTransform[0]

newLight = cmds.directionalLight(rgb=(0.2, 0.2, 0.2),
name="BackLight")
lightTransform = cmds.listRelatives(newLight, parent=True)
backLight = lightTransform[0]

cmds.move(0, 0, offsetAmount, keyLight)
cmds.move(0, 0, 0, keyLight + ".rotatePivot")
cmds.rotate(-lightRotation, lightRotation, 0, keyLight)

cmds.move(0, 0, offsetAmount, fillLight)
cmds.move(0, 0, 0, fillLight + ".rotatePivot")
cmds.rotate(-lightRotation, -lightRotation, 0, fillLight)

cmds.move(0, 0, offsetAmount, backLight)
cmds.move(0, 0, 0, backLight + ".rotatePivot")
cmds.rotate(180 + lightRotation, 0, 0, backLight)

rigNode = cmds.group(empty=True, name="LightRig")

cmds.parent(keyLight, rigNode)
cmds.parent(fillLight, rigNode)
cmds.parent(backLight, rigNode)

cmds.select(rigNode, replace=True)

createLightRig()
```

Run the preceding code, and you'll see that you're left with three lights created—two spotlights and one directional light.

How it works...

We'll be creating three lights—two spotlights and one directional light. To simplify the positioning, we'll create a few helper variables:

```
offsetAmount = 10
lightRotation = 30
```

The offsetAmount variable will be the amount by which each of the lights is moved away from the origin, and lightRotation will control the amount by which the lights are rotated. Next, we create the first of our lights—the key light:

```
newLight = cmds.spotLight(rgb=(1, 1, 1), name="KeyLight")
```

Creating the light is easy enough; we just call the spotLight command. While we're at it, we'll use the rgb flag to set the color of the light (full intensity white), and we'll set the name to easily identify the light later. We store the result to a newLight variable.

One slight complication arises in that the light creation command returns the name of the shape node, rather than the transform. Because setting up the position and rotation requires making changes to the transform, we'll use the listRelatives command to grab the associated transform node:

```
lightTransform = cmds.listRelatives(newLight, parent=True)
```

As we've seen in previous examples, we have to account for the fact that the listRelatives command always returns a list of nodes, even if there's at most one possible node (as is the case with the parent flag). We store the first entry to a variable that we'll use to identify our light for the rest of the script:

```
keyLight = lightTransform[0]
```

At this point, we've created the first of our three lights. We'll do the exactly same thing to create a second spotlight for our fill light, with the only difference is that we start it off with something a bit less than full white:

```
newLight = cmds.spotLight(rgb=(0.8, 0.8, 0.8), name="FillLight")
lightTransform = cmds.listRelatives(newLight, parent=True)
fillLight = lightTransform[0]
```

Finally, we set up our back light. We start it out with a dark gray light, and we create a directional light rather than a spot:

```
newLight = cmds.directionalLight(rgb=(0.2, 0.2, 0.2),
name="BackLight")
lightTransform = cmds.listRelatives(newLight, parent=True)
backLight = lightTransform[0]
```

Now that we have all of our lights created, we're ready to set their positions and rotations to give us a nice default three-light setup. To do this, we'll be taking the following steps for each light:

1. Move the light a set distance away from the origin along the z-axis.
2. Move the light's rotational pivot back to the origin.
3. Set the light's rotation to give us the position we want.

We could also calculate the light positions directly using some trigonometry, but having the lights each rotate around the origin will not only make the script more straightforward, but will also make it easier to change after creation.

First off, we move the light along the z-axis:

```
cmds.move(0, 0, offsetAmount, keyLight)
```

Once we've done this, we want to move the rotate pivot back to the origin. We'll use the move command for that as well:

```
cmds.move(0, 0, 0, keyLight + ".rotatePivot")
```

Note that we append `.rotatePivot` to the name of the light so that we move just the pivot and not the light itself. Also note that we're moving it to (0,0,0). This will end up giving us what we want because the move command defaults to absolute coordinates. So, moving by (0,0,0) is actually telling Maya to move the object in question to the origin.

Once we've done it, we can use the rotate command to rotate the light in question around the origin. For the key light, we'll rotate it around the x-axis to move it up and around the y-axis to move it to the right. Note that we negate the value for the x-axis so that the light is rotated counter-clockwise rather than clockwise around the x-axis. This will ensure that the light moves up, rather than down, relative to the *X-Z* plane:

```
cmds.rotate(-lightRotation, lightRotation, 0, keyLight)
```

We repeat the preceding code two more times to set up our fill and back lights with default positions:

```
cmds.move(0, 0, offsetAmount, fillLight)
cmds.move(0, 0, 0, fillLight + ".rotatePivot")
cmds.rotate(-lightRotation, -lightRotation, 0, fillLight)
```

The fill light is rotated around the x-axis by the same amount as the key light, but in the opposite direction around the y-axis:

```
cmds.move(0, 0, offsetAmount, backLight)
cmds.move(0, 0, 0, backLight + ".rotatePivot")
cmds.rotate(180 + lightRotation, 0, 0, backLight)
```

And the back light is rotated around the *x-axis* by 180 degrees (to place it behind the origin) plus our `lightRotation` value to move it above the origin.

At this point, we have three lights with default settings and positions, but we'll want to make the entire rig easier to manipulate. To do this, we'll create a new transform node and add all three lights as children.

To create the new transform node, we'll use the group command with the `empty` flag, to allow us to create an empty group. We'll also be sure to set the base name with the name flag:

```
rigNode = cmds.group(empty=True, name="LightRig")
```

Once we've done this, we use the parent command to make all three lights the children of the `LightRig` node:

```
cmds.parent(keyLight, rigNode)
cmds.parent(fillLight, rigNode)
cmds.parent(backLight, rigNode)
```

As a final touch, we make sure that we have the parent node selected, with a call to select, with the `replace` option:

```
cmds.select(rigNode, replace=True)
```

It's always a good practice, when creating new nodes or groups of nodes, to leave the newly created object(s) selected at the end of your script so that the end user can easily make further changes as necessary (such as moving the entire rig around).

There's more...

In this example, we set the color of the lights to different values to make the fill and back lights have less of an effect. Alternatively, we could set all of the lights to be a single color and use the intensity to provide variation. This might end up looking like the following:

```
keyLightShape = cmds.spotLight(rgb=(1, 1, 1), intensity=1,
name="KeyLight")
fillLightShape = cmds.spotLight(rgb=(1,1,1), intensity=0.8,
name="FillLight")
backLightShape = cmds.directionalLight(rgb=(1,1,1),
intensity=0.2, name="BackLight")
```

The preceding code would give us three lights that are all white, but at varying intensities. If you want to set the intensity of a light after creating it, you can do so with the `setAttr` command. For example, if we wanted to change the intensity of `keyLight` after the fact, we could do the following:

```
cmds.setAttr(keyLightShape + ".intensity", 0.5)
```

One nice possible addition to the script might be to better account for varying scales of geometry. In the current version, we can use the scale of that parent group to increase or decrease the spacing of the lights. A slightly better way would be to pass in a value for the offset amount to our function. We could also pass in a value for the rotation amount to support a wider range of use cases.

Doing this would lead us to take the following code:

```
def createLightRig():
    offsetAmount = 10
    lighRotation = 30
    newLight = cmds.spotLight(rgb=(1, 1, 1), name="KeyLight")
    # rest of script
```

It will be changed to:

```
def createLightRig(offsetAmount, lightRotation):
    newLight = cmds.spotLight(rgb=(1, 1, 1), name="KeyLight")
    # rest of script
```

Creating GUI to control all lights

Most scenes will end up containing multiple lights, and controlling them all can get to be a real hassle. In this example, we'll be creating GUI that will present the user with an easy way to control the colors of all the lights in the scene.

Running the script with three lights in the scene would result in something like the following:

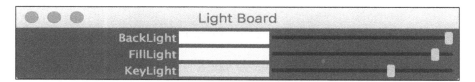

Getting ready

Make sure that you have at least a few lights in your scene. Alternatively, use the three-point lighting example above to quickly set up a system of lights.

How to do it...

Create a new file and add the following code:

```
import maya.cmds as cmds
from functools import partial

class LightBoard():

    def __init__(self):

        self.lights = []
        self.lightControls = []
        self.lightNum = 0

        if (cmds.window("ahLightRig", exists=True)):
            cmds.deleteUI("ahLightRig")

        self.win = cmds.window("ahLightRig", title="Light Board")
        cmds.columnLayout()

        lights = cmds.ls(lights=True)

        for light in lights:
            self.createLightControl(light)

        cmds.showWindow(self.win)

    def updateColor(self, lightID, *args):
        newColor =
        cmds.colorSliderGrp(self.lightControls[lightID],
        query=True, rgb=True)
        cmds.setAttr(self.lights[lightID]+ '.color', newColor[0],
        newColor[1], newColor[2], type="double3")

    def createLightControl(self, lightShape):

        parents = cmds.listRelatives(lightShape, parent=True)
        lightName = parents[0]

        color = cmds.getAttr(lightShape + '.color')
        changeCommandFunc = partial(self.updateColor,
        self.lightNum)
```

```
newSlider = cmds.colorSliderGrp(label=lightName,
rgb=color[0], changeCommand=changeCommandFunc)

self.lights.append(lightShape)
self.lightControls.append(newSlider)

self.lightNum += 1

LightBoard()
```

Run the preceding script, and you'll get a new window with a control for each light in the scene. The control will provide both a color swatch and a slider, and changing it will cause the relevant light's color to update.

How it works...

The first thing to note is that we're adding a second import statement:

```
import maya.cmds as cmds
from functools import partial
```

The functools library provides capabilities to create functions and work with them as variables. This will come in handy later when we're wiring up our controls.

The next thing to note is that we're once again setting up a proper class for this example. Because we're going to need to maintain a list of all the lights in the scene (as well as a list of the controls for each one), wrapping our script in a proper class is the best way to go.

Having said this, let's move onto our __init__ function. We start off by initializing some member variables—one to hold a list of lights, one to hold a list of controls, and one to help us link the proper light to the proper control:

```
def __init__(self):

    self.lights = []
    self.lightControls = []
    self.lightNum = 0
```

We then perform our boilerplate initialization work for a new window—creating a window, setting its title, and adding a column layout. Before we create the window, we first delete the previous one (if it exists):

```
if (cmds.window("ahLightRig", exists=True)):
    cmds.deleteUI("ahLightRig")
```

Once we've done this, we create our window, being sure to pass in the same name we checked for:

```
self.win = cmds.window(("ahLightRig", title="Light Board")
cmds.columnLayout()
```

Now we're ready to set up our controls. We'll need to create one for each light in the scene, which means we first have to get a list of all the lights. Luckily for us, the ls command makes that easy. All we have to do is to set the `lights` flag to `true`:

```
lights = cmds.ls(lights=True)
```

Note that there are a few different flags (`lights`, `cameras`, and `geometry`) that can be used with the `ls` command to grab specific types of objects. If you want to grab nodes of a type that doesn't have a specific flag, you can do that too; just use either the `type` or `exactType` flags and specify the type of node you're looking for.

Once we have a list of all the objects in the scene, we run through the list and create a control for each one, using our `createLightControl` method, which we'll get to next.

Once all the controls have been created, we show the window to the user:

```
for light in lights:
    self.createLightControl(light)

cmds.showWindow(self.win)
```

Before we dive into actually creating our controls, we'll need to have a function that can be used to update a given light to the color in a given slider. For that, we create the following function:

```
def updateColor(self, lightID, *args):
    newColor = cmds.colorSliderGrp(self.lightControls[lightID],
    query=True, rgb=True)
    cmds.setAttr(self.lights[lightID]+ '.color', newColor[0],
    newColor[1], newColor[2], type="double3")
```

The function looks like it takes three arguments, but only one really matters. First, since we're building this script as a class, we have to account for the fact that Python will pass the class instance to every member function, which we do with the self argument. Next is the thing we actually care about, in this case, an integer representing which control/light to work with. Finally, we have a catch-all in `*args`.

Using `*args` will provide a way to grab a variable number of arguments into a single array. This is necessary, as many UI controls will pass extra data to functions that they call. We don't actually want to make use of that in this case, but if we left out the `*args`, we would end up with Maya passing three arguments in to a function that only takes two, generating an error.

The argument that we *do* care about, `lightID`, tells us which light/control to work with. Both the lights and the controls are stored in class member variables—`self.lights` and `self.lightControls`. In order to set a given light to a given slider, we have to first get the current value of the slider by running the `colorSliderGrp` command in query mode, as follows:

```
newColor = cmds.colorSliderGrp(self.lightControls[lightID],
query=True, rgb=True)
```

Note that we pass in an entry in our `self.lightControls` array to specify the control, we run the command in query mode, and we set the `rgb` flag to `True` to tell Maya that it's the specific attribute that we're querying.

Once we've done it, we use `setAttr` to set the color of the corresponding light to the given red, green, and blue values. We'll use `setAttr` to do that, but we'll need to make sure that we specify the type because we'll be using multiple values.

```
cmds.setAttr(self.lights[lightID]+ '.color', newColor[0],
newColor[1], newColor[2], type="double3")
```

Okay, so at this point, we have a function that we can call to update a given light to the current color value of a given slider. So, if we were to call the function, we would set the first light to the current color of the first slider:

```
self.updateColor(0)
```

That's a big part of what we need, but we'll want to make sure that this gets called every time a slider's value is changed.

On to creating an individual control. We create a function that takes a given light and does the following:

► Stores a reference to the light so we can later alter its properties
► Creates a new `colorSliderGrp` control for the light

The function will pass the light we want to create a control for, and we'll once again need to account for the fact that Python passes in the class instance itself, giving us the following function signature:

```
def createLightControl(self, lightShape):
```

Within the function, we'll start out by grabbing the transform node associated with the light. That's not strictly necessary because the node that we'll want to alter (to set color) is the actual shape node. However, it's a lot nicer to have our controls labeled something like `Key Light` rather than `keyLightShape`. Grabbing the transform is done in the same way that we did it in the previous example:

```
parents = cmds.listRelatives(lightShape, parent=True)
lightName = parents[0]
```

Before we create the control, there are a few things we'll want to do first. We'll want to make sure that the colorSliderGrp starts out with the same color value as the light. To do it, we'll need to grab the light's current color with the getAttr (get attribute) command:

```
color = cmds.getAttr(light + '.color')
```

The getAttr command is a real workhorse, and (as is the case with many other commands) it always returns an array because some of the uses to which it can be put will return multiple values. What's a bit surprising about its behavior in this specific case is that we'll end up with a one-element array, with that one element being itself a three-element list of the red, green, and blue values. So, when we make use of the color variable, we'll need to use color[0], instead of (as you would likely suspect) just color.

The next thing that we'll want to do is to create the function that gets called when the slider has its value changed. In the case of a colorSliderGrp control, this includes both moving the slider or clicking on the color swatch to select a color. In either case, we'll want to respond by running some code to update our light's color value.

Here's where it gets tricky because the function we call will need to be aware of the specific UI control to grab data from, as well as the specific light to apply changes to.

We'll create the slider with the colorSliderGrp command, which provides a flag, changeCommand, which can be used to specify a command that should be run every time the slider's value changes.

If we wanted the slider to run a function that took zero arguments when it changes, we could do the following:

```
newSlider = cmds.colorSliderGrp(label=lightName, rgb=color[0],
changeCommand=self.someFunction)
```

However, in this case, we want to call our updateColor function, while passing in an integer to specify which light/control to update. You might be tempted to do something like the following:

```
newSlider = cmds.colorSliderGrp(label=lightName, rgb=color[0],
changeCommand=self.updateColor(0))
```

Unfortunately, it's not quite that simple. The preceding code would cause Python to actually run the updateColor function at the time we create the control. As a result, the actual value of the changeCommand flag would be whatever the return value of self.updateColor is (in this case, None).

That's where the partial command, included in the `functools` library, comes in. We can use the `partial` function to create a copy of a function with specific arguments baked in. It's almost as if we had written a separate function for each light and slider combo. We'll use the `partial` command to create a copy of our `self.updateColor` command, with a number representing the current light baked in, as follows:

```
changeCommandFunc = partial(self.updateColor, self.lightNum)
```

The first argument to partial is a function. Note the lack of parentheses after `self.updateColor`, indicating that we're making use of the function itself, rather than running it. After the function, we can pass in one or more arguments to bind to the function. For example, if we had the following function:

```
def printANum(number):
    print(number)
```

And we used partial in the following way:

```
newFunction = partial(printANum, 23)
```

The value of `newFunction` would itself be a new function with exactly the same behavior as if we had called `printANum(23)`.

So, at this point in the script, our `changeCommandFunc` variable holds a new function that will have identical behavior to calling our `updateColor` function with a specific input. With this, we're ready to create our slider:

```
newSlider = cmds.colorSliderGrp(label=lightName, rgb=color[0],
changeCommand=changeCommandFunc)
```

We use our `lightName` variable to label the slider and pass in our color variable (note the `[0]`, since it's an array) to make sure that the slider starts with the current color of the light.

We're almost done, except for a bit of bookkeeping. We'll want to make sure that we maintain references to both the slider and the light to which it corresponds. To do this, we insert the light's shape node (originally passed in to the `createLightControl` function) into the class member variable, lights. We also insert the newly created slider into the `lightControls` list:

```
self.lights.append(light)
self.lightControls.append(newSlider)
```

Finally, we increment our `lightNum` variable by one so that the next time through the function, we'll pass the correct value into the `partial` command:

```
self.lightNum += 1
```

And that's it! We're done creating our class, and finish off our script with a command to create an instance:

```
LightBoard()
```

There's more...

In this example, we created controls to alter the color of the lights in the scene. It's likely that you would also want to control the intensity of the lights as well. That could be done easily enough by creating an additional control (likely either `floatField` or `floatSlider`) in the `createLightControl` function. Either way, you would want to:

1. Create a separate class member variable to hold references to the intensity controls.

2. Make sure that changing the value on the intensity slider also calls the `updateColor` function.

3. In the `updateColor` function, make sure that you grab the current value of the control and use it to set the intensity of the light with the `setAttr` command.

Creating cameras from code

In this example, we'll be looking at how to use code to create cameras. We'll create a collection of four orthographic cameras, suitable for use in rendering out multiple views of an object for use as assets for an isometric game.

Isometric games have a long history and are characterized by using 2D assets to create a three-quarters overhead view of a game environment. This approach was very common before full 3D games became the norm, and it still shows up often in web and mobile games. Creating assets for isometric games often means rendering out a view for each side of an object and making sure that there is no perspective distortion in the rendering, which is exactly what we'll be doing in this example.

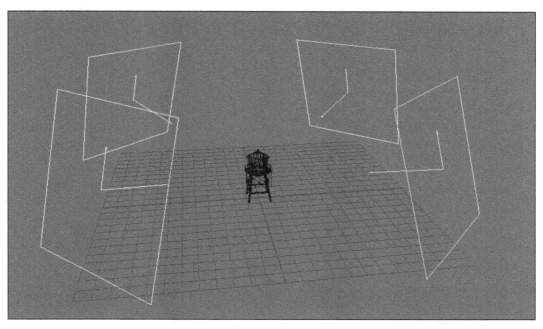

The result of the script-four orthographic cameras, all pointed at the origin

Getting ready

For best results, make sure that you have some geometry in your scene, placed at the origin.

How to do it...

Create a new file and add the following code:

```
import maya.cmds as cmds

def makeCameraRig():
    aimLoc = cmds.spaceLocator()

    offset = 10

    for i in range(0, 4):
        newCam = cmds.camera(orthographic=True)
        cmds.aimConstraint(aimLoc[0], newCam[0], aimVector=(0,0,-
        1))
```

```
        xpos = 0
        ypos = 6
        zpos = 0

        if (i % 2 == 0):
            xpos = -offset
        else:
            xpos = offset

        if (i >= 2):
            zpos = -offset
        else:
            zpos = offset

        cmds.move(xpos, ypos, zpos, newCam[0])

    makeCameraRig()
```

Run the script, and you should have four isometric cameras, all looking at the origin.

How it works...

Making a camera is easy enough; all we need to do is to use the `camera` command. However, there's no direct way to create a camera and aim setup with code. Instead, we have to manually create an aim constraint for each of the cameras we create.

We start our script by creating a locator to serve as the target for the aim constraint.

```
    aimLoc = cmds.spaceLocator()
```

The locator will be positioned at the origin by default, which is fine for our purposes. Now that we have an aim object, we're ready to create our cameras. We kick off a for loop to create four cameras, one for each of the diagonal directions.

Actually, creating the camera is simple; we just call the `camera` command. In this case, we'll want to have orthographic cameras, so we'll set the `orthographic` flag to `true`:

```
for i in range(0, 4):
    newCam = cmds.camera(orthographic=True)
```

Next, we'll set up the aim constraint. To create an aim constraint, we need to pass in two transform nodes, with the first being the target and the second being the one that will have its rotations controlled. Note that because both the `spaceLocator` and `camera` commands return two nodes (one transform, one shape), we'll need to specify the first index of the variables we used to hold the results.

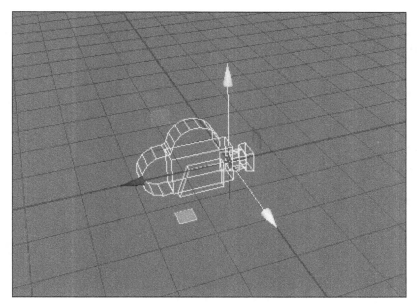

A default camera, pointed down the negative z-axis

We'll also want to make sure that our cameras look down their axis at the locator by setting the proper aim vector. Because the default position of a camera will have it looking along the z-axis in the negative direction, we'll want to use (0, 0, -1) as the aim vector.

Putting this all together gives us the following line to create the `aim` constraint:

```
cmds.aimConstraint(aimLoc[0], newCam[0], aimVector=(0,0,-1))
```

Now we just need to move the camera to the proper location. Because the aim constraint will take care of the rotations, all we have to worry about is the position. In this case, we want to make sure that each camera lies on a line that is some multiple of 45 degrees from the origin. To do this, we'll want to make sure that the *X* and *Z* positions have the same magnitude, with only the signs changing from camera to camera.

First off, we'll create variables for each of the x, y, and z positions, with the `ypos` variable being set to a default value:

```
xpos = 0
ypos = 6
zpos = 0
```

For X and Z, we'll want to have values for each of the four quadrants- (+,+), (+,-), (-,-), and (-,+). To do this, we'll have one of the values be negative when our index is odd, and the other be negative when the index is greater than or equal to 2:

```
if (i % 2 == 0):
    xpos = -offset
else:
    xpos = offset

if (i >= 2):
    zpos = -offset
else:
    zpos = offset
```

Note that we're making use of the `offset` variable, which was set outside of the loop.

Having done this, we use the `move` command to position the camera at the proper location.

```
cmds.move(xpos, ypos, zpos, newCam[0])
```

And with this, we're done!

There's more...

In this example, we created an `aim` constraint to replicate the behavior that one gets when creating a *Camera and Aim* from Maya's UI. The nice thing about this is that we can move the locator in order to change the look at location.

If all we wanted was to have the camera look at a given location though, we could do it with the `viewPlace` command, which can both move a camera and rotate it to look at a given location. For example, if we wanted to have a camera positioned at (5,6,5) and looking at a point slightly above the origin (let's say 0,2,0), we could do the following:

```
newCam = cmds.camera()
cmds.viewPlace(newCam[0], eye=(5,6,5), lookAt=(0, 2, 0))
```

We also only scratched the surface of what can be done when creating cameras; you'll often want to set things such as the near/far clip planes, depth of field, and so on. You can either set such things directly on creation or use `setAttr` to alter them after the fact. For more details, be sure to consult the documentation for the `camera` command.

Rendering a sprite sheet

In this example, we'll be building a tool to render out multiple views of an object to a single image. This could be used to create a sprite sheet for use in an isometric game.

In the course of the example, we'll use both Maya's Python library (to render out frames) and the **Python Imaging Library** (**PIL**) to combine them into a single image.

Four views rendered out and combined into a single image

Getting ready

Make sure that you have an object in your scene and it is at the origin. Also make sure that you have some number of cameras set up. You can either do it manually, or refer to the previous example on how to create cameras from script.

You'll also want to make sure that you have PIL installed on your system. The best way to do that is to grab Pillow (a fork of PIL). More information on Pillow can be found at `http://pillow.readthedocs.io/en/3.2.x/`.

In order to install Pillow in a (relatively) painless way, you'll probably want to grab PIP, which is a robust package manager for Python. For more information on PIP, check `https://pypi.python.org/pypi/pip`.

How to do it...

Create a new file and add the following code:

```python
import maya.cmds as cmds
import os
from PIL import Image

FRAME_WIDTH = 400
FRAME_HEIGHT = 300

def renderSpriteSheet():
    allCams = cmds.listCameras()

    customCams = []
```

```
        for cam in allCams:
            if (cam not in ["front", "persp", "side", "top"]):
                customCams.append(cam)

        # make sure we're rendering TGAs
        cmds.setAttr("defaultRenderGlobals.imageFormat", 19)

        # create a new image
        fullImage = Image.new("RGBA", (FRAME_WIDTH*len(customCams),
        FRAME_HEIGHT), "black")

        # run through each camera, rendering the view and adding it to
        the mage
            for i in range(0, len(customCams)):
            result = cmds.render(customCams[i], x=FRAME_WIDTH,
            y=FRAME_HEIGHT)
            tempImage = Image.open(result)
            fullImage.paste(tempImage, (i*FRAME_WIDTH,0))

        basePath = cmds.workspace(query=True, rootDirectory=True)
        fullPath = os.path.join(basePath, "images", "frames.tga")
        fullImage.save(fullPath)

    renderSpriteSheet()
```

Run the script, and you should get a new image, named `frames.tga` in the `images` directory of your project folder, containing a view from each of the (nonstandard) cameras. If you haven't set up a project, the images will be in the default project directory. If you want them to be in a specific location, be sure to set your project before running the script.

How it works...

First off, we're importing a few additional libraries to make the script work. First is the `os` library, to let us combine paths and file names in a safe, cross-platform way. Then, we also import the Image module from PIL, which we'll use to create our combined image:

```
import maya.cmds as cmds
import os
from PIL import Image
```

Next, we define a couple of variables that we'll use to set the size of our rendered images. We'll use that both to set the render size, as well as to calculate the size of the combined image:

```
FRAME_WIDTH = 400
FRAME_HEIGHT = 300
```

Note that the variables are all caps, that is by no means necessary. Capitalized variables are often used to indicate constants that are used in multiple places and don't vary during the course of a script. The dimensions of the frames to render are a good example of that kind of variable, so I've given them all-caps names, but feel free to use a different style if you so choose.

Now we're ready to get started rendering out images. To do it, we'll want to first get a list of all the cameras in our scene, then filter out the default views. We *could* use the ls command to do it, but it's easier to use the listCameras command:

```
allCams = cmds.listCameras()
```

To ignore the default camera views, we'll start by creating a new (empty) list, then running through our allCams list. Each camera that is *not* in the list of defaults gets added, leaving us with a handy list of all the nondefault cameras in the scene.

```
customCams = []

for cam in allCams:
    if (cam not in ["front", "persp", "side", "top"]):
        customCams.append(cam)
```

At this point, we have a list of all the cameras that we'll want to render out. Before we render anything, we'll want to make sure that we're rendering the proper image format. In this case, we'll render out Targa files because they're both uncompressed and include an alpha channel:

```
cmds.setAttr("defaultRenderGlobals.imageFormat", 19)
```

To set the image type, we use the setAttr command, but the value is less clear than we might like. It just so happens that the targa format happens to correspond to 19. Other common formats include JPG (8), PNG (32), and PSD (31). To check the value of any given format, open the render globals window, select the desired format from the dropdown, and observe the output in the script editor.

Before we start rendering our images, we'll want to use PIL to create a larger image to hold all of the frames. We'll create a single image that has the same height as our render size and a width equal to the render width multiplied by the number of cameras. We'll also set up the image to default to black:

```
fullImage = Image.new("RGBA", (FRAME_WIDTH*len(customCams),
FRAME_HEIGHT), "black")
```

Note that we pass in RGBA to set the image mode to full color plus alpha. With our base image created, we're ready to run through our cameras and render each frame.

For each camera, we'll want to:

▶ Render the current view at our specified width and height

▶ Paste the rendered image into the combined image

To render out a given view, we use the `render` command with three arguments-the camera to render from, followed by the width and the height for the rendered image:

```
result = cmds.render(customCams[i], x=FRAME_WIDTH, y=FRAME_HEIGHT)
```

We store the result of the `render` command into a result variable for later use. It's important to note that the output isn't the image itself, but rather the path to the image (something like `/Documents/maya/projects/default/images/tmp/MyScene.tga`).

Now that we've rendered out the image, we'll want to use PIL to create the second `Image` object from the specified path:

```
tempImg = Image.open(result)
```

We use `Image.open` instead of `Image.create` because we want to create an image from a given file, rather than a new blank image. Finally, we copy the new image into our combined image with the `paste` command:

```
fullImage.paste(tempImg, (i*FRAME_WIDTH,0))
```

PIL's paste command allows one image to be pasted into another at a specific location. In this case, we call it on our `fullImage` image and pass in the image we just rendered out (`tempImg`), as well as a tuple for the location. The *Y* location is locked to 0 in all cases, and the *X* location is set to `FRAME_WIDTH` multiplied by the loop index so that our images are placed in an orderly horizontal line.

Once we've finished that loop, we're ready to save out the combined image. There are any number of places we could put it, but it probably makes sense to put it somewhere in our project directory. To do that, we'll need to first grab the current project directory using the `workspace` command in the query mode as follows:

```
basePath = cmds.workspace(query=True, rootDirectory=True)
```

Where you save the image is up to you, but in this case, I decided to go with saving it out as `frames.tga` in the `images` folder of the project directory. We could build up the path by adding strings, but using Python's `os` library to join the path guarantees that our script will have better cross-platform support:

```
fullPath = os.path.join(basePath, "images", "frames.tga")
```

Finally, we call `Image.save` on our `fullImage` variable and pass in the path we just created:

```
fullImage.save(fullPath)
```

There's more...

Although there is certainly a wide range of options offered by Maya's rendering capabilities, some things may be easier to achieve by postprocessing after the fact. The PIL is quite powerful and well worth digging into. If you ever find yourself needed to perform 2D operations on your renders, it's quite possible that doing so with the PIL could be a good choice.

This script, or something like it, could easily be used to build a robust asset pipeline for an isometric game. You could easily add the ability to send the combined image to a central server along with metadata on the particular structure or object. We'll look at sending data across the Web in *Chapter 9, Communicating with the Web*.

See also

PIL is capable of a great deal more than what we used it for in this example. For more details, you'll want to dig into the documentation on *effbot.org* (`http://effbot.org/imagingbook/pil-index.htm`).

8

Working with File Input/Output

In this chapter, we'll be looking at ways to get custom data in and out of Maya via scripting:

- ▶ Using the fileDialog2 command to navigate the file system
- ▶ Reading text files
- ▶ Writing text files
- ▶ Writing binary data
- ▶ Reading binary data
- ▶ Reading multiple types of files

Introduction

Although Maya is an incredibly powerful tool, it's almost always just one step in a larger toolchain. Whether you're using Maya to create prerendered animation for film and video or creating assets for use in real-time applications, you'll generally always need to interface Maya or the content you create within it, with other applications. Very often, this takes the form of either reading or writing data of a specific format.

In this chapter, we'll be looking at how to work with custom data formats, both text-based and binary, and to both read and write data.

Using the fileDialog2 command to navigate the file system

Loading and saving files will almost always require prompting the user for a file location. In this example, we'll look at how to do that. We'll also see how to work with directories, including creating new ones.

We'll create a script that will allow the user to browse the files in a `customData` folder within the current project directory. If that folder doesn't exist, it will be created the first time the script is run.

How to do it...

Create a new file and add the following:

```python
import os
import maya.cmds as cmds

def browseCustomData():

    projDir = cmds.internalVar(userWorkspaceDir=True)

    newDir = os.path.join(projDir, 'customData')

    if (not os.path.exists(newDir)):
        os.makedirs(newDir)

    cmds.fileDialog2(startingDirectory=newDir)


browseCustomData()
```

You'll be presented with a file browser dialog. And, while the dialog won't actually do anything just yet, if you check your project directory, you'll find that it now contains a folder named `customData`.

How it works...

The first thing to note about this script is that we add an additional import statement to the start of the script:

```python
import os
```

The os library (short for "operating system") offers a variety of functionality related to the operating system of the host machine, including the ability to work with directories. We'll be using both to check to see whether a directory exists and to create it if it doesn't exist. More on this will be explained later.

For this script, we'll want to start by finding out what the current project directory is. For that, we can use the `internalVar` command. The `internalVar` command can be used to get access to various directories related to the current user's environment. It cannot be used to set any of those directories, only to query them. However, note that we don't actually use it in the query mode (Maya's commands aren't always the most consistent). Instead, we set the value of the flag we want the value of to true.

In this case, we're asking for the `userWorkspaceDir`, which will provide us with the current project directory:

```
projDir = cmds.internalVar(userWorkspaceDir=True)
```

Next, we want to test to see if there's the `customData` folder within the current workspace. To do this, we'll start by creating the full path to that directory (if it exists) by adding "customData" to the value that `internalVar` returned. We *could* do it with string manipulation, but that gets a bit tricky, since different platforms can use different characters to indicate separations between directories. Linux-based platforms (including Macintosh) use "/", whereas Windows machines use "\". A safer (and therefore better) way to go about it is to use Python's `os.path.join` method, which is guaranteed to be safe, as follows:

```
newDir = os.path.join(projDir, 'customData')
```

Now we have the full path to the `customData` folder, but it might not actually exist. We can use another function from `os.path`, `os.path.exists`, to check that, and to create it if it doesn't:

```
if (not os.path.exists(newDir)):
```

If we find that the path, in fact, does not exist, we use `os.makedirs` to create it:

```
    os.makedirs(newDir)
```

At this point, we can finally invoke the `fileDialog2` command to present the user with a file browser dialog. In order to make sure that it starts out in the `customData` directory, we set the `startingDirectory` flag to our `newDir` variable:

```
cmds.fileDialog2(startingDirectory=newDir)
```

Note that we use `fileDialog2`, which might look a bit odd. There is also a `fileDialog` command, but it's deprecated (along with the `fileBrowserDialog` command). As a result, we're left needing to use the somewhat awkwardly named `fileDialog2`.

There's more...

The `fileDialog2` command has a number of other options that we'll see in later examples. The `internalVar` command also has a number of additional locations that it can provide. One that is often useful is the `userScriptDir` option, which will provide the user's script directory.

If you wanted to get a list of all of the scripts currently in the user's script directory, for example, you could use the following snippet:

```
def listScripts():
    scriptDir = cmds.internalVar(userScriptDir=True)
    print(os.listdir(scriptDir))
```

The `os.listdir` command will provide an array of all the files in a given directory. In this case, we might want to create GUI with a button for each script, providing an easy way for users to select and run scripts.

Reading text files

In this example, we'll be reading a text file and using the contents to create some geometry in our scene.

Getting ready

In order to do any kind of file input/output, the first thing you'll need to do is to understand the file format that you're wanting to read (or create). In both this example and the one involving writing to text files, we'll be using an example file format—the "foo" file. "Foo" files are text-based files, and each line represents a geometric primitive of a given type, at a given location. The type of geometric primitive is represented by a three-letter string, with "spr" meaning a sphere and "cub" meaning a cube. The type string is then followed by three numbers representing the X, Y, and Z position of the item. So, an example `.foo` file might look something like the following:

```
spr    0    0    0
cub    -2   0    -2
```

Although this is certainly not a particularly useful format, it shares similarities with many common text-based formats. The OBJ format, for example, is a common standard for 3D models that uses a similar approach—each line consists of an identifier for the type of information it holds, followed by details on that entry. For example, a line indicating that there is a vertex located at 2, 3, and 4 would look like the following:

```
v 2 3 4
```

So, our "foo" files, while intentionally very simple, will be read and processed in much the same way as many *real* file formats.

Before you run the script for this example, make sure that you've created a .foo file. To do that, create a new text file and add some number of lines that:

- ▶ Begin with either "spr" (for sphere) or "cub" (for cube)
- ▶ Are followed with three numbers (for X, Y, and Z positions), each separated by a space

Be sure to save the file as a .foo file, rather than .txt.

How to do it...

Create a new file and add the following code:

```python
import maya.cmds as cmds

def processFooLine(line):

    parts = line.split()

    if (len(parts) < 4):
        cmds.error("BAD DATA " + line)

    x = float(parts[1])
    y = float(parts[2])
    z = float(parts[3])

    if (parts[0] == "spr"):
        cmds.sphere()
    elif (parts[0] == "cub"):
        cmds.polyCube()

    cmds.move(x, y, z)


def readFooFile():
    filePath = cmds.fileDialog2(fileMode=1, fileFilter="*.foo")

    fileRef = open(filePath[0], "r")
```

```
        line = fileRef.readline()
        while (line):
            processFooLine(line)
            line = fileRef.readline()

        fileRef.close()

    readFooFile()
```

Run the file, and you will be presented with a file dialog that will let you find a `.foo` file. Once you specify a file with valid FOO file data, you should see some number of spheres and cubes created.

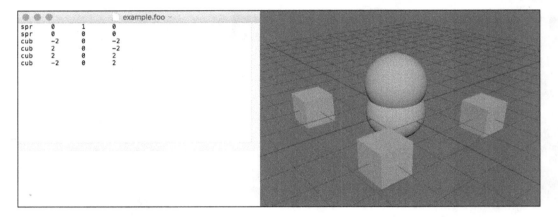

How it works...

The first thing we do in the script is to invoke the `fileDialog2` command in order to let the user specify a file. We set the `fileMode` flag to 1 to indicate that we want to read (rather than write) a file. We also make use of the `fileFilter` flag in order to point the user at our custom file format. This is totally optional, but it can be a nice way to prevent the user from giving you the wrong kind of data. To do that, we'll want to provide Maya with two things:

▸ A short description of the file type to show the user, and

▸ One or more file extensions, with a wildcard character ("*")

So in this case, we'll want to limit the user to "FOO files", and we'll identify those as anything that ends in either `.foo` or `.fo`. The final value of the string to pass in looks like:

```
"FOO files (*.foo *.fo)"
```

Note that we could also allow the user to open other kinds of files as well, by separating the strings for each with a double semicolon. Let's say that we wanted to allow the user to open text (.txt) files as well. For that, our call to fileDialog2 would look like the following:

```
cmds.fileDialog2(fileMode=1, fileFilter="FOO files (*.foo *.fo);;Text
files (*.txt)")
```

If you allow the user to open files of more than one type, each type will be available in the dropdown in the bottom of the file dialog. By selecting an option from the dropdown, the user can change which types of files the dialog will accept. Now that we've covered specifying the file type, let's go back to our regularly scheduled example.

We store the output of the fileDialog to a variable. We also check to make sure that the variable is not None before proceeding. This way, we'll ensure that we don't proceed with the script if the user has clicked on the "cancel" button:

```
    filePath = cmds.fileDialog2(fileMode=1, fileFilter="FOO files
(*.foo *.fo);;Text files (*.txt)")

    if (filePath == None):
        return
```

Now we're ready to actually open the file. To do it, we use Python's open command, with the first argument being the full path to the file we want to open, and the second argument indicating the mode to open the file in, with "r" meaning "read":

```
    fileRef = open(filePath[0], "r")
```

Note that filePath is an array, so we'll need to feed in the first element into the open command. The return value of open, which we store in our fileRef variable, is a reference to the file that we can use to read in data.

For most types of text-based files (with FOO files being no exception), we'll want to read the file in line by line. We'll start by reading a single line from our file reference:

```
    line = fileRef.readline()
```

Once we've done that, we want to:

1. Process the information in the line we just read
2. Read the next line from the file
3. Continue until we've read the entire file

That's easily done with a while loop. The processing will be handled by a separate function, which we'll get to next:

```
while (line):
    processFooLine(line)
    line = fileRef.readline()
```

Once we get to the end of the file, our line variable will be empty, and the while loop will terminate. The last thing we do is a bit of housekeeping, that is, we close the reference to the file:

```
fileRef.close()
```

Now, let's take a closer look at how we process the data, in our `processFooLine` function. We start off by breaking the line up into parts, using Python's `split` function. That will take the input string and break it up into an array of strings, separated (by default) based on whitespaces:

```
parts = line.split()

if (len(parts) < 4):
    cmds.error("BAD DATA " + line)
```

Because our FOO file specification states that each line should be a short string, followed by three numbers, we throw an error if our parts array has fewer than four entries. If it does have at least four, we convert the second, third, and fourth entries to floats and store them into variables for the x, y, and z position:

```
x = float(parts[1])
y = float(parts[2])
z = float(parts[3])
```

Now we create the object, either a sphere or a cube based on the first entry in the parts array:

```
if (parts[0] == "spr"):
    cmds.sphere()
elif (parts[0] == "cub"):
    cmds.polyCube()
```

Finally, we move the object we just created to the position indicated in our x, y, and z variables:

```
cmds.move(x, y, z)
```

There's more...

Although the FOO format specification is intentionally simplistic, we could easily extend it to store more information or possibly optional information. For example, we might also have an optional fifth entry to indicate the size of the object to be created (for example, face width for cubes and radius for spheres). If you would like to see what a format that is superficially similar to FOO files, but more useful, looks like, I encourage you to take a look at the OBJ file format. Not only is it widely used in 3D, but it's also a relatively simple format to understand and as such is a great introduction to file parsing.

Writing text files

In the previous example, we looked at how to read a custom data file format and use it to create geometry in a scene. In this example, we'll do the inverse, in that we'll examine our scene for polygonal cubes and NURBS spheres, and write the position of each one we find out to a new FOO file. In the process, we'll see how to write data to custom text-based formats.

Getting ready

Before running this example, make sure that you have a scene with some number of (NURBS) spheres and polygonal cubes in it. Make sure that you create the cubes and spheres with construction history enabled, otherwise our script won't be able to correctly identify the geometry.

How to do it...

Create a new file and add the following code:

```python
import maya.cmds as cmds

def checkHistory(obj):
    history = cmds.listHistory(obj)

    geoType = ""

    for h in history:

        if (h.startswith("makeNurbSphere")):
            geoType = "spr"

        if (h.startswith("polyCube")):
            geoType = "cub"
```

```
        return geoType


def writeFOO():

    filePath = cmds.fileDialog2(fileMode=0, fileFilter="FOO files
(*.foo)")

    if (filePath == None):
        return

    fileRef = open(filePath[0], "w")

    objects = cmds.ls(type="transform")

    for obj in objects:
        geoType = checkHistory(obj)

        if (geoType != ""):

            position = cmds.xform(obj, query=True, translation=True,
worldSpace=True)
            positionString = " ".join(format(x, ".3f") for x in
position)

            newLine = geoType + " " + positionString + "\n"
            fileRef.write(newLine)

    fileRef.close()


writeFOO()
```

How it works...

We start off by prompting the user to specify a file. As in the file reading example, we set the `fileFilter` flag so that the dialog is limited to .foo files. This time, though, we set the `fileMode` flag to 0 to indicate that we want to write a file (instead of a value of 1, indicating reading):

```
filePath = cmds.fileDialog2(fileMode=0, fileFilter="FOO files
(*.foo)")
```

If the result of the `fileDialog2` command is empty (indicating that the user canceled), we stop. Otherwise, we continue with the script and open the specified file for writing. Again, note that the `fileDialog2` command returned an array, meaning that we need to pass in its first entry to the open command. We also set the second argument to `"w"`, indicating that we want to write to the file:

```
if (filePath == None):
    return

fileRef = open(filePath[0], "w")
```

Next, we need to find all of the cubes and spheres in our scene. To do that, we start off by getting all of the transform nodes in the scene.

```
objects = cmds.ls(type="transform")
```

For each object, we want to find out if it's a sphere or a cube. One way to do it is to examine the construction history of the object and see if there's a `makeNurbSphere` or `polyCube` node. To keep things nice and neat, we'll wrap that in a separate function, `checkHistory`.

To get the history for a given object, we can use the `listHistory` command, which will give us the construction history as an array:

```
def checkHistory(obj):
    history = cmds.listHistory(obj)
```

Once we've done that, we're ready to run through the history and see if we can find the geometry that we're looking for. But first, we set up a variable to hold the geometry type and initialize it to an empty string:

```
geoType = ""
```

If the object in question *is* one of the types we're looking for, it will have either the `makeNurbSphere` or `polyCube` node in its history. However, in either case, the node will have a number at the end of its name. So, we'll need to use Python's `startswith` command to perform the check, instead of just testing for direct equality.

If we find either of the geometry creation nodes we're looking for, we'll set our `geoType` string to the appropriate abbreviation (based on the FOO file format specification):

```
for h in history:

    if (h.startswith("makeNurbSphere")):
        geoType = "spr"

    if (h.startswith("polyCube")):
        geoType = "cub"
```

Finally, we return the `geoType` variable:

```
return geoType
```

The upshot of all that is that we'll have either "spr" or "cub" for the objects that we want to export, and an empty string for everything else. With this, we can turn our attention back to our main function.

Armed with out `checkHistory` function, we're now ready to loop through all of the objects in the scene, testing each one to see if it's the geometry we're interested in:

```
for obj in objects:
    geoType = checkHistory(obj)

    if (geoType != ""):
```

If the value returned from `checkHistory` is *not* an empty string, we know that we have something that we want to write out to our file. We already know the geometry type, but we still need to get the world-space position. For that, we use the `xform` command, in query mode.

```
position = cmds.xform(obj, query=True, translation=True,
worldSpace=True)
```

Now we're finally ready to write our data out to our file. We'll want to build up a string with the following format:

```
[geometry type ID] [x position] [y position] [z position]
```

We'll start by creating a string from the position we received from `xform`. The position starts out as an array of floating-point numbers, which we'll want to convert into a single string. This means that we need to do two things:

1. Convert the numbers to strings.
2. Join the strings together into a single string.

If we have an array of strings, we can join them together using Python's `join` command. The syntax for that is a bit odd, but it's easy enough to use; we start with a string that holds whatever it is that we would like to use as a separator. In this case (as in most cases), we'll want to use a space. We then call join on that string, passing in the list of elements that we want to join. So, if the position array contained strings, we could do the following:

```
positionString = " ".join(position)
```

However, it's not quite that easy because the position array contains floating-point values. So, before we can run join, we need to first convert the numerical values to strings. If that's all we want to do, we could do the following:

```
positionString = " ".join(map(str, position))
```

In the preceding code, we use Python's `map` function to apply the first argument (the `str` or string function) to each element of the second (the position array). That translates the position array into an array of strings, which can then be passed to the join function.

However, we may want more control over the formatting of our floats, which brings us to the line that we're actually using, namely:

```
positionString = " ".join(format(x, ".3f") for x in position)
```

This is a bit similar to the map-based example, in that we apply a function to the position array before passing the contents into the join function. However, in this case, we use the `format` function, which allows us more control over the specifics of how floats are formatted. In this case, we're limiting the precision of the values to three decimal places.

At this point, we have the full position of the object at hand as a string. To finish it off, we need to add the geometry type identifier (as specified in our FOO file format spec). We'll also want to add a newline (\n) character at the end, to ensure that each piece of geometry has a separate line for its data.

Note that if you open the created file in notepad on a Windows machine, you'll see that all of your data appear as a single line. That's because unix-like systems (including Mac) use \n as the newline character, whereas Windows uses \r\n. The \r is the carriage return character, whereas \n is the newline character. Using both is a byproduct of the old days when typewriters would perform two actions to move to the next line—move the paper all the way to the right (\r) and move it up (\n). If you're working on Windows, you might want to add \r\n instead of just \n.

This gives us the following:

```
newLine = geoType + " " + positionString + "\n"
```

Now we're finally ready to write the data to our file. That's easily done with a call to `write()` on our file:

```
fileRef.write(newLine)
```

Once we've finished our loop through all the objects and saved out all our data, we finish off by closing the file reference:

```
fileRef.close()
```

There's more...

The example presented in this section may seem a bit artificial, but exporting positional data is a fairly common need. Very often, it can be easier for your art team to use Maya to position objects that are later used in some programmatic way, such as (in the case of games) spawn points or item pickup locations.

In this example, we identified the objects to export by examining their construction history. This can work, but it's easily broken if construction history is ever deleted. Because deleting history is a common thing to do, it's good to have alternative means to identify nodes for export.

One very reliable way to go about it is to add a custom attribute to nodes that should be exported and to use that when looping through objects. For example, we might be using polygonal cubes to indicate where certain types of item pickups are in a game level. To better prepare for exporting the data, we could add a `pickupType` attribute to each cube.

We could easily wrap that in a nice function to add the attribute and set its value, as in the following:

```
def markAsPickup(obj, pickupType):
    customAtts = cmds.listAttr(obj, userDefined=True)

    if ("pickupType" not in customAtts):
        cmds.addAttr(obj, longName="pickupType", keyable=True)

    cmds.setAttr(obj + ".pickupType", pickupType)
```

The preceding code would add a keyable `pickupType` attribute to a given object and set its value. Note that we check to see whether the `pickupType` attribute exists on the node before adding it because adding an attribute that already exists will generate an error. To check for the attribute, we first get a list of all the user-defined attributes, then test to see if `pickupType` exists in that array.

When we're ready to export our data, we can use the same trick to identify the objects for which we want to export data. If we wanted to write out data for every object that possesses the `pickupType` attribute, we could do the following:

```
def listPickups():
    pickups = []
    objects = cmds.ls(type="transform")

    for obj in objects:
        customAtts = cmds.listAttr(obj, userDefined=True)
        if (customAtts != None):
```

```
if ("pickupType" in customAtts):
    print(obj)
    pickups.append(obj)

return pickups
```

We start by creating a new list to hold our pickups, then grabbing all of the transform nodes in the scene. For each transform, we grab all of the custom attributes added to it and check to see whether any of them are named `pickupType`. If that's the case, we add the object to our list. Once we've finished with the loop, we return the list, for use elsewhere (perhaps to write out their locations).

See also

For a quick overview of the FOO file format, be sure to take a look at the previous example regarding reading text-based data.

Writing binary data

So far in this chapter, we've looked at reading and writing text-based data formats. This will allow you to work with many types of data (and to easily create your own formats), but it's only half of the picture. In this example, we'll look at the other half-binary formats.

Getting ready

In this example, we'll be writing out a binary version of our FOO file. We'll call such files FOB (foo, binary). As was the case with FOO files, FOB files are a scaled-down example of the types of things that are often encountered in real formats. FOB files will contain the same data we saw in FOO files, namely a list of object types and positions, but stored in a way common to binary formats.

Most binary files consist of two main parts:

- A header, which is a fixed-size chunk that describes the nature of the rest of the document.
- Entries that are read according to the data layout specified in the header.

In the case of our FOB files, our header will contain the following:

- An integer (1 byte) that specifies how many characters are used for the geometry type specification per entry (our "spr" or "cub").
- An integer (1 byte) that specifies the maximum number of attributes per object (X, Y, and Z position at a minimum, possibly more data).
- An integer (1 byte) that specifies the number of bytes per attribute.

So, a specific FOB file might say that we're using three bytes for the geometry type, with a maximum number of four data values (X, Y, Z position and size), each of which uses four bytes. This would give us a header like the following:

```
3  4  4
```

After the header, there would be some number of entries, each of which would consist of 19 bytes (3 for the geometry type, plus 4 * 4, or 16 bytes for the data).

Before you run the example, make sure that you have one or more NURBS spheres and/or polygonal cubes in your scene and that they were created with construction history enabled (the default option).

How to do it...

Create a new file and add the following code:

```python
import maya.cmds as cmds
import struct


def checkHistory(obj):
    history = cmds.listHistory(obj)

    geoType = ""

    for h in history:

        if (h.startswith("makeNurbSphere")):
            geoType = "spr"

        if (h.startswith("polyCube")):
            geoType = "cub"

    return geoType


def writeFOBHeader(f):
    headerStr = 'iii'
    f.write(struct.pack(headerStr, 3, 3, 4))

def writeObjData(obj, geoType, f):
```

```
        position = cmds.xform(obj, query=True, translation=True,
    worldSpace=True)

        f.write(geoType)

        f.write(struct.pack('fff', position[0], position[1], position[2]))


    def saveFOBFile():
        filePath = cmds.fileDialog2(fileMode=0, fileFilter="FOO Binary
    files (*.fob)")

        if (filePath == None):
            return

        fileRef = open(filePath[0], "wb")

        writeFOBHeader(fileRef)
        objects = cmds.ls(type="transform")

        for obj in objects:
            geoType = checkHistory(obj)

            if (geoType != ""):

                writeObjData(obj, geoType, fileRef)
                # positionString = " ".join(format(x, ".3f") for x in
    position)

        fileRef.close()


    saveFOBFile()
```

How it works...

The first thing to note is that we have an additional import statement at the start of the script:

```
import struct
```

The `struct` library provides functions that we'll be using to properly format data to write to binary. More on that in a bit. Onto the script itself...

First off, we ask the user to specify a file, just as we've done in the previous examples. The only difference is that we change the `fileFilter` argument a bit to specify files of type "FOO Binary", with a `.fob` extension:

```
filePath = cmds.fileDialog2(fileMode=0, fileFilter="FOO Binary files
(*.fob)")
```

We check to make sure that our `filePath` variable has an actual value (that the user didn't cancel out) and stop the script if it doesn't. We then open the file for writing:

```
fileRef = open(filePath[0], "wb")
```

Note that we're using `"wb"` instead of `"w"` as an argument to the open command; this tells Python that we want to open the file for writing (`"w"`) in binary mode (`"b"`).

Now we're ready to start writing to our file. Before we can write any data though, we'll need to write the header. In the case of FOB files, all that is three integers—one to hold the number of characters for the geometry identifier, one to hold the number of data points per object, and one to hold the number of bytes per data points.

To actually write the data, we'll use the pack function of the `struct` library. The pack function will create a sequence of bytes containing data of a given format, as specified in a format string. The format string is a sequence of characters, with each one representing the type of data that is to be written. The characters can be any of the following as well as many others:

i	integer
f	float
c	char

For a full list, refer to Python's documentation.

In this case, we'll want to store three integers, so our format string will need to consist of three Is, as in:

```
headerStr = 'iii'
```

We pass the format string into the `struct.pack` function, followed by the values we want to encode (in this case, three integers). In this case, we'll want three characters for our geometry identifier length (to accommodate "spr" and "cub"), three points of data (the X, Y, and Z positions), and four bytes for each piece of data. Putting that all together gives us the following:

```
struct.pack(headerStr, 3, 3, 4)
```

Once we have the data packed up, we write it to our file with `write`. We wrap all of that in a nice function as follows:

```
def writeFOBHeader(f):
    headerStr = 'iii'
    f.write(struct.pack(headerStr, 3, 3, 4))
```

Now that we've written our header to the file, we're ready to write the data for our objects. We run through the scene and find all of the spheres and cubes in exactly the same way that we did in the example on saving text data. For each object we find, we write the data to our file.

```
for obj in objects:
    geoType = checkHistory(obj)

    if (geoType != ""):
        writeObjData(obj, geoType, fileRef)
```

Our `writeObjData` function takes the object itself, the object type string (as determined by our `checkHistory` function from the text output example and a reference to the file we're writing to.

Within the `writeObjData` function, we start out by grabbing the position of the object in world space using the `xform` command:

```
position = cmds.xform(obj, query=True, translation=True,
worldSpace=True)
```

We then write the geometry type identifier (either "spr" or "cub") to the file. Writing text to binary files is easy—we just write the values directly. This will result in a single byte for each character being written to the file.

```
f.write(geoType)
```

Finally, we write the position data to the file, once again using the struct.pack function. This time, however, we want to write floating-point values, so we use three fs as the format string:

```
f.write(struct.pack('fff', position[0], position[1], position[2]))
```

Finally, and back in our main function, we close our file, which now contains both the header and all of our data.

```
fileRef.close()
```

There's more...

We could easily write out more than just position data for each object. If we wanted to write out a radius value for each sphere, we would need to do a few things, namely:

1. Change our header to specify four values per object, instead of just three.
2. Change the format string passed in to pack to have four fs instead of three.

Note that even though a radius value doesn't make sense in the case of a cube, we would still need to write *something* in that place in order to ensure that each entry occupies the same number of bytes. Since binary files are generally processed by reading in a set number of bytes at a time, having a byte width that changes from entry to entry would interfere with that.

If you think that it's a limitation, you're right. Binary formats tend to be much stricter than text-based formats, and they are generally only worth it if you really need to create very compact files. In general, if you're considering creating a custom format, text is almost always going to be a better choice. Reserve binary output for situations where you find yourself having to output data to an existing format that happens to be binary.

Reading binary data

In this example, we'll look at how to read in binary data. We'll use our same example format, the "FOO binary" format, which consists of a header with three integers, followed by one or more entries, each of which has a string identifying a type of object and three or more numbers indicating its position (and possibly additional data).

Getting ready

In order to run this example, you'll need to have a .fob file at the ready. Creating binary files manually is a bit of a hassle, so I recommend using the example explained earlier to generate one for you.

How to do it...

Create a new file and add the following code:

```
import maya.cmds as cmds
import struct

def makeObject(objType, pos):

    newObj = None
```

```
    if (objType == "spr"):
        newObj = cmds.sphere()
    elif (objType == "cub"):
        newObj = cmds.polyCube()

    if (newObj != None):
        cmds.move(pos[0], pos[1], pos[2])



def readFOBFile():
    filePath = cmds.fileDialog2(fileMode=1, fileFilter="FOO binary
files (*.fob)")

    if (filePath == None):
        return

    f = open(filePath[0], "rb")

    data = f.read()

    headerLen = 12

    res = struct.unpack('iii', data[0:headerLen])

    geoTypeLen = res[0]
    numData = res[1]
    bytesPerData = res[2]

    objectLen = geoTypeLen + (numData * bytesPerData)

    numEntries = (len(data) - headerLen) / objectLen

    dataStr = 'f'*numData

    for i in range(0,numEntries):
        start = (i * objectLen) + headerLen
        end = start + geoTypeLen

        geoType = data[start:end]

        start = end
        end = start + (numData * bytesPerData)
```

```
        pos = struct.unpack(dataStr, data[start:end])
        makeObject(geoType, pos)

    f.close()


    readFOBFile()
```

Run the script, point it at a valid .fob file, and you should see some number of spheres and/or cubes in your scene.

How it works...

In this example, we'll also be using the struct library (to unpack our data), so we need to make sure that we import it:

```
import struct
```

We start out by using the `fileDialog2` command to prompt the user to specify a .fob file and exiting the script if nothing was given:

```
filePath = cmds.fileDialog2(fileMode=1, fileFilter="FOO binary files
(*.fob)")

if (filePath == None):
    return
```

If we have a file to open, we open it using the `open` command, passing in `"rb"` for the mode (`"r"` for reading and `"b"` for binary):

```
f = open(filePath[0], "rb")
```

Once we have the file open, we grab all of the data at once, using the `read` function:

```
data = f.read()
```

This will result in data holding an array of all of the bytes in the file. Once we've done that, we're ready to start parsing our content. For each bit of data we read, we'll be doing the following:

1. Reading some number of bytes from our data variable.
2. Passing the bytes into `struct.unpack`, along with a format string indicating what type of data it should be interpreted as.

The first thing we'll need to do is to read the file's header. In the case of .fob files, that's guaranteed to always be exactly 12 bytes—3 integers, at 4 bytes each. So, we start by reading the first 12 bytes in the data array and passing that to `struct.unpack`. The format string we use will be "iii", indicating that the bytes should be interpreted as three integers:

```
headerLen = 12
res = struct.unpack('iii', data[0:headerLen])
```

The output of the `unpack` function is an array containing the data. In this case, we have the number of bytes per geometric identifier, the number of data points per entry, and the number of bytes per data point. To make things easier on ourselves (and the code more readable), we store each element in its own, named variable:

```
geoTypeLen = res[0]
numData = res[1]
bytesPerData = res[2]
```

Once we've done that, we do one more thing for the sake of clarity in what comes next—we calculate the total number of bytes per entry as follows:

```
objectLen = geoTypeLen + (numData * bytesPerData)
```

Once we have that, we can determine the total number of entries in the file by dividing the total number of bytes (minus those consumed by the header) by the number of bytes per entry:

```
numEntries = (len(data) - headerLen) / objectLen
```

There's one more detail to take care of before we read the data; we'll want to create a format string for use with `struct.unpack`. In the case of `.fob` files, everything after the geometric identifier string will be a float, but we want to make sure that we take into account the number of entries, as specified in the header. So, if we have three entries per object, we'll want "fff", but if we have four, we would want "ffff". Python makes creating a string from a given number of repeated characters as easy as multiplying, which gives us the following:

```
dataStr = 'f'*numData
```

And with that, we're done with the prep work and we're ready to move on to actually reading our data. We start with a loop that runs for the number of entries that we found earlier:

```
for i in range(0,numEntries):
```

The math to calculate the indices we'll need to read isn't particularly complicated, but it would get confusing, so we use a couple of variables to break it out onto separate lines.

The starting byte for each entry is simply the number of entries we've read so far multiplied by the total length per entry and offset by the length of the header. The end index is the start plus the length of the header:

```
start = (i * objectLen) + headerLen
end = start + geoTypeLen
```

Reading the geometric identifier is easy, since it's just text, with each byte corresponding to a single letter:

```
geoType = data[start:end]
```

Now we set out start and end variables to new values to read the position (and possibly other) data. We set the start to the previous value of end. This works, because when reading a range of indices from a Python array, the values read start at the first number and read up to (but not including) the second.

The ending index for the data is the start plus the total number of bytes for the data (numData * bytesPerData):

```
start = end
end = start + (numData * bytesPerData)
```

And with this, we can finally read our object's data. We index into our data array and pass the result to struct.unpack, along with our previously created format string (dataStr):

```
pos = struct.unpack(dataStr, data[start:end])
```

Once we have both the geometry type (geoType) and the position (pos), we pass both into a function to actually create the geometry we want:

```
makeObject(geoType, pos)
```

The makeObject function is pretty straightforward—we use the geoType argument to create one of two possible objects and, if that worked, we move the created object to the position given in the pos array:

```
def makeObject(objType, pos):

    newObj = None

    if (objType == "spr"):
        newObj = cmds.sphere()
    elif (objType == "cub"):
        newObj = cmds.polyCube()

    if (newObj != None):
        cmds.move(pos[0], pos[1], pos[2])
```

There's more...

Till now, we've only read (or written) binary data of a single type, such as integers (for our header) and floats (for the data). The `struct.pack` and `struct.unpack` functions can also be used with mixed types, as long as you use the proper format string. For example, if we knew that our header contained three floats and one integer, we could use the following to read it in:

```
struct.unpack('fffi', data[0:16])
```

Note that the preceding code uses 0 and 16 as the start and end indices, which might seem like we're grabbing 17 bytes. However, Python interprets ranges as from the start up to (but not including) the second. So, what we're really saying is to use indices from 0 to (16-1), or 15.

Reading multiple types of files

Sometimes, you might want to have a single script that is capable of reading in multiple file types. For example, if you were building a complex system to build character rigs, you might want to have one custom format that holds information about default bone layouts and another type that stores information about animation settings, allowing the user to mix and match any two files.

In such cases, you might want your script to handle files with multiple extensions—one for each type of data. In this example, we'll look at how to do that by creating a script that can be used to read either FOO (our example text-based format) or FOB (our example binary format).

Getting ready

Make sure that you have at least one file of each type. For FOO files, you can just create them directly in a text editor. For FOB files, it's best to use the script in the writing binary files example.

How to do it...

Create a new file and add the following code:

```
import maya.cmds as cmds
import struct
import os

def readMultipleTypes():
```

```
        fileRes = cmds.fileDialog2(fileMode=1, fileFilter="FOO files(*.
foo);;FOO binary files (*.fob)")

    if (fileRes == None):
        return

    filePath = fileRes[0]

    pathParts = os.path.splitext(filePath)
    extension = pathParts[1]

    if (extension == ".foo"):
        readFOOFile(filePath)
    elif (extension == ".fob"):
        readFOBFile(filePath)
    else:
        cmds.error("unrecognized file type")

    readMultipleTypes()
```

Note that the preceding code makes use of two functions that we haven't defined, namely `readFOOFile` and `readFOBFile`. I've left those out for the sake of brevity, but they both use the same code as we discussed in the previous examples on reading text and binary files, respectfully.

If you run the script, you'll be able to select FOO files or, by selecting "FOO binary files" from the drop-down list of file types, FOB files. Either way, you should see the corresponding collection of spheres and cubes added to the scene.

How it works...

The first thing that we have to do in order to read multiple files is to add two or more types to the `fileFilter` argument, separating them with a double semicolon, as in:

```
FOO files(*.foo);;FOO binary files (*.fob)
```

Other than this, the `fileDialog2` command is used as we've used it in the past. Once we have the result from the command, we store the first entry (the path the used selected) into a `filePath` variable.

Once we've done that, we want to examine the file extension of the file chosen by the user. We could do that with string functions, but it's a bit safer to rely on Python's `os.path.splitext` function, which is specifically designed to separate extensions from paths, with the return being an array consisting of first the path (including filename) and then the extension:

```python
filePath = fileRes[0]

pathParts = os.path.splitext(filePath)
extension = pathParts[1]
```

Once we have the extension, we test it against all of the types we want to process, calling the appropriate function for each:

```python
if (extension == ".foo"):
    readFOOFile(filePath)
elif (extension == ".fob"):
    readFOBFile(filePath)
else:
    cmds.error("unrecognized file type")
```

For each file type, we invoke a function to handle the actual processing, passing in the path to the file. We finish off by throwing an error, in the event that the user somehow managed to choose a file of a type that we don't handle.

There's more...

You can certainly extend this approach to handle a wide range of file types in a single script, though if you have a large number of types, selecting the proper one from the dropdown might prove tiring for the user.

In such cases, you might want to just leave out the `fileFilter` altogether, and just allow the script to accept all file types, relying on the extension-filtering logic to filter out any types that you didn't want to process.

In practice, however, if you're really dealing with a large number of different file types, it's likely that your script is trying to do too many things. Consider breaking it up into smaller components, with each one focused on a specific subset of the process you're building them for.

9

Communicating with the Web

In this chapter, we'll be looking at the following ways to get your scripts talking to the outside world by sending and receiving web requests:

- ▶ Opening a web page from script
- ▶ Grabbing data from a server
- ▶ Working with XML data
- ▶ Working with JSON data
- ▶ Sending POST data to a web server from Maya

Introduction

In the previous chapter, we looked at how to read and write data to disk, which can be a great way to build up toolchains and pipelines for your teams. However, you will almost always be working as part of a team (or working to support a team as a TD), which means that you'll generally want to read and write data to some central repository.

And in order to do it, you'll probably need to communicate with a web server of some kind. In this chapter, we'll be looking at how to do just that—how to pull data from and push data onto the Web.

Opening a web page from script

If you find yourself writing a complex script, it can often be helpful to provide documentation for your script in the form of a web page. A great way to do that is to include an easy way to show that page to the user. In this example, we'll create a simple script that will open a given URL in the user's default web browser.

How to do it...

Create a new script and add the following code:

```
import maya.cmds as cmds

def showHelp():
    cmds.showHelp("http://www.adrianherbez.net", absolute=True)

showHelp()
```

Run the script, and you'll see the specified URL appear in your default browser.

How it works...

All we're really doing here is using the showHelp command. It's a bit misleading, as the showHelp command is also used to show Maya's documentation for a specific command. However, as long as you specify the absolute flag to true, you can pass in a full path to the URL you would like to open:

```
cmds.showHelp("http://www.adrianherbez.net", absolute=True)
```

Note that there are a few deprecated commands that you might come across that no longer work. In older versions of Maya, there was a webBrowser command that would allow for the inclusion of web content in script-based UIs. Unfortunately, that command has been removed, necessitating the use of showHelp to open content in the browser.

There's more...

It's highly likely that if you have a script that is complex enough to warrant a page of documentation, it also includes (possibly complex) UI. Rather than just having a button to show help, it's easy enough to implement a proper "Help" menu, as is commonly seen in other programs.

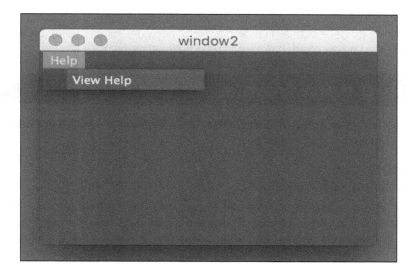

This is easily done with the menu and `menuItem` commands. Here's a full listing to produce the preceding result:

```
import maya.cmds as cmds

class helpWin():

    def __init__(self):
        self.win = cmds.window(menuBar=True, width=300, height=200)
        cmds.menu(label="Help", helpMenu=True)
        cmds.menuItem(label="View Help", command=self.showHelp)
        cmds.columnLayout()
        cmds.showWindow(self.win)

    def showHelp(self, args):
        cmds.showHelp("http://www.adrianherbez.net", absolute=True)

helpWin()
```

We start by creating a window, just as we've done in previous examples. Then, we add a new menu with the `menu` command. The label is the text that will appear as the top of the menu, and specifying `helpMenu=True` ensures that this particular menu will be treated as a help menu (displayed to the far right of all menu options).

Once we have a menu, we can add menu items to it. This is a lot like adding a button, in that we specify a label and a command that will be executed when the item is selected.

Note that the new `menuItem` will be added to the most recent menu. To add menu items in different menus (to have both a "File" and a "Help" category, for example), be sure to call `cmds.menu` to start a new menu before adding additional items.

Grabbing data from a server

In this example, we'll look at the simplest possible way to grab data from a given URL, using Python's built-in `urllib2` library.

Getting ready

You'll want to make sure that you have a URL to grab. You can use any website you like, but for the sake of testing, it can be helpful to have a minimal page served on your local machine. If you want to do that, start by creating a simple html file, something like the following:

```
<html>
    <head>
        <title>
            Maya scripting chapter 9
        </title>
    </head>
    <body>
        HELLO FROM THE WEB
    </body>
</html>
```

Once you've done that, you'll want to have that served as a page on your own machine. Python offers a really simple way to do just that. Open a command line (terminal on a mac) and navigate to wherever you saved your html file. From there, enter the following command:

```
python -m SimpleHTTPServer
```

This will cause Python to serve the contents of the current directory as a website on localhost. The -m flag tells python to include a given module (in this case, `SimpleHTTPServer`) when running the interpreter. It's the equivalent of using the following at the beginning of a Python script:

```
import SimpleHTTPServer
```

By default, the contents of the current directory will be served on port 8000, meaning that you can access the contents by opening a browser and going to:

```
http://localhost:8000/
```

How to do it...

Create a new file and add the following code:

```
import maya.cmds as cmds
import urllib2

def getWebData():
    url = 'http://localhost:8000'

    print('grabbing web data from ', url)

    try:
        web = urllib2.urlopen(url)

    except Exception as e:
        print("ERROR: ", e)
        return

    print(web.getcode())
    print(web.info())
    print(web.read())



    getWebData()
```

Make sure that you've created an `index.htm` (or html) file somewhere and that you've run `python -m SimpleHTTPServer` from that same directory. If you've done that, running the preceding script should output something like the following followed by the entire contents of your `index.htm` file:

```
200
Server: SimpleHTTP/0.6 Python/2.7.10
Date: Tue, 26 Apr 2016 19:08:08 GMT
Content-type: text/html
Content-Length: 113
Last-Modified: Wed, 13 Apr 2016 06:31:18 GMT
```

How it works...

First off, we have to make sure to import the `urllib2` library in addition to our standard `maya.cmds`:

```
import maya.cmds as cmds
import urllib2
```

This will give us access to the commands we'll need to load data from a given URL. We start by setting up a variable to hold the URL we're loading, and printing a message indicating that we're about to attempt to load it:

```
def getWebData():
    url = 'http://localhost:8000'

    print('grabbing web data from ', url)
```

Now we're ready to actually attempt to load the data. When loading data from a URL, it's important that you never assume that the URL is accessible. There are any number of things that can go wrong either on the server side (the server could be down or not responding to requests) or on the client side (the indicated URL could be blocked by a firewall, the Ethernet cable could be unplugged, and so on) any one of which would prevent the URL from loading.

As such, we'll wrap our attempt to fetch the URL in a try/catch block. If anything goes wrong in the loading of the URL, we'll print out the error and return:

```
    try:
        web = urllib2.urlopen(url)

    except Exception as e:
        print("ERROR: ", e)
        return
```

If we manage to actually retrieve the URL in question, we're left with a "file-like object". This means that we can use all the functions that we would use when opening a file, such as `read()` to get the contents. The specific file-like objects returned by `urllib2.urlopen` also implement a couple of additional functions, which we make use of here. First, we get the HTTP code:

```
    print(web.getcode())
```

If everything went as expected, that *should* print out "200", indicating a successful request. Next, we retrieve some information about the URL:

```
    print(web.info())
```

This will display the information in the headers (server type, time of last modification, and so on):

```
print(web.info())
```

Finally, we'll get the actual data at the web address with the `read()` function. Calling `read()` without specifying a number of bytes to read will grab the entire contents of the file (or in this case, the website).

There's more...

In this example, we loaded the entirety of a website. While you generally wouldn't want to do that for most websites, it makes a lot of sense when requesting data from a web API, where the result will typically be a small(ish) amount of formatted data (either XML or JSON).

If what you want is to just display a full website (rather than retrieving data via an API), see the previous example where we use the `showHelp` command to display a given website.

Working with XML data

When grabbing data from a web server, it's highly likely that you'll receive it in a structured format of one kind or another, with XML and JSON being the most common options. In this example, we'll look at how to make use of data served up as XML.

Getting ready

To use this example, you'll need to have an XML file available on a server somewhere. The easiest way to do this is to create a file locally on your machine, then run the following:

```
python -m SimpleHTTPServer
```

From the same directory as the file, provide access to it via localhost. Here's the file that I'll be using as the example:

```
<xml version="1.0">
    <object type="cube">
        <x>0</x>
        <y>2</y>
        <z>3</z>
        <size>3</size>
    </object>

    <object type="sphere">
        <size>2</size>
        <x>0</x>
```

```
        <y>0</y>
        <z>0</z>
    </object>
</xml>
```

The file is pretty simple, but will allow us to look at iterating over XML nodes and parsing both attributes and elements.

How to do it...

Create a new file and add the following code:

```python
import maya.cmds as cmds
import urllib2
import xml.etree.ElementTree as ET

def makeObjectAt(type, position, size):

    if (type == 1):
        cmds.polyCube(height=size, width=size, depth=size)
    elif (type == 2):
        cmds.sphere(radius=size/2)

    cmds.move(position[0], position[1], position[2])

def loadXML():
    url = 'http://localhost:8000/data.xml'

    try:
        webData = urllib2.urlopen(url)

    except Exception as e:
        print("ERROR: ", e)
        return

    data = ET.parse(webData)
    root = data.getroot()

    for item in root:

        objectType = 1
        objectSize = 1
        pos = [0,0,0]
```

```
        if (item.attrib['type'] == "sphere"):
            objectType = 2

        for details in item:
            tagName = details.tag
            tagValue = float(details.text)

            if (tagName == "size"):
                objectSize = tagValue
            elif (tagName == "x"):
                pos[0] = tagValue
            elif (tagName == "y"):
                pos[1] = tagValue
            elif (tagName == "z"):
                pos[2] = tagValue

        makeObjectAt(objectType, pos, objectSize)


    loadXML()
```

Be sure to point the URL at the proper location for your XML file, and run the script; you should see a cube and a sphere appear.

How it works...

First off, we add another library `xml.etree.ElementTree` to our imports and give it a shorter name to make it easier to work with:

```
import maya.cmds as cmds
import urllib2
import xml.etree.ElementTree as ET
```

Next, we create a simple function to create either a sphere or a cube of a given size and move it to a given position. This is pretty straightforward and probably seems quite familiar at this point:

```
def makeObjectAt(type, position, size):
    if (type == 1):
        cmds.polyCube(height=size, width=size, depth=size)
    elif (type == 2):
        cmds.sphere(radius=size/2)
    cmds.move(position[0], position[1], position[2])
```

Next, we grab the data from the specified URL, as we have in the previous examples this chapter:

```
def loadXML():
    url = 'http://localhost:8000/data.xml'

    try:
        webData = urllib2.urlopen(url)

    except Exception as e:
        print("ERROR: ", e)
        return
```

Now we're ready to move onto the meat of the example—the actual XML parsing. First off, we parse the data we received from the Web into an XML tree with the `xml.etree.ElementTree` parse command.

```
data = ET.parse(webData)
```

The parse command can accept either a string or a file-like object. Because we receive a file-like object from the `urllib2.urlopen` command, we can pass the result straight in.

Once we've done that, we have a proper tree of XML nodes, and we're ready to start traversing the tree and parsing our data. To get started parsing, we first need to grab the root node, which we do with the `getroot()` command:

```
root = data.getroot()
```

The actual parsing will be a bit different, depending on the nature of your XML schema. In this case, we have some number of <object> nodes, each of which containing a "type" attribute and several child nodes for the x, y, and z positions as well as the size.

We'll want to start by iterating through all of the child nodes of the root to give us all of the object nodes. The `ElementTree` library makes that really easy—we can simply use a for loop to get all the child nodes. For each object we find, we'll start by setting variables for object type, position, and size to default values:

```
for item in root:

    objectType = 1
    objectSize = 1
    pos = [0,0,0]
```

In this case, our local `item` variable represents a node that is a direct child of the root. Given the structure of our example XML document, that means we have an <object> node. First off, we'll want to examine the `type` attribute to see if we should be making a cube or a sphere.

The attributes of a given node are stored as a dictionary in the node's `attrib` attribute. We can index into that to grab the value, and if we find that it's equal to `sphere`, we set our `objectType` to `2`:

```
if (item.attrib['type'] == "sphere"):
    objectType = 2
```

Now we need to look at the children of our current node to get the *x, y, z* positions and the size. We'll use the same trick as before, iterating over the children of a given node with a for loop. For each child we find, we want to know two things:

► The name of the tag.

► The value contained within the tag, as a float.

The name of a given node can be accessed via its tag property, and any text contained within it can be grabbed via the text property. For our purposes, we want to ensure floating point values, so we'll be sure to cast the text to a float. Putting all that together gives us the following:

```
for details in item:
    tagName = details.tag
    tagValue = float(details.text)
```

All that's left is to make use of the tag that we found and set the appropriate variable to our `tagValue`:

```
if (tagName == "size"):
    objectSize = tagValue
elif (tagName == "x"):
    pos[0] = tagValue
elif (tagName == "y"):
    pos[1] = tagValue
elif (tagName == "z"):
    pos[2] = tagValue
```

Having done all of that, we pass our data into our `makeObjectAt` function to produce the object.

```
makeObjectAt(objectType, pos, objectSize)
```

Working with JSON data

In this example, we'll look at the other format you're likely to want to use—JSON. JSON can model data just as well as XML, but is considerably more compact. As such, it has been growing in popularity in recent years and has all but replaced XML for many tasks.

Getting ready

Once again, you'll want to make sure that you have a file being served by a server that you have access to, but this time you'll want to make sure that it's JSON data. Once again, we'll create some number of cubes and spheres, but this time, we'll specify the data as an array of JSON objects.

The full listing for the example document is as follows:

```
[
    {"type": "cube", "size": 3, "x": 0, "y": 2, "z": 3},
    {"type": "sphere", "size": 1, "x": 0, "y": 0, "z": 0}
]
```

The square brackets indicate an array, and the curly brackets indicate an object. Within an object, there can be any number of named values. Arrays and objects can also be nested, allowing us to have an array *of* objects, as we do here. For more information on how to structure JSON data, be sure to have a look at http://www.json.org/.

How to do it...

Create a new script and add the following code:

```
import maya.cmds as cmds
import urllib2
import json

def makeObjectAt(type, position, size):

    if (type == 1):
        cmds.polyCube(height=size, width=size, depth=size)
    elif (type == 2):
        cmds.sphere(radius=size/2)

    cmds.move(position[0], position[1], position[2])

def loadJSON():
    url = 'http://localhost:8000/data.json'
```

```
try:
    webData = urllib2.urlopen(url)

except Exception as e:
    print("ERROR: ", e)
    return

data = json.loads(webData.read())

for item in data:

    objectType = 1
    objectSize = 1
    position = [0,0,0]

    if ('type' in item and item['type'] == "sphere"):
        objectType = 2
    if ('x' in item):
        position[0] = item['x']
    if ('y' in item):
        position[1] = item['y']
    if ('z' in item):
        position[2] = item['z']
    if ('size' in item):
        objectSize = float(item['size'])

    print(objectType, position, objectSize)
    makeObjectAt(objectType, position, objectSize)

loadJSON()
```

Make sure that you have a JSON file formatted in the same way as the example and that it's accessible via a URL, localhost, or otherwise. Run the script, and you should have some number of cubes and spheres appear on your scene.

How it works...

Most of the script is the same as our previous example of parsing XML data. The first difference is that we change the import statements slightly, removing the `xml.etree.ElementTree` library and adding the JSON library instead:

```
import maya.cmds as cmds
import urllib2
import json
```

Next up, we have the same function as was used in the XML example to create either a sphere or a cube of a given size and move it to a specified position. I'll omit the details because it's identical to the function from the previous example.

In the function responsible for actually loading the data, we start off grabbing the URL as we have in the previous examples in this chapter:

```
def loadJSON():
    url = 'http://localhost:8000/data.json'

    try:
        webData = urllib2.urlopen(url)

    except Exception as e:
        print("ERROR: ", e)
        return
```

The new functionality comes in the form of a call to the `loads()` or "load string" function, which will load data from a string into a proper JSON object. By passing the result of `webData.read()` into that function, we will be left with the full contents of our file into an object:

```
data = json.loads(webData.read())
```

Once we've done that, we'll want to step through the entries in the data. The result of parsing JSON in Python will translate arrays into lists and objects into dictionaries. Because our JSON data was in the form of an array of objects, we are left with a list of dictionaries after loading.

We start our parsing by stepping through the array and grabbing the data for each object. As in the XML example, we set up placeholder variables with default values for `objectType`, `objectSize`, and `position`, as follows:

```
    for item in data:

        objectType = 1
        objectSize = 1
        position = [0,0,0]
```

Within the loop, we'll grab the values for each of our attributes by first checking to see if they're present in the current dictionary and, if so, set the value of the corresponding variable. We have the following code:

```
        if ('type' in item and item['type'] == "sphere"):
            objectType = 2
        if ('x' in item):
            position[0] = item['x']
        if ('y' in item):
```

```
        position[1] = item['y']
if ('z' in item):
        position[2] = item['z']
if ('size' in item):
        objectSize = float(item['size'])
```

Note that we cast `objectSize` to a float. That's necessary, since we divide it by 2 in our `makeObjectAt()` function. If we happen to have an integer input, dividing it by 2 would result in an integer result, possibly giving us a bad value (if we pass in 1, we would get 0 instead of 0.5, for example).

Finally, we pass in the retrieved values to our `makeObjectAt()` function:

```
makeObjectAt(objectType, position, objectSize)
```

There's more...

You'll probably note that JSON data is a bit easier to work with than XML—with JSON, we end up with standard Python lists and dictionaries, whereas XML requires that we walk up and down a series of nodes.

That's true not only in Python, but in many other languages as well. If you happen to be working in JavaScript, there's often no actual parsing required, as JSON is a subset of JavaScript itself (JSON is short for JavaScript Object Notation).

There are still good reasons to use XML, but if all that's needed is a way to move structured data from one place to another, JSON tends to be easier to parse, and just as easy to read.

See also

If you're new to JSON, it's a good idea to have a look at the official docs, available at `http://www.json.org/`. You'll find that for all its flexibility, it's actually a pretty simple format.

Sending POST data to a web server from Maya

So far, everything we've looked at involves pulling data from the Web into Maya. In this example, we'll look at how to send data to a server from within Maya.

There are two main ways to send data to a server—GET and POST. Using GET involves adding arguments onto a URL directly. It has the benefit of being able to be bookmarked (since the arguments are in the URL), but has limitations on the amount of data that can be sent. POST requests are more flexible and will usually be what you want to use to build tool pipelines in a production environment.

In this example, we'll implement two different examples of sending POST data. First, we'll look at sending summary data about a scene (the name of the file and the number of objects). Then, we'll look at using POST requests to send a selected model to a server as an OBJ file. This could form the backbone of an asset management pipeline.

Getting ready

We'll be using the requests library for this example, so make sure to install it. For details on how to do that, visit `http://docs.python-requests.org/en/master/user/install/#install`.

In order to make the most of this example, you'll need to have a server that can respond to GET and POST requests. Setting that up is beyond the scope of this book, and there are any number of ways to go about it (and any number of languages you can use to do so). Luckily, there's an easy way to test your requests in the form of `http://httpbin.org/`. The httpbin site can be used to test a wide range of HTTP requests, and will return whatever data is passed to it.

Also, since we're going to be sending actual model data, you'll need to have at least one polygonal mesh in your scene.

How to do it...

Create a new file and add the following code:

```python
import maya.cmds as cmds
import os
import requests
import json

DATA_URL = "http://httpbin.org/post"

def sendFileData():
    fullname = cmds.file(query=True, sceneName=True)
    filename = os.path.basename(fullname)

    data = {}
    data['fileName'] = filename
    data['numObjects'] = len(cmds.ls(geometry=True))

    result = requests.post(DATA_URL, json=data)

    if (result.status_code == 200):
        responseData = json.loads(result.text)
        print("SENT DATA: ")
```

```
            print(responseData['data'])
        else:
            error("HTTP Error")


def polygonSelected():
    objs = cmds.ls(selection=True)
    if (len(objs) < 1):
        return False

    objectToExport = objs[0]

    shapeNode = cmds.listRelatives(objectToExport, shapes=True)
    if (cmds.nodeType(shapeNode[0]) != "mesh"):
        return False

    return True

def saveSelectionAsOBJ(path):
    cmds.loadPlugin("objExport", quiet=True)

    if (not cmds.file(path, query=True, exists=True)):
        f = open(path,"w")
        f.close()

    cmds.file(path, type="OBJ", force=True, exportSelected=True, optio
ns="groups=0;ptgroups=0;materials=0;smoothing=1;normals=1")


def sendModelAsPost(fileName):

    if not polygonSelected():
        cmds.error("Please select a polgonal object to export")

    baseDir = cmds.workspace(query=True, directory=True)
    path = os.path.join(baseDir, fileName)

    saveSelectionAsOBJ(path)

    data = {}
    data['filename'] = path
    modelFile = {'file': open(path, "rb")}
```

```
        result = requests.post(DATA_URL, json=data, files=modelFile)

        responseData = json.loads(result.text)
        print("FILE SENT: ")
        print(responseData['files'])


    sendFileData()
    sendModelAsPost("widget4.obj")
```

Select a polygonal mesh and run the script. Both of the examples will send data to httpbin
and output the result that gets parroted back from the site. You should see something like
the following:

```
# requests.packages.urllib3.connectionpool : Starting new HTTP
connection (1): httpbin.org #
SENT DATA:
{"numObjects": 2, "fileName": "widgt.ma"}
# requests.packages.urllib3.connectionpool : Starting new HTTP
connection (1): httpbin.org #
FILE SENT:
{u'file': u'# OBJ file data'}
```

How it works...

We start off the script with importing everything we need—maya.cmds as always,
plus the following:

 ▶   - requests: This provides nicer tools for working with requests and sending data

 ▶   - os: This is needed to work with paths

 ▶   - json: This is needed to parse the response that we'll get from httpbin.org

We also set a global variable to hold the URL that we'll be sending data to, in this case,
httpbin.org/post:

```
import maya.cmds as cmds
import os
import requests
import json

DATA_URL = "http://httpbin.org/post"
```

Now we're ready to implement our first example—sending some summary data about our scene. In this case, we'll send the name of the scene and the number of objects it contains. To get the name of the current scene, we use the file command in query mode, and setting the sceneName flag.

This will give us the full path to the current scene, which we'll pass into os.path.basename to retrieve just the filename itself:

```
def sendFileData():
    fullname = cmds.file(query=True, sceneName=True)
    filename = os.path.basename(fullname)
```

Next, we'll get the total number of objects in the scene by using the ls command and setting the geometry flag to true. The length of that list will give us the total number of (geometric) objects:

```
    numObjects = len(cmds.ls(geometry=True))
```

At this point, we have all of the data that we want to send. In order to prep it for sending, we'll need to create a new dictionary and create an entry for each value we want to send:

```
    data = {}
    data['fileName'] = filename
    data['numObjects'] = numObjects
```

Actually, sending the data is very straightforward, thanks to the requests library. All that we need to do is to call requests.post with our desired URL, and with our data variable passed in as the value for the JSON option. We'll be sure to save the result to a variable so that we can examine the response from the server:

```
    result = requests.post(DATA_URL, json=data)
```

Once we've sent the request, we'll want to examine whether or not it was successful. To do that, we examine the status_code attribute of the result, checking it against 200. If the request went through, we parse the actual response into a JSON object and print the data attribute. Otherwise, we display an error, as in the following code:

```
    if (result.status_code == 200):
        responseData = json.loads(result.text)
        print("SENT DATA: ")
        print(responseData['data'])
    else:
        error("HTTP Error")
```

Since `httpbin.org/post` will echo back any data sent to it, we should see something like the following:

```
SENT DATA:
{"numObjects": 2, "fileName": "widget.ma"}
```

This indicates that the data was successfully sent to the server and returned to us as a response.

Now, let's look at a slightly more involved example. We'll create a function that will save a selected polygonal object as an OBJ, then send that file to a server as POST data. We'll build that up from a few smaller functions, starting with one to test whether or not the current selection is a polygon mesh.

```python
def polygonSelected():
    objs = cmds.ls(selection=True)
    if (len(objs) < 1):
        return False

    objectToExport = objs[0]

    shapeNode = cmds.listRelatives(objectToExport, shapes=True)
    if (cmds.nodeType(shapeNode[0]) != "mesh"):
        return False

    return True
```

This is similar to what we've done in previous examples; we get the current selection and start by checking to see if at least one object is selected. If that succeeds, we use the `listRelatives` command to retrieve the shape node associated with the selected object and test its node type. If it's anything other than "mesh" (indicating a polygonal object), we return false. If we pass through both checks, we return true.

Next, we implement a function to save the currently selected object as an OBJ. Since exporting OBJs requires that the OBJ export plugin be loaded, we start our function with a call to `loadPlugin` to make sure that it is. See the following:

```python
def saveSelectionAsOBJ(path):
    cmds.loadPlugin("objExport", quiet=True)
```

We pass in `objExport` as the plugin to load, and we set the quiet flag to true, which will prevent Maya from displaying a message if the plugin was already loaded.

To export the model, we'll need to use the `file` command, but before doing that, we'll want to make sure that the file exists. That's needed in order to avoid a quirk of the file command, which can cause it to error out if saving to a file that doesn't exist.

We start by using the `file` command in the query mode to see if a file of the given name exists. If not, we create one by opening it in write mode, then immediately closing it, as follows:

```
if (not cmds.file(path, query=True, exists=True)):
    f = open(path,"w")
    f.close()
```

Now we're ready to actually write out the OBJ file, using the file command once again:

```
cmds.file(path, exportSelected=True, type="OBJ", force=True,
    options="groups=0;ptgroups=0;materials=0;smoothing=1;normals=1")
```

The first argument is the full path to where we want to save the file. After that, we set `exportSelected` to true to indicate the main operation that should be performed, in this case, exporting only the currently selected object. Next, we specify that we want to save it as an OBJ, and we set force to true to avoid prompting the user for a file overwrite confirmation. Finally, we set the options for the OBJ export as a single string, with semicolons to separate out each of the parts. In this case, we'll turn everything off except `normals`.

Now that we've created both of our helper functions, we're ready to move to the function to put them together and send the model to a server. We start by running the check for polygonal geometry and throwing an error if it fails:

```
def sendModelAsPost(fileName):

    if not polygonSelected():
        cmds.error("Please select a polygonal object to export")
```

Once we've done that, we build up the path to save the file by first using the workspace command to retrieve the current workspace location and using `os.path.join` to append the desired filename:

```
baseDir = cmds.workspace(query=True, directory=True)
path = os.path.join(baseDir, fileName)
```

With the full path, we can save out the model using our `saveSelectionAsOBJ()` function:

```
saveSelectionAsOBJ(path)
```

Now we're ready to send the file. In order to send files via POST data, we'll need to send a "multipart" request in order to send the file data as its own part. Luckily for us, the requests library handles all of that for us. It ends up looking quite similar to our previous example of sending simple POST data, in that we start by setting up our data in a dictionary.

```
modelFile = {'file': open(path, "rb")}
```

In this case, we have only a single entry, named `file`, which we set equal to the output of the `file open` command:

```
modelFile = {'file': open(path, "rb")}
```

Once we've done that, all we need to do to actually send the file is to call `requests.post` with the desired URL, and pass in our `modelFile` dictionary as the value for the `files` attribute:

```
result = requests.post(DATA_URL, files=modelFile)
```

Just as with the simple example, we'll check the `result.status_code` and, if we find 200, parse the response as JSON and output some of it, though in this case, we output the `files` attribute instead of data. We have the following code:

```
if (result.status_code == 200):
    responseData = json.loads(result.text)
    print("FILE SENT: ")
    print(responseData['files'])
else:
    error("File send error")
```

There's more...

While we sent data and files in two separate requests for the sake of the examples, you can certainly send both at the same time. For example, if you wanted to build an asset management pipeline for an MMO, you might want to send the models to a central server, along with some metadata, such as which textures they use or what their in-game attributes are.

10

Advanced Topics

In this chapter, we'll look at the following few advanced topics that can be used to take your scripts farther:

- ▸ Wrapping Python functionality in MEL
- ▸ Creating custom tools using contexts
- ▸ Using script jobs to trigger custom functionality
- ▸ Using script nodes to embed code in scenes
- ▸ Combining script jobs and script nodes

Introduction

In this chapter, we'll look at a few advanced topics that can be used to give your scripts extra polish and make them easier to use for your teammates. We'll see how to make your scripts work like Maya's built-in tools using contexts, trigger custom functionality in response to events using script jobs, and embed code into a scene using script nodes.

Finally, we'll look at a tool that can be used to embed custom functionality in a scene and trigger it when a specific object is selected (very useful for invoking complex UIs for character rigs, for example).

Wrapping Python functionality in MEL

Although Python is definitely the preferred way to go about scripting for Maya, there are some features that still require you to use MEL. We'll be seeing several of those features in this chapter, but first we'll need to look at how to call Python code from MEL.

Getting ready

First off, we'll need a Python script to call. You can either use something you've already written or make something new. For the sake of this example, I'll use a new script that simply creates a NURBS sphere at the origin, as follows:

```
# listing of pythonFromMel.py
import maya.cmds as cmds

def makeSphere():
    cmds.sphere()
```

How to do it...

In this example, we'll create an MEL script that will in turn call our Python script. Create a new file and add the following code, being sure to save it with a `.mel` extension. In this case, we'll create a file named `melToPython.mel`:

```
global proc melToPython()
{
    python "import pythonFromMel";
    python "pythonFromMel.makeSphere()";
}
```

Note that the function defined in the file has the same name as the file itself; this is a standard practice when creating MEL scripts, and it is used to indicate the entry point for the script. You can certainly have multiple functions within the script, but there should generally always be one with the same name as the file, and that function should be the starting point for your script.

Be sure to save the script to one of Maya's default script locations. On a Mac system, that means:

```
/Users/Shared/Autodesk/Maya/(Version)/scripts
```

And on a PC, it means:

```
\Documents and Settings\<username>\My Documents\maya
```

Once you've done this, you'll need to make sure that Maya is aware of the new script, which means calling the rehash MEL command from within Maya. Switch your command line to MEL by clicking to the left of the text field, where it says **Python**. Alternatively, switch to the **MEL** tab in the script editor and enter your code there.

The rehash command forces Maya to re-examine its list of known script locations and take note of any new MEL scripts that have been added. This happens automatically every time Maya starts up, but if you make a new script with Maya open and attempt to run it without first calling rehash, Maya will give you an error.

Once you've run rehash, you can run our new MEL script by entering the name of the script into either the command line or the script editor. Doing so should result in a new NURBS sphere appearing at the origin.

How it works...

The MEL script is pretty straightforward. Note that functions are defined in a slightly different manner, with a few minor differences. The `proc` keyword (short for *procedure*) serves the same purpose as `def` in Python, indicating a named block of code. Also, instead of having a colon after the parentheses, curly brackets are used to enclose the actual code.

The `global` keyword indicates that this particular function is meant to be called from outside the script. It is very common practice when writing MEL to have a global procedure with the same name as the file, which serves as the entry point for the script.

We're mainly interested in getting this script to invoke some Python functionality, though. To do that, we rely on the `python` MEL command. The `python` command takes a string as an argument and will attempt to run that string as a line of Python.

For example, if we wanted to invoke Python's `print` command from MEL, we could do the following:

```
python "print('hello from Python')"
```

Note that MEL differs from Python in that arguments to built-in functions are *not* enclosed in parentheses. So, in the previous example, the `python` command receives a string as its single argument. That string is passed to the Python interpreter and, in this case, results in some text being printed.

To actually run a Python script from MEL, we'll need to do two things:

- ▶ Use the import statement to load the script
- ▶ Invoke a function from within the script

That means that we need to call MEL's `python` command twice. Importing is fairly simple:

```
python "import pythonFromMel";
```

The second line requires a bit of explanation. When we use the `import` command to load a script, the script is loaded as a module. Each of the functions defined in the script are attributes of the module. So, to invoke a function defined the script, we'll want to use the following syntax:

```
moduleName.functionName()
```

Wrapping that in a string and passing it to MEL gives us the following for the `makeSphere()` function defined in the `pythonFromMel` script:

```
python "pythonFromMel.makeSphere()";
```

We could optionally combine both the `import` statement and the call to `makeSphere` into a single line. To do that, we'll need to separate out the two statements with a semicolon. While Python doesn't *require* semicolons at the end of statements, it does allow them. In most cases, that's not necessary, but if you need to have multiple statements on a single line, it can be useful.

If we did that, we would end up with the following:

```
python "import pythonFromMel; pythonFromMel.makeSphere()";
```

This will prove useful later, when we need to pass in MEL commands to invoke Python functionality as a single line.

There's more...

It should be mentioned that Maya provides a built-in utility for creating MEL scripts from a given Python script, in the `createMelWrapper` command, defined as part of the `maya.mel` library.

If we wanted to invoke that on the `makeSphere` function that we used in this example, we could do that by running the following code in the **Python** tab of the script editor:

```
import maya.mel as mel

maya.mel.createMelWrapper(pythonFromMel.makeSphere)
```

That would prompt you for a place to save the created MEL script. If you open the created script, you'll see something like the following:

```
global proc makeSphere () {
    python("from pythonFromMel import makeSphere");

    python("makeSphere()"); }
```

Differences in formatting aside, the generated script is almost identical to what we wrote. The only real difference is that it explicitly imports just the `makeSphere` command, rather than the entire `pythonFromMel` module.

Creating custom tools using contexts

Many of Maya's tools are used in an interactive manner, with the user specifying inputs as needed, and actions taking place either when the necessary number of inputs have been provided, or the user hits the *Enter* key.

So far, none of our scripts have worked this way—it has been necessary to have the user explicitly run the script, or press a button. That works fine for many things, but providing interactive input can add a lot of polish to a script. In this example, we'll be doing exactly that.

We'll create a script that, once invoked, prompts the user to select two or more objects. When they press the *Enter* key, we'll create a locator at the average position of all of the objects. To do that, we'll need to create a custom context to implement our very own tool.

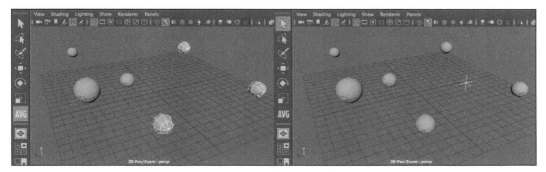

Our custom tool in action. Left image is the tool while it's being used (notice the custom "AVG" icon on the left), and right image shows the result—a new locator at the average position of the selected objects

Getting ready

The script as presented makes use of a custom icon. While it's not required, it's a nice bit of polish. If you want to do that as well, create a 32 by 32 pixel transparent PNG, and save it to the icons folder. On a mac, that would be:

```
/Users/Shared/Autodesk/Maya/icons/
```

...and on a PC, it means:

```
\Documents and Settings\<username>\My Documents\maya\icons\
```

How to do it...

Create a new file and add the following code. Be sure to name it `customCtx.py`.

```python
import maya.cmds as cmds

def startCtx():
    print("starting context")

def finalizeCtx():
    objs = cmds.ls(selection=True)

    numObjs = len(objs)
    xpos = 0
    ypos = 0
    zpos = 0

    for o in objs:
        # print(o)
        pos = cmds.xform(o, query=True, worldSpace=True,
        translation=True)
        # print(pos)
        xpos += pos[0]
        ypos += pos[1]
        zpos += pos[2]

    xpos /= numObjs
    ypos /= numObjs
    zpos /= numObjs

    newLoc = cmds.spaceLocator()
    cmds.move(xpos, ypos, zpos, newLoc)

def createContext():
    toolStartStr = 'python("customCtx .startCtx()");'
    toolFinishStr = 'python("customCtx .finalizeCtx()");'

    newCtx = cmds.scriptCtx(i1='myTool.png', title='MyTool',
    setNoSelectionPrompt='Select at least two
    objects',toolStart=toolStartStr,
    finalCommandScript=toolFinishStr, totalSelectionSets=1,
    setSelectionCount=2, setAllowExcessCount=True,
    setAutoComplete=False, toolCursorType="create")

    cmds.setToolTo(newCtx)

createContext()
```

If you run the script, you'll see that Maya activates your new icon in the left UI, just like is the case with any of the other tools. *Shift*-select at least two objects, and press the *Enter* key. You'll see a new locator appear at the averaged position of the selected objects.

As an additional feature, you'll find that the *Y* hotkey, which can be used to re-invoke the most recently used tool, will also start your script over again.

How it works...

First off, we create a couple of functions that will be used by the new context, one that gets called when it starts, and another that gets called when it ends. The `start` script is very simple (just prints some text) and is just included for demonstration purposes.

```
def startCtx():
    print("starting context")
```

The function that gets called at the end is a bit more involved, but still nothing too complex. We start by grabbing the currently-selected objects, and setting up a few variables—one to hold the number of objects, and one each for the x, y, and z position that we'll create the locator at.

```
def finalizeCtx():
    objs = cmds.ls(selection=True)

    numObjs = len(objs)
    xpos = 0
    ypos = 0
    zpos = 0
```

Next, we run through all of the objects and grab their position using the `xform` command in query mode. We add each of the x, y, and z positions to our variables to create a running tally of positions.

```
for o in objs:
    # print(o)
    pos = cmds.xform(o, query=True, worldSpace=True,
    translation=True)
    xpos += pos[0]
    ypos += pos[1]
    zpos += pos[2]
```

We then divide each of the position variables by the number of objects to average the positions, create a new locator, and move it to the averaged position.

```
xpos /= numObjs
ypos /= numObjs
zpos /= numObjs

newLoc = cmds.spaceLocator()
cmds.move(xpos, ypos, zpos, newLoc)
```

Now for the fun part—actually setting up a custom context. We start by creating MEL strings that can be used to invoke our two functions. In both cases, they simply call one of the functions defined as part of our script.

```
def createContext():
    toolStartStr = 'python("customCtx .startCtx()");'
    toolFinishStr = 'python("customCtx .finalizeCtx()");'
```

Note that we're not explicitly importing `customCtx` before invoking the functions (as we did in the previous example). That's because we're using functionality defined within the same script, so if this code is executing at all, the `customCtx` script must have already been imported.

Now we're ready for the main event- creating a new context using the `scriptCtx` command.

```
newCtx = cmds.scriptCtx(i1='myTool.png', title='MyTool',
setNoSelectionPrompt='Select at least two
objects',toolStart=toolStartStr, finalCommandScript=toolFinishStr,
totalSelectionSets=1, setSelectionCount=2,
setAllowExcessCount=True, setAutoComplete=False,
toolCursorType="create")
```

As you can see, this is a pretty big command, so let's go through the arguments. First off, we use the `i1` flag to specify the icon to use for the tool. You can leave this out, but if you do, Maya will highlight a blank spot in the UI while your tool is active. Be sure to make the icon 32x32 pixels, and to put it in the icons folder (see *Getting ready*, above).

Next, we set the title. This is also optional, but will make the text that appears a bit more useful for the user. Similarly, we could leave out the `setNoSelectionPrompt` flag, but it's best to leave it in. Setting both the title and `setNoSelectionPrompt` flag will cause helpful text to show up in bottom of Maya's interface.

Now we get to the meat of the command, with the `toolStart` and `finalCommandScript` flags. Both have to be passed a single string that corresponds to a MEL command that should be run either at the start of the script, or when *Enter* is pressed. We pass in the MEL strings that we created for each, which will in turn invoke Python functionality.

The next set of flags all have to do with the specifics of the selection. First off, we set the number of selection sets to 1, meaning that we want a single collection of items. After that, we use the `setSelectionCount` flag to specify that there should be at least two items selected for the tool to function. In this case, we also want to allow for the user to select more than two objects, so we set the `setAllowExcessCount` flag to `true`. Since we want to allow the user to specify a variable number of objects, and not finish the command until they press *Enter*, we need to set `setAutoComplete` to `false`. Setting it to `true` would cause the final command script to be run as soon as the user had selected objects equal to the `setSelectionCount` number. That's certainly useful in some cases, but isn't what we want here.

Finally, we set the `toolCursorType` flag to `create`. That will set the cursor that gets used during the tool. Maya offers a number of different options, and choosing the best one for your purposes can be a great way to add a professional touch to your tool (as well as give the user some quality feedback). For the list of options, be sure to check the documentation for the `scriptCtx` command.

Whew—that was a lot of flags, but we're done, and ready to wrap things up. At this point in the script, we've created the new context, but it is not yet active. To actually invoke the tool, we need to use the `setToolTo` command, and pass in the output of the call to `scriptCtx`.

```
cmds.setToolTo(newCtx)
```

And with that, we've added a brand-new tool to Maya.

There's more...

In this example, we created our own, custom tool. You can also invoke Maya's built-in tools by using the appropriate command to create a context of that type, and then switching to it using `setToolTo`.

For example, you might be creating a script to allow users to create character rigs in a semi-automated way. You might, as a part of that, want to have the user create some bones that are then manipulated further by your system. You could have that process begin with the user creating some bones using the joint tool. To drop them straight into bone creation after invoking your script, you could use the following:

```
makeBoneCtx = cmds.jointCtx()
cmds.setToolTo(makeBoneCtx)
```

There are a large number of contexts that you can create—consult the Maya documentation for the full list.

Something else you might find useful is the ability to reset the current context, which will discard any input so far and reset the current tool. You can do that with either your own custom tools or with those built into Maya. Either way, reset the current tool with the following:

```
cmds.ctxAbort()
```

Contexts are a great way to add polish to your scripts, but should only really be used when it makes sense to have the user add input in an interactive way, or if you expect the user to want to use your tool more than once in rapid succession. If you have a script that you only expect the user to use once, with a limited (and fixed) number of inputs, it's likely easier to just provide a button. However, if your script needs to work with a variable number of inputs and or be called again on a new set without re-invoking the script, you may want to consider creating a context. Another way to look at it is that you should only use contexts when they would offer a net *reduction* in work (as measured in number of clicks) for the user.

Using script jobs to trigger custom functionality

Script jobs offer another alternative to explicitly calling scripts, or pressing buttons, to invoke your functionality. By using script jobs, it is possible to trigger custom functionality based on either a specific condition or a specific event.

In this example, we'll create a script job that will respond to the selection changed event by printing the name and type of the selected object to the console.

Getting ready

One of the things that makes script jobs so useful is the fact that they persist (as opposed to just running once). However, that can make developing scripts that use them a bit difficult, since if you change your code and re-run your script, you'll end up with multiple script jobs in your scene. For that reason, it's good to give yourself a way to easily clear out all existing script jobs. The following script will do just that:

```
import maya.cmds as cmds

def killAll():
    cmds.scriptJob(killAll=True, force=True)
    print('KILLED ALL JOBS')

killAll()
```

Running the `scriptJob` command with the `killAll` flag will clear out all normal script jobs in the scene. However, script jobs can also be created as either `protected` or `permanent`. Adding the force flag will also clear out protected script jobs as well, but be careful with that, as Maya uses `scriptJobs` to implement some of its UI functionality. To be totally safe, leave off the `force=True` flag and make sure that the `scriptJobs` you create are not protected.

Permanent script jobs will persist until you create a new scene, but that shouldn't come up in development. Even if you really do want a permanent script job, it's best to develop it with default priority and upgrade it to permanent only once you're certain that you're getting the functionality you want.

Be sure to have the above script (or similar) available before you start working with script jobs, as it will definitely make your life a lot easier.

How to do it...

Create a new script and add the following code. Be sure to name the file selectionOutput.py:

```
import maya.cmds as cmds
import sys

def selectionChanged():
    objs = cmds.ls(selection=True)

    if len(objs) < 1:
        sys.stdout.write('NOTHING SELECTED')
    else:
        shapeNodes = cmds.listRelatives(objs[0], shapes=True)
        msg = objs[0]
        if (len(shapeNodes) > 0):
            msg += ": " + cmds.nodeType(shapeNodes[0])

        sys.stdout.write(msg)

def makeEventScriptJob():
    cmds.scriptJob(event=["SelectionChanged", selectionChanged],
    killWithScene=True)

makeEventScriptJob()
```

Run the above script, and you should see text appear in the bottom of Maya's UI every time you select (or deselect) an object.

How it works...

First off, note that we're importing the sys (or system) library in addition to our standard maya.cmds. That's to allow us to print text to the command line, so that it will be visible to the user even if they don't have the script editor open. More on that in a bit.

Before we create the `scriptJob`, we'll want to create the code we want it to call. In this case, we'll be triggering code every time the selection changes, and we want that code to examine the currently-selected object(s). We start, as we have in other examples, by using ls to grab the selection:

```
def selectionChanged():
    objs = cmds.ls(selection=True)
```

Then, if we find that there is nothing selected, we output some text to the command line.

```
if len(objs) < 1:
    sys.stdout.write('NOTHING SELECTED')
```

And here's where that `sys` library comes in—by using `sys.stdout.write`, we are able to output text directly to the command line. That can be a good way to provide feedback to the users of your scripts, since you shouldn't expect them to have the script editor open. Note that we *could* have used either the error or warning commands as well, but since this text is simply output, and neither an error nor a warning, it is better to use `stdout.write`.

The rest of the `selectionChanged` function is pretty straightforward. The only slightly tricky thing is that if we look at the node type for the selected nodes themselves, we're guaranteed to get nothing but transforms. To avoid that, we first check to see if there are any shape nodes connected to the node in question. If there are, we append the node type for the shape to the name of the object, and output that to the command line.

```
else:
    shapeNodes = cmds.listRelatives(objs[0], shapes=True)
    msg = objs[0]
    if (len(shapeNodes) > 0):
        msg += ": " + cmds.nodeType(shapeNodes[0])

    sys.stdout.write(msg)
```

Now we're ready for the fun part—actually making `scriptJob`. All `scriptJobs` require that we specify either an event or a condition, along with some code to execute when the event is triggered, or when the condition assumes a given value (true, false, or when it changes).

It's important to note that the events and conditions must correspond to those that are built into Maya. In this case, we'll be using the `SelectionChanged` event as our trigger. This will fire every time the selection changes for any reason, and no matter how many objects are selected (including zero).

To actually create the `scriptJob`, we use the `scriptJob` command.

```
cmds.scriptJob(event=["SelectionChanged", selectionChanged],
killWithScene=True)
```

In this case, we use the event flag to tell Maya that this `scriptJob` should be event-based (as opposed to being based on a condition). The value that we pass into the flag needs to be an array, with the first element being a string that corresponds to the event we want to watch for, and the second being a function to call in response.

In this case, we want to call our `selectionChanged` function in response to the `SelectionChanged` event. We also include the `killWithScene` flag, which will cause `scriptJob` to be destroyed when we leave the current scene, which is generally a good idea. There are certainly valid reasons to have `scriptJob` persist from scene to scene, but unless you're sure that that's what you want, it's usually a good idea to prevent that from happening.

And that's it! We will now have our custom function called each time the selection changes.

There's more...

In the *Getting ready* section, we covered a simple script to delete *all* `scriptJobs`. That's fine during testing, but can be a bit heavy-handed sometimes. There are many situations where you might want to delete only a specific `scriptJob`—possibly because the functionality it is being used to implement is no longer necessary. That's easily done, but requires you specify which `scriptJob` you want to delete.

When creating a new script job, the `scriptJob` command will return an integer that can be used as the ID of the created script job. Later, you can use that number to delete that specific script job while leaving any other script jobs in the scene intact. If you want to delete a script job later, make sure to save the output to a variable as in:

```
jobID = cmds.scriptJob(event=["SelectionChanged",
selectionChanged], killWithScene=True)
```

Then, to delete the script job, call the `scriptJob` command again, but with the kill flag, and passing in the ID, as in:

```
cmds.scriptJob(kill=jobID)
```

If the script job you're trying to delete is protected, you'll need to also set the `force` flag to `true`, as in:

```
cmds.scriptJob(kill=jobID, force=True)
```

You can also use the `scriptJob` command to get a list of all of the script jobs currently active. To do that, run it with the `listJobs` flag set to `True`. For example:

```
jobs = cmds.scriptJob(listJobs=True)

for j in jobs:
        print(j)
```

...which would result in something like the following:

```
0:    "-permanent" "-event" "PostSceneRead"
"generateUvTilePreviewsPostSceneReadCB"
1:    "-permanent" "-parent" "MayaWindow" "-event" "ToolChanged"
"changeToolIcon"
```

...as well as a long list of other script jobs used by Maya, as well as any that you have added. The number on the left is the ID of the job, and can be used to delete it (as long as it isn't *permanent*).

As an alternative to deleting all jobs, or deleting individual jobs by ID, you can also have Maya delete a script job when a given piece of UI is deleted. For example, if we wanted to have a script job that would only exist as long as a given window was open, we could do something like the following:

```
def scriptJobUI():
    win = cmds.window(title="SJ", widthHeight=(300, 200))

    cmds.scriptJob(parent=win, event=["SelectionChanged",
    respondToSelection])

    cmds.showWindow(win)
```

Notice the addition of the `parent` flag in the call to `cmds.scriptJob`. You can include that flag to tie the script job to a specific piece of UI. In this case, we tie the script job to the window.

Using script nodes to embed code in scenes

All of the examples we've seen so far exist as scripts, separate from the actual scene that they are run in. That's fine for tools, but means that if you create a script that is tightly tied to a particular scene (such as a custom control UI for a character rig), you have to be careful to make sure that the script file is always distributed along with the Maya file.

For such situations, Maya offers a better way. Script nodes can be used to bake scripts directly into a scene, allowing them to be run without any external dependencies. Furthermore, script nodes can be created with code.

In this example, we'll create a script that will prompt the user for a Python file, and will then create a script node with the contents of the file, and set it up so that the script will be executed each time the file is opened.

Getting ready

To use the script we'll be creating, we'll need to have a script ready to embed. For the sake of the example, I'll be using a simple script that shows a window containing a single button to create a NURBS sphere.

The full script is as follows:

```
import maya.cmds as cmds

def testUI():
    win = cmds.window(title="Script Node", widthHeight=(300,200))
    cmds.columnLayout()
    cmds.button(label="Make Sphere", command="cmds.sphere()")
    cmds.showWindow(win)

testUI()
```

How to do it...

Create a new script and add the following code:

```
import maya.cmds as cmds

def createScriptNode():
    filePath = cmds.fileDialog2(fileMode=1, fileFilter="Python
    files (*.py)")

    if (filePath == None):
        return

    f = open(filePath[0], "r")

    scriptStr = ""

    line = f.readline()
    while (line):
        scriptStr += line
        line = f.readline()

    f.close()

    cmds.scriptNode(sourceType="python", scriptType=2,
    beforeScript=scriptStr)

createScriptNode()
```

Run the script, and point the resulting file browser at the script that you want to embed. Save your file, and re-open it. You should see your embedded script run automatically.

How it works...

The first thing that we do is to invoke the `fileDialog2` command to prompt the user to provide a Python file.

```
def createScriptNode():
    filePath = cmds.fileDialog2(fileMode=1, fileFilter="Python
    files (*.py)")
```

If the user cancels out of the dialog without specifying a file, `filePath` will be empty. We check for that and end the script early if it is.

```
if (filePath == None):
    return
```

If we *do* have a file, we open it for reading, in text mode.

```
f = open(filePath[0], "r")
```

At this point, we're ready to prep the script for embedding. The `scriptNode` command will be expecting a single string for the code that makes up the script node, so we'll need to create such a string. To do that, we'll start out with a blank string, and add each line of the python file specified by the user.

```
scriptStr = ""

line = f.readline()
while (line):
    scriptStr += line
    line = f.readline()
```

At this point, the `scriptStr` variable holds the entire contents of the specified script. Since we're done with the file, we close it.

```
f.close()
```

Now we're ready to actually create the script node. Creating a script node requires that we specify a few different things. First off, we need to specify whether the script is MEL or Python, which we do with the `sourceType` flag.

We also need to specify the conditions under which the code in the script node will be run, which requires that we specify both a condition and whether the code should be executed either before or after it. In this case, we'll be using what is probably the most standard option, in that we'll have the script run once when the scene is first loaded.

To do that, we want to use the **Execute on file load** option, and set our code using the `beforeScript` flag. Putting it all together gives us the following:

```
cmds.scriptNode(sourceType="python", scriptType=2,
beforeScript=scriptStr)
```

The `scriptType` flag specifies the condition, and needs to be an integer between 0 and 7. Using a value of 2 will tie the node to the opening of the scene when not in batch mode. If you wanted to have the script run on opening even in batch mode, use 1 instead. Using a value of 0 will only run the code when it is explicitly invoked—more on that in a bit. The other options are less commonly used—see the documentation for details.

Note that there is also an `afterScript` flag which can be used to tie code execution to after the given event. If you use that with either of the file load options (1 or 2), it will cause the code to be executed when the file is closed. You can specify scripts for both the `beforeScript` and `afterScript` flags if you want.

There's more...

You can also use `scriptNodes` to embed functionality that doesn't execute on its own, but is triggered directly. To do that, specify a value of 0 for the `scriptType` (corresponding to the **Execute on demand** option). Then, when you want to invoke the code, call it in the following way:

```
cmds.scriptNode("scriptNodeName", executeBefore=True)
```

... to run the "before" script, or..

```
cmds.scriptNode("scriptNodeName", executeAfter=True)
```

...to run the "after" script.

As you work with script nodes, it can be helpful to verify that they have been created without directly triggering them. To do that, go to **Windows | Animation Editors | Expression Editor**. From the expression editor, go to **Select Filte**r **| By Script Node Name**. You'll see the interface change, and a list of the script nodes in your scene appear. Clicking on any of them will allow you to alter its properties and view or edit the corresponding code.

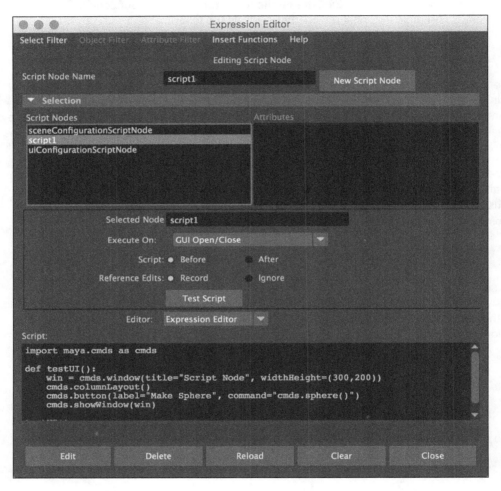

You can also delete script nodes from this window, if you need to.

Combining script jobs and script nodes

One of the great things about script jobs, and script nodes, is that you can use script nodes to ensure that a given script job travels along with your scene. For example, you might want to use a script job to trigger a custom character rig UI any time the user selects a certain object in the scene.

In this example, we'll create a script that will make it really easy to set such things up. Our script will perform the following:

- It will ask the user to point it at a Python file with one or more functions to create UI
- It will present the user with a list of all functions defined in the file in a scroll list
- It will allow the user to select an object in the scene and a named function from the file
- It will embed the contents of the function into the scene as a script node, along with a script job that will run the function every time the specified object is selected

Getting ready

To use the script we'll be writing, you'll need to have a script with at least one top-level function definition. Note that the current form of the script cannot parse functionality that is part of a class, and will only deal with a single function at a time, so make sure that all of your functionality is self-contained in a single function. For best results, make sure your input file looks something like this:

```
import maya.cmds as cmds

def testUI():
    win = cmds.window(title="Script Node", widthHeight=(300,200))
    # add some features here
    cmds.showWindow(win)

def otherUI():
    win = cmds.window(title="Other UI", widthHeight=(300,200))
    # add some features here
    cmds.showWindow(win)
```

How to do it...

Create a new script and add the following:

```python
import maya.cmds as cmds

class EmbedUI():

    def __init__(self):
        self.win = cmds.window(title="Embed UI",
        widthHeight=(300,400))
        self.commandList = {}

        cmds.columnLayout()

        self.loadButton = cmds.button(label="Load Script",
        width=300, command=self.loadScript)
        self.makeNodeBtn = cmds.button(label="Tie Script to
        Current Object", width=300, command=self.makeNode)

        self.functionList = cmds.textScrollList(width=300,
        numberOfRows=10, selectCommand=self.showCommand)

        cmds.showWindow(self.win)

    def loadScript(self, args):

        self.commandList = {}

        filePath = cmds.fileDialog2(fileMode=1, fileFilter="Python
        files (*.py)")

        if (filePath == None):
            return

        f = open(filePath[0], "r")

        functionName = ""
        functionStr = ""

        line = f.readline()

        while (line):
            parts = line.split()
```

```python
        if (line.startswith("import")):
            pass

        elif (line.startswith("def")):
            if (functionName != "" and functionStr != ""):
                self.commandList[functionName] = functionStr

            functionName = parts[1].replace("():", "")
            functionStr += line

        elif (line.strip() == ""):
            # possibly blank line, check for tab
            if (line.startswith("\t") == False):
                # blank line, see if we have a function
                if (functionName != "" and functionStr != ""):
                    self.commandList[functionName] =
                    functionStr
                    functionName = ""
                    functionStr = ""
        else:
            functionStr += line

        line = f.readline()

    f.close()
    self.updateList()

def updateList(self):
    cmds.textScrollList(self.functionList, edit=True,
    removeAll=True)

    for function in self.commandList:
        cmds.textScrollList(self.functionList, edit=True,
        append=function)

def showCommand(self):
    command = cmds.textScrollList(self.functionList,
    query=True, selectItem=True)[0]

def makeNode(self, args):
    command = cmds.textScrollList(self.functionList,
    query=True, selectItem=True)[0]
```

```
            objectName = ""
            objs = cmds.ls(selection=True)

            if (len(objs) > 0):
                objectName = objs[0]

            if (command != "" and objectName != ""):
                print("Tying " + command + " to " + objectName)

                nodeStr = "import maya.cmds as cmds\n\n"

                nodeStr += self.commandList[command] + "\n\n"

                nodeStr += 'def testSelection():\n'
                nodeStr += '\tobjs = cmds.ls(selection=True)\n'
                nodeStr += '\tif (len(objs) > 0):\n'
                nodeStr += '\t\tif (objs[0] == "' + objectName +
                '"):\n'
                nodeStr += '\t\t\t' + command + '()\n\n'

                nodeStr += 'cmds.scriptJob(killWithScene=True,
                event=["SelectionChanged", testSelection])'

                cmds.scriptNode(sourceType="python", scriptType=2,
                beforeScript=nodeStr)

        else:
            cmds.error("Please select a script and an object")


    EmbedUI()
```

How it works...

First off, we create a class for our UI, in order to make it easier to pass data around.

In the __init__ function, we add three items:

▶ A button to load and parse a source file

▶ A button to tie a specific function to the selection of a specific object

▶ A textScrollList command to hold the function names and allow the user to select them

We also give ourselves a `commandList` variable, which is a dictionary that we'll be using to hold the commands found in the file. The index of each element will be the name of the function, and the value will be the entire source code for that function.

> Dictionaries are one of Python's built-in data structures, and are equivalent to what are sometimes called **associative arrays** in other languages. The big difference between dictionaries and lists is that, in lists, you specify entries by a numerical index, while with dictionaries you specify entries by name.
>
> For example, you can create a simple dictionary with `myDict = {'foo':1, 'bar':2}`.
>
> ...which would create a dictionary with two entries—one for `foo` and another for `bar`. Accessing those values looks a lot like indexing into a list, just with the name instead of a number, as in `print(myDict['foo']  # would print 1`.

Putting that all together gives us the following:

```
class EmbedUI():

    def __init__(self):
        self.win = cmds.window(title="Embed UI",
widthHeight=(300,400))
        self.commandList = {}

        cmds.columnLayout()

        self.loadButton = cmds.button(label="Load Script", width=300,
command=self.loadScript)
        self.makeNodeBtn = cmds.button(label="Tie Script to Current
Object", width=300, command=self.makeNode)

        self.functionList = cmds.textScrollList(width=300,
numberOfRows=10, selectCommand=self.showCommand)

        cmds.showWindow(self.win)
```

Next up, we implement the `loadScript` function. We start by clearing out our `commandList` variable, in case the user is specifying a new file, then ask them to point us at a Python source file to load.

```
def loadScript(self, args):
    self.commandList = {}
    filePath = cmds.fileDialog2(fileMode=1, fileFilter="Python
    files (*.py)")
```

If we find a file, we open in in read mode.

```
if (filePath == None):
    return

f = open(filePath[0], "r")
```

Now we're ready to actually read the file. We start by creating two variables—one to hold the human-friendly function name, which we'll display in the `textScrollList` command, and another to hold the actual source code.

```
functionName = ""
functionStr = ""
```

Once we've done that, we start parsing the file. We loop through the file in the same way that we've done in previous examples, reading each line in turn—the only difference is how we parse the contents. Setting aside the handling of the file contents for a moment, the outer part of our parsing should look familiar:

```
line = f.readline()
while (line):
    # code to handle contents
    line = f.readline()
```

Onto the parsing—what we want to do is to capture all of the text for each function. That means we want everything from the line that defines the function to the function's end. Finding the end of the function requires some thought, however. What we're looking for is not only a blank line but, more specifically, a blank line that does *not* have a tab character.

We start by ignoring the import statement. We test to see if the current line starts with `import` and if so, we use the pass statement to skip doing anything.

```
while (line):
    if (line.startswith("import")):
        pass
```

Note that we could use the `continue` statement to skip the rest of the loop, but that would also skip the line responsible for reading in the next line of the file, leaving us with an infinite loop.

Next, we check to see if the line starts with `def`, indicating that it represents a new function definition.

```
elif (line.startswith("def")):
```

If it does, we want to start collecting the code for the new function, but first we want to save the function that we were previously stepping through, if one exists. To do that, we check to see if our `functionName` and `functionStr` variables are blank. If they both have contents, it is because we were previously saving another function, which we insert into our function list as follows:

```
if (functionName != "" and functionStr != ""):
    self.commandList[functionName] = functionStr
```

This would happen if the file that we're parsing had a new function definition on the line directly below a previous function, with no blank lines in between.

Now that we've dealt with the previous function (if there was one), we're ready to start storing our new function. We'll start by getting a more human-friendly form of the function name by discarding the `def` keyword, as well as the parentheses and colon.

To do that, we first use the split function to break the line up into an array by spaces, giving us `def` in the first index and something like `myFunction():` in the second. We then use replace to remove the `():`. That gives us:

```
parts = line.split()
functionName = parts[1].replace("():", "")
```

Finally, we set our `functionStr` variable to the entire line. As we continue to parse the file, we'll add additional lines to this variable. When we encounter either a new `def` statement, or truly empty (no tab character) lines, we'll store the entire `functionStr` into our list of commands.

```
functionStr = line
```

Speaking of blank lines, that's the next thing that we check for. If the line contains nothing but whitespace characters, running it through the `strip()` function will give us an empty string. If we do find an empty string, we might be at the end of the current function, but we'll want to make sure by testing to see if the current line starts with a tab.

```
elif (line.strip() == ""):
    # possibly blank line, check for tab
    if (line.startswith("\t") == False):
```

If we do have a truly blank line (no tabs), and we've been building up a function, now's the time to store it to our list. Once again, we check to make sure that both our `functionName` and `functionStr` variables have contents, and if they do, we store the function code into our `commandList`.

```
if (functionName != "" and functionStr != ""):
    self.commandList[functionName] = functionStr
    functionName = ""
    functionStr = ""
```

In order to prevent the script from storing the same function more than once (in the event of multiple blank lines), we also reset both our `functionName` and `functionStr` variables to be blank.

If none of the above code has been triggered, we know that we have a non-blank line that starts with neither `import` or `def`. We'll assume that any such line is a valid line of code, and is part of the current function. As such, we simply add it on to our `functionStr` variable.

```
else:
    functionStr += line
```

And with that, we're done parsing our file, and we close it. At this point, our `commandList` dictionary will have an entry for each function in the file. We'll want to show those functions to the user by adding them to our scroll list, which we do in our `updateList` function.

```
f.close()
self.updateList()
```

In the `updateList` function, we want to first clear out the contents of `scrollList`, and then add an entry for each of the functions we found. Both are easily done by calling the `textScrollList` command in edit mode. First, we clear it out:

```
def updateList(self):
    cmds.textScrollList(self.functionList, edit=True,
    removeAll=True)
```

Then we run through our list of commands and add the name of each to the list with the `append` flag:

```
for function in self.commandList:
    cmds.textScrollList(self.functionList, edit=True,
    append=function)
```

Now all that's left is to implement the function that will actually create the script node. First, we want to make sure that the user has selected both a command from the scroll list and an object in the scene. To get the currently selected item in the scroll list, we use the `textScrollList` command once again, but this time in query mode.

```
command = cmds.textScrollList(self.functionList, query=True,
selectItem=True)[0]
```

Note that we have a `[0]` at the end of the `textScrollList` command. That's necessary, since `textScrollList` widgets can allow for multiple item selection. As a result, the output of querying `selectItem` may have multiple values, and is returned as an array. Adding the `[0]` gives us the first element (if there is one).

Our code for grabbing the selected object is simple, and should look very familiar indeed:

```
objectName = ""
objs = cmds.ls(selection=True)

if (len(objs) > 0):
    objectName = objs[0]
```

If we have *both* an object and a command, we're ready to dive into the script node creation. If we don't, we display an error message to the user.

For our script node, what we want is code that will perform the following:

 ▸ Run on the start of the scene.

 ▸ Include the definition of the selected function.

 ▸ Include the definition of a function that can be run every time the selection changes. That function will need to compare the currently selected object to the target object and, if there's a match, invoke the trigger function

 ▸ Create a script job tied to the `SelectionChanged` event.

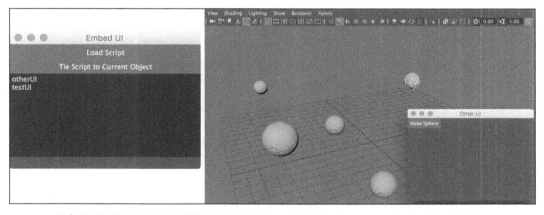

Left: the UI displaying a list of functions in the input file. Right: the result- selecting the specified sphere triggers a custom UI.

That's a number of steps, but ultimately it all amounts to constructing a big string that has all of the features listed above. We start off by setting our string to the `import maya.cmds as cmds` line that we've been using in all of our scripts.

```
if (command != "" and objectName != ""):
    print("Tying " + command + " to " + objectName)
    nodeStr = "import maya.cmds as cmds\n\n"
```

Note that there are two newline characters at the end of the line. That will make things more readable, and make it easier to check the results in the expression editor in case there are problems.

Next, we add the code for the command we want to trigger. This is really easy, since we have all of the code stored in our `commandList` dictionary. All we need to do is to index into it using the command name that the user selected.

```
nodeStr += self.commandList[command] + "\n\n"
```

Now we need to create the code for the function responsible for checking the current selection against the target object and running the target script. To do that, we'll need to string together some boilerplate code and the specific names (of the object and function) that we happen to have.

In situations like this, it's generally helpful to write out what the result should look like given a specific input first. Let's say that we wanted to trigger a function named `myFunction` if an object named `triggerObject` was selected. To do that, we could use the following function:

```
def testSelection():
    objs = cmds.ls(selection=True)
    if (len(objs) > 0):
        if (objs[0] == "triggerObject"):
            myFunction()
```

Easy enough, right? All we need to do is to add the above text to our `nodeStr` variable, making sure that we replace the object and function name, and that we add proper tabs (`\t`) and newline characters (`\n`) so that we follow proper Python whitespace rules.

That ends up giving us the following:

```
nodeStr += 'def testSelection():\n'
nodeStr += '\tobjs = cmds.ls(selection=True)\n'
nodeStr += '\tif (len(objs) > 0):\n'
nodeStr += '\t\tif (objs[0] == "' + objectName + '"):\n'
nodeStr += '\t\t\t' + command + '()\n\n'
```

All that's left is to add the code that will create a script job to properly tie our `testSelection` method to the `SelectionChanged` event. We add one final line to our `nodeStr` variable to do just that, as follows:

```
nodeStr += 'cmds.scriptJob(killWithScene=True,
event=["SelectionChanged", testSelection])'
```

We're very close to done, but what we have is still just a big chunk of text. To actually make it into a script node, we'll need to pass it into the `scriptNode` command as the `beforeScript` value, with `scriptType=2` in order to have it run at scene startup.

```
cmds.scriptNode(sourceType="python", scriptType=2,
beforeScript=nodeStr)
```

And that's it! We now have a way to embed arbitrary UI code into a scene and have it trigger when a given object is selected.

There's more...

As it stands, this example is more of a proof of concept than a proper tool. In the interest of brevity, I was forced to leave out several things that one would want, but the script could easily be extended to include all of them.

First off, the script only deals with single functions. For a proper character rig UI, it would be likely that we would want to include a collection of functions, possibly bundled together into one or more classes. In order to support that, the script would need to be changed to either copy the entire contents of a source file to the script node, or to have more sophisticated parsing of the file contents to include multiple functions.

Also, the script as written would not work as desired if it was used more than once in the same scene, since every pairing of function and object uses the same name (`testSelection`) for the function tied to the script job.

To fix that, we would want to ensure that each script job gets its own uniquely-named function to test the selection. One way to do that would be to append the name of the function that we ultimately want to trigger to the `testSelection` function name, as in:

```
selectionFunctionName = "testFor" + command

nodeStr += 'def ' + selectionFunctionName + '():\n'
nodeStr += '\tobjs = cmds.ls(selection=True)\n'
nodeStr += '\tif (len(objs) > 0):\n'
nodeStr += '\t\tif (objs[0] == "' + objectName + '"):\n'
nodeStr += '\t\t\t' + command + '()\n\n'

nodeStr += 'cmds.scriptJob(killWithScene=True,
event=["SelectionChanged", ' + selectionFunctionName + '])'
```

Index

G

geometric data
  accessing, in NURBS objects 52-54
  accessing, in polygonal models 49-51
GUI
  creating, for controlling lights 149-155

I

input
  retrieving, from controls 25-30
inverse kinematics (IK)
  setting up, with script 112-118

J

JSON
  URL 209
JSON data
  working with 206-209

K

keyframes
  about 121
  setting 133-135

L

lights
  creating 143-148
  editing 143-148

M

Maya Embedded Language (MEL)
  about 2, 47
  Python functionality, wrapping in 217
Maya's built-in Python functionality
  importing 6-8
MEL script
  calling, with Python 17, 18
menus
  adding, to UIs 40-44

N

nested layouts
  using 33-36
new modifiers (noise)
  creating 61-64
new polygonal faces
  creating 58-60
ngons 61
node type
  checking 46-49
novel primitives (tetrahedron)
  creating 64-72
NURBS objects
  geometric data, accessing 52-54

O

object-oriented programming (OOP) 33
objects
  shaders, applying to 86-89

P

Pillow
  reference 161
polygonal models
  geometric data, accessing 49-51
POST data
  sending, to web server from Maya 209-215
Python
  reference 161
Python functionality
  wrapping, in MEL 217-220
Python Imaging Library (PIL) 161
  reference 165

Q

Query flag 10, 11

S

script
expressions, creating via 136-141
skeletons, creating with 95-102
script editor
about 2
code, running from 5, 6
used, for investigating functionality 2-4
script jobs
and script nodes, combining 235-245
used, for triggering custom
functionality 226-230
script nodes
used, for embedding code in scenes 230-234
script path
custom folders, adding to 12, 13
scrolling
using 36-39
selected objects
working with 46-49
server
data, grabbing from 198-201
set-driven key relationships
setting up, with script 103-106
shaders
applying, to objects 86-89
shading networks
creating, with code 82-85
shading nodes
using, for non-shading tasks 90-92
skeletons
creating, with script 95-102
sprite sheet
rendering 161-165

T

tabs
using 36-39
text files
reading 170-174
writing 175-181

U

user interface
basic window, creating 20-22
button, creating 23-25
classes, for organizing UI logic 30-33
creating 19
input, retrieving from controls 25-30
menus, adding 40-44
nested layouts, using 33-36
scrolling, using 36-39
tabs, using 36-39
UV data
querying 73-76
UVs
laying out, with Python 77-81

W

web page
opening, from script 196-198
Wolfram MathWorld
URL 58

X

XML data
working with 201-205

www.ingramcontent.com/pod-product-compliance
Lightning Source LLC
Chambersburg PA
CBHW060534060326
40690CB00017B/3485